EDUCATION
An Interdisciplinary Look at Art in the Curriculum

About NAEA

The National Art Education Association is the world's largest professional visual arts education association and a leader in educational research, policy, and practice for art education. NAEA's mission is to advance visual arts education to fulfill human potential and promote global understanding.

Membership includes elementary and secondary art teachers, middle school and high school students in the National Art Honor Society programs, artists, administrators, museum educators, arts council staff, university professors, and students from the United States and 25 other countries. It also includes publishers, manufacturers, and suppliers of art materials; parents; students; retired art educators; and others concerned about quality art education in our schools.

National Art Education Association
901 Prince Street, Alexandria, VA 22314

All rights reserved. No part of this book may be reproduced in any form by any electronic or mechanical means (includes photography, recording, or information storage and retrieval) without permission in writing from the author and publisher.

To order a copy of this book or obtain additional information, contact National Art Education Association: www.arteducators.org or 800-299-8321.

ISBN: 978-1-890160-77-7

Copyedited by Katherine V. Holland
Book and cover design by Jamie Klinger-Krebs

STEAM EDUCATION

An Interdisciplinary Look at Art in the Curriculum

EDITED BY:
Tracey Hunter-Doniger
and Nancy Walkup

NATIONAL ART EDUCATION ASSOCIATION

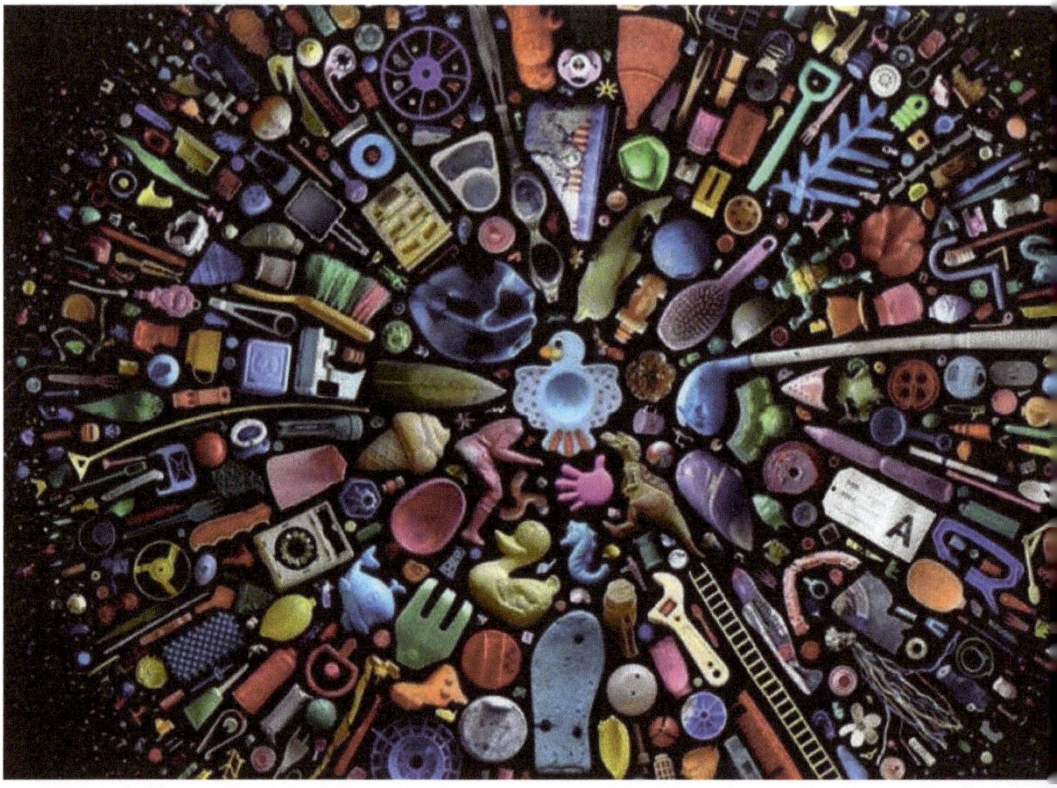

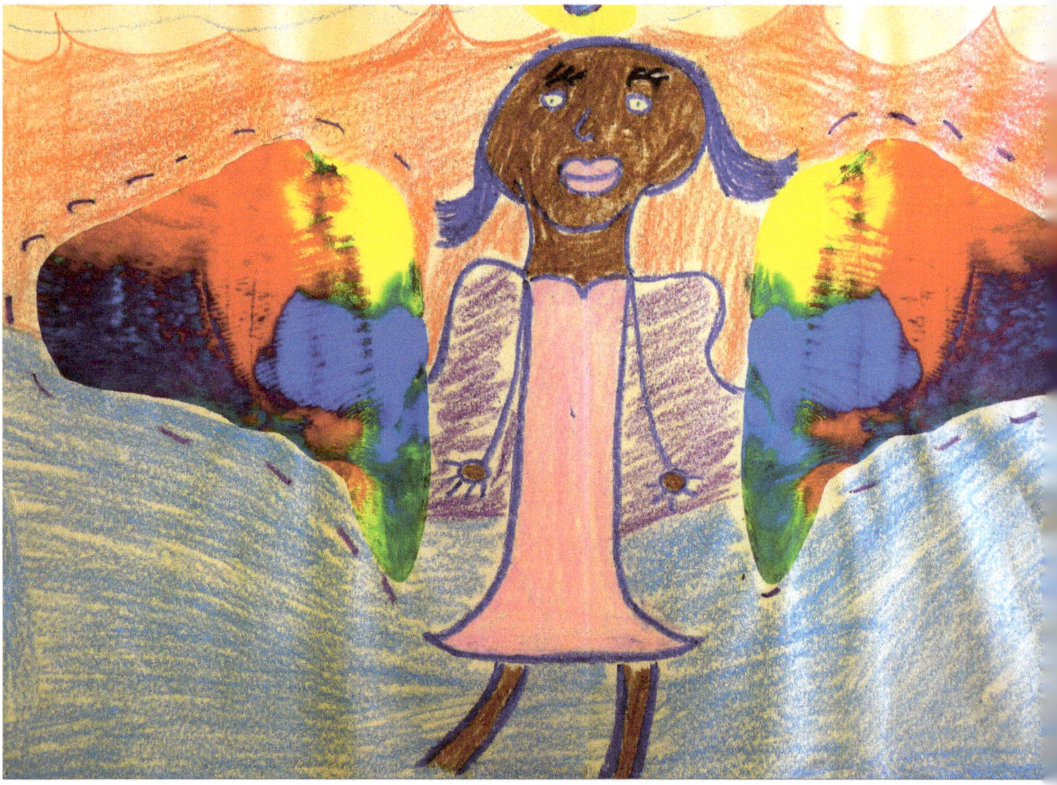

TABLE OF CONTENTS

Acknowledgments
Tracey Hunter-Doniger ix

Introduction/Foreword: STEAM and Interdisciplinarity
Tracey Hunter-Doniger x

Section I: Conducive Environments for STEAM Education

Chapter 1 | Art Infusion: Ideal Conditions for STEAM
Tracey Hunter-Doniger 2

Chapter 2 | STEAM Team: A Cross-Curricular Adventure
Pamelia D. Valentine 14

Section II: Science

Chapter 3 | What if We Crank It Up a Notch?
Samantha Melvin 24

Chapter 4 | A Model for High School STEAM Activities: Science and Visual Art
Pam Stephens 36

Chapter 5 | The Process of Building an Art Installation With Plastic Waste
Tina Hirsig 44

Chapter 6 | Culturally Relevant STEAM
Tracey Hunter-Doniger, Courtney A. Howard, Rénard Harris, & Cyndi Hall 54

Section III: Technology

Chapter 7 | I Am Here Too! Career and Technical Education Digital Arts & Design Cluster and STEAM Integration
Indira Bailey 66

Chapter 8 | Art-Based Makerspaces: *Making* the Connection to STEAM
Melissa Negreiros 80

Chapter 9 | Digital Technology in the Art Room: Breakfast Cereal Box Design
Rachel Wintemberg 88

Chapter 10 | Virtual Reality Art Education
Jeremy Blair 100

Section IV: Engineering/Design

Chapter 11 | Engineering Joy: Toying With Process in Expanded Media Arts
Sean Justice 118

Chapter 12 | Building Forts at Recess: When Student-Initiated Creativity Becomes STEAM Learning
David Rufo 130

Chapter 13 | Engineering Intersections of STEAM: Maker-Centered Learning to Support Teachers' Engineering Confidence and Connections Between Design Processes
Shaunna Smith 136

Chapter 14 | How Might We Make This Work? Using Design Thinking to Engineer Kinetic Sculptures in the Art Room
Kristin Vanderlip Taylor 152

Section V: Art (Performing Arts)

Chapter 15 | COVID-19 Leads to Powerful STEAM Lessons in Music
Rodney Harshbarger 166

Chapter 16 | When the "A" Stands for Dance: Transdisciplinary STEAM Education That Dances to Connect Disciplines
Alison E. Leonard 174

Chapter 17 | "But What About the Eyeballs?": Devised Theatre as Interdisciplinary Knowledge-Generation Tool
Vivian Appler & Emily Pears 186

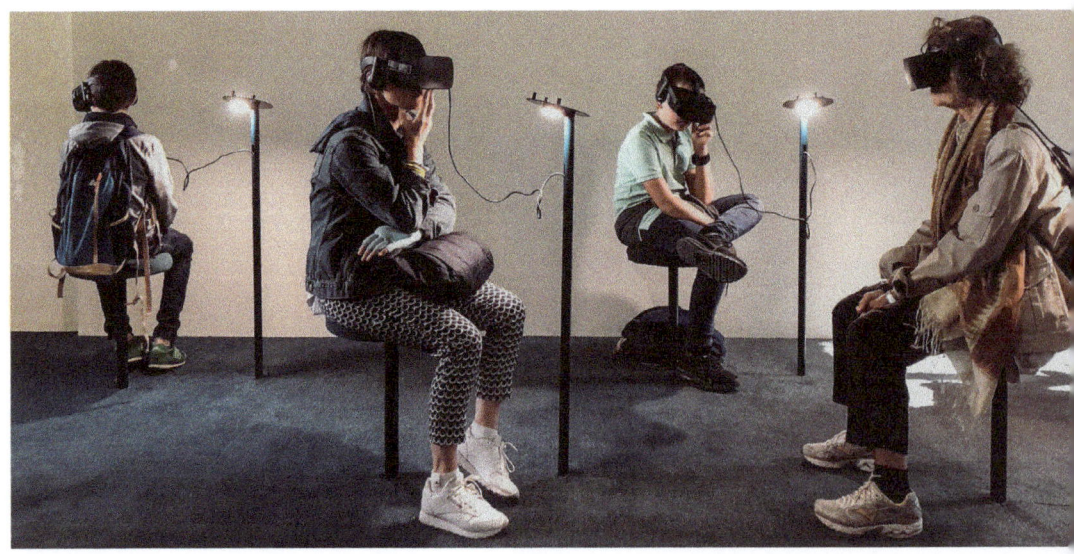

Section VI: Mathematics

Chapter 18 | Connecting Mathematics to Verbal–Visual Art
Punya Mishra & Danah Henriksen 200

Chapter 19 | Guitar Makers on the Border: Bilingual Elementary Students Learning Math by Designing and Building Guitars
Daniel A. Tillman & Song A. An 214

Chapter 20 | Providing a Compass for STEAM With M.C. Escher and Tessellations
Melody Weintraub 224

Chapter 21 | Imagination, Color Theory, and Symmetry
Nancy Walkup 238

Closing
Tracey Hunter-Doniger & Nancy Walkup 243

About the Authors

Tracey Hunter-Doniger is an associate professor at the College of Charleston, and the department chair of the Teacher Education Department in the School of Education. She serves as the chair of the National Art Education Association (NAEA) Research Commission's Professional Learning through Research (PLR) Working Group. Hunter-Doniger is also the director of Camp Art Attack, a STEAM camp; director of Project Inspire, an arts-integrated ecological program for underserved schools; and the former director of the Teaching Fellows & Teacher Cadets. As a lifelong advocate for education and the arts, Hunter-Doniger taught 15 years as a visual arts teacher in public schools for Grades K–8 in the United States. Her research investigates art infusion, forest schools, and STEAM education. Hunter-Doniger has received two National Art Education Foundation Research Grants (2017 and 2023). She was also the recipient of the South Carolina Art Education Association High Education Art Teacher of the Year Award in 2019. She has authored several peer-reviewed journal articles and a textbook, *Experiencing the Art: Creative Arts in Education*, written for nonarts educators learning to infuse the arts in their classrooms.

Nancy Walkup has been the editor of *SchoolArts*, a magazine for art educators published since 1901, since 2005. She was also a contributing author, along with Marilyn Stewart, Eldon Katter, and Laura Chapman, for the first edition of Explorations in Art, Davis Publications's elementary textbook series. She is also coauthor of *Bridging the Curriculum Through Art: Interdisciplinary Connections* with Pam Stephens, and an author of interdisciplinary Take 5 Study Prints for Crystal Productions. Her more than 30 years of teaching experience covers all grade levels from kindergarten through university, where she has always taught with an interdisciplinary approach. Since 2005, she has been the editor in chief of *SchoolArts* magazine, published for art educators preK–12 since 1901.

Her honors include serving as an invited teacher at an elementary school in Beijing, China; selection for the Japanese Fulbright Memorial Teacher program; and being named 2007 Teacher of the Year for her elementary campus. She has won numerous awards from the art education associations of Louisiana and Texas, as well as NAEA. She was the conference chair for the 2001 NAEA National Convention, held in New York City. She was named Texas Elementary Art Educator of the Year in 2010. From 2013 to 2015, she served as the Elementary Director of NAEA and was recently named a Distinguished Fellow by NAEA. In 2016 she received the NAEA Western Region Art Educator Award. In 2019 she was named a Distinguished Fellow by the Texas Art Education Association.

Acknowledgments

Tracey Hunter-Doniger

Acknowledgements from Tracey Hunter-Doniger:

I would like to thank the following people for their assistance and inspiration:

Nancy Walkup: Thank you for agreeing to work with me on this project. It is a labor of love, but it has been a true pleasure to work with such an icon in art education.

To the National Art Education Association: Thank you for all the amazing opportunities for art educators, including the ongoing advocacy for art education. I appreciate all that you do for art teachers and our students.

Thank you to each and every chapter author who made this book possible and a work of art. This holds true as a testament of your dedication and expertise in art education.

To all the art teachers in the world: You make a tremendous difference to so many students. You are the reason some get out of bed and go to school. You bring the light to education, not through fluff but with ongoing rigor and commitment. You need to know you make a difference in so many ways. Thank you.

Larry Barnfield: Thank you for taking me under your wing and helping me navigate through this higher ed art education adventure. I aspire to one day be like you.

Lily (Ian) and Drew Doniger: Keep dreaming, keep being who you are, and never settle for less. You are the solution to all my problems and happiness, and you make me so proud.

Steve Doniger: My fabulous husband, thank you for being my rock, and a biggest fan. You have stood by me through everything, but most importantly taught me to LIVE LIFE!!!

Introduction

STEAM and Interdisciplinarity

Tracey Hunter-Doniger & Nancy Walkup

Visual and performing arts have made significant connections with STEM (science, technology, engineering, and mathematics) subjects, creating the acronym "STEAM." The arts have been known to transcend the strict disciplinary borders of other subject areas. As such, educational leaders are looking toward ways to incorporate STEAM into the curriculum. This book, *STEAM Education: An Interdisciplinary Look at Art in the Curriculum*, is a comprehensive guide to STEAM. Its central point is inspired by the interest in STEAM-based education and pedagogical practices.

This book is compiled into sections that address STEAM and each specific discipline of science, technology, engineering, art, and math. Each section has two to four chapters that discuss interdisciplinary education and how blurring the curricular lines can enhance learning in all areas. The main theme of this book is to explore STEAM education and how it can be used in classrooms to advance learning through interdisciplinary education and to promote the utility and effectiveness of STEAM education. It provides a rich discussion on STEAM and interdisciplinary collaboration through art alongside examples of successful STEAM lessons in each discipline. The chapter authors discuss their significant contributions to STEAM education and how they have successfully integrated an interdisciplinary approach in their own work. In order to bring a broad perspective to STEAM, the chapters are written by a diverse group of authors that include in-service and retired art educators; music, dance, and theatre instructors; academics; people from a variety of ethnic backgrounds; researchers; a former principal; a member of NASA; an associate dean; and a private school teacher. This book is designed to systematically outline the ways art interacts with different disciplines. The content is a valuable resource for preservice teachers, practitioners, researchers, and administrators seeking to implement STEAM in their own practices.

Relevance of STEAM Education

There is a growing body of evidence regarding the positive education that stems from learning in nontraditional settings (Hunter-Doniger, 2019, 2021, 2022). "Expanded learning programs can assist and support children and youth with opportunities to learn and grow so they can succeed educationally and lead productive lives" (Peterson, 2013, p. 439). Creating inspiring learning environments is essential to the learning process (Sandberg &

Ärlemalm-Hagsér, 2011; Wells, 2000). There is a need for alternative learning experiences, especially provided that so many students' educational needs are not being met. As educators, we have an obligation to serve all students equally and to the best of our abilities. Focusing on rote memorization ultimately devalues the power of the learning process to produce meaningful and creative intellectual skills (Hunter-Doniger, 2019). Hetland (2013) argued that there must be a shift in the role of education away from gaining knowledge and toward the process of acquiring understanding. To provide equity and enrich educational experiences, teachers can take advantage of children's natural tendency to create art and to explore their world and surroundings through artmaking (Eisner, 2002; Lowenfeld, 1957; Vygotsky, 1974). By investing in nontraditional education programs, we can give young people the power to participate in the world with an open mind, self-awareness, confidence, and understanding (Eisner, 1997). STEAM is a way to break down the academic silos and connect subject areas in a way that mirrors real life. STEAM encourages divergent ways of thinking and creating using a multidisciplinary approach to learning (Sousa & Pilecki, 2013). By making purposeful connections through STEM and the arts, skills in all areas are strengthened and students gain a richer learning experience (Riley, 2012). Employing STEAM in a classroom provides students with creativity, maintaining their engagement in learning subjects like science, engineering, and math. STEAM has a positive impact on math and literacy development, engagement, school attendance, and graduation rates (Eisner, 2002; Hunter-Doniger & Sydow, 2016). When infusing the arts through STEAM education, children have been able to reach new heights in engagement and learning outcomes (Hartle et al., 2015).

What Is STEAM?

While there has been a noticeable trend in education to place an emphasis on STEM subjects, merely adding an "A" for the arts to make STEAM is not an accurate definition. Admittedly, grant foundations, job creators, policy makers, and even government officials in the United States are discussing the importance of STEM education (Johnson, 2012; Peterson, 2013). However, while STEM subjects are important, it has become increasingly evident that creativity and the arts are equally important and should be treated as such (Hetland, 2013; Hunter-Doniger, 2021). Throughout the chapters found in this book there is a spectrum of definitions of STEAM, yet one consistent thread they share is that the arts must not be used as a prop but taught at an equal level of importance when considering standards and assessments.

Additionally, we, the authors, believe it is necessary to provide full transparency in the STEAM debate. Some traditionalists in the STEM subject areas reject the integration of the arts within the STEM fields. Likewise, not all art educators subscribe to the concept of STEAM education and believe that art should be taught for art's sake rather than as an add-on to entertain students as they learn nonart subjects (Eisner, 2002; Hetland, 2013). The National Art Education Association (NAEA, 2014/2022) defines *STEAM* as a pedagogical approach to infusing the arts, as well as design concepts and techniques, into STEM instructional learning. NAEA suggests that this approach values all STEAM disciplines equally, is implemented through a wide variety of approaches, encourages creativity and innovation, and acknowledges the rigor found in the arts. This approach allows the learner to be engaged and helps them understand that disciplines across the curriculum are interwoven and, at times, rely on skills applied in other areas. For STEAM to be successful, arts integration needs to be clearly defined.

Arts Integration Continuum

STEAM education works under the assumption that nonart subjects will integrate the arts, or the arts will integrate the nonarts subjects. But what does that mean exactly? There is a larger varying spectrum of how the arts are used in tandem with other disciplines, ranging from the serendipitous to the fully planned team-taught art infusion. The Arts in Basic Curriculum (ABC, 2005) Project created a clear continuum to define art infusion. This continuum has five separate levels: Arts Basic, Arts Enhanced, Initial Arts Integration, Developed Arts Integration, and Arts Infusion (Table 1).

Table 1. Arts Integration Continuum

	Not adequate for STEAM			Acceptable for STEAM	Best practice for STEAM
Arts Basic	**Arts Enhancement**	**Initial Arts Integration**	**Developed Arts Integration**	**Arts Infusion**
Serendipitous art experiences. Arts integration that is not planned. Disciplines are confined to their designated time and space.	Some art–nonart connections are made, but there is still a clear separation between disciplines.	There are deliberate connections between art and nonart disciplines, but the arts are used as a prop or a way to maintain engagement.	Significant integration is evident, and connections between disciplines are made. However, the arts are not assessed.	Knowledge is constructed through arts and nonarts disciplines concurrently. Teachers from each discipline plan and teach the lesson, and all areas are assessed.

Source: ABC, 2005.

The first level is Arts Basic, where the arts are taught separately in a specialized room. If art is integrated at the basic level, it is a happy accident and not intentional. The second level is Arts Enhancement. At this level, the art exposure is planned but superficial and as a separate subject. Initial Arts Integration is the third level, which is where preliminary connections are made between arts and nonarts subjects. This level is where STEAM might be introduced, but the tendency is to use the arts as a prop or a way to engage students. Developed Arts Integration is the fourth level, where STEAM makes significant interdisciplinary connections. The fourth level is where the disciplines support one another. Standards from all areas are addressed but with the emphasis placed on the nonarts subjects. While the arts are intentionally included, the arts standards are not assessed. The fifth and final level in the continuum is Arts Infusion. At this level, STEAM education has the most potential for meaning-making across the disciplines. Knowledge is constructed through the integrated study of arts and nonarts, all disciplines mutually support and enhance each other, and all areas are assessed. At the Arts Integration level, students are challenged to think reflectively and solve creative problems. This is a result of continuous planning on the part of teachers from all areas. But how do STEAM and arts integration correlate to interdisciplinary learning?

Interdisciplinarity

Defining interdisciplinarity requires deconstructing the word. *Inter-* is a Latin prefix meaning "among" or "between." This involves two or more objects, entities, or concepts. *Disciplinarity* refers to the expertise of a discipline, including the understanding of the methodology and best practices, and the capacity to obtain, analyze, and employ specialized knowledge. Therefore, *interdisciplinarity* is teaching across the curriculum and fully understanding the relationship between the disciplines to enhance the learning process. This concept empowers each discipline as they are infused. There is not a competition for importance between the subjects, but a coexistence that supports learning in all areas. Table 2 provides some definitions of a variety of educational approaches to learning for comparison.

Interdisciplinarity is a structure in which STEAM education can thrive, as it gives a framework that requires critical thinking and a plurality of perspectives among several disciplines at the same time while making connections within each area.

Table 2. Educational Approaches, Definitions, and Examples

Educational approach	Definition	Examples
Cross-Disciplinary	Examines one discipline through the lens of another discipline.	A lesson on the influence of jazz on African American history.
Multidisciplinary	Extracts knowledge from two or more disciplines side by side without interaction and provides varying perspectives.	Learning about birds in science class and drawing birds in the art room.
Interdisciplinary	**Integrates or infuses disciplines around common themes, issues, or problems for a deep understanding of the interrelationships of the subject areas.**	STEAM education; art infusion.
Transdisciplinary	A holistic experience that is similar to interdisciplinary learning, as it spans across multiple subject areas, but this method explores a relevant concept, issue, or problem simultaneously.	An entrepreneurial project to raise money that designs an exhibit for a history museum that includes content, artifacts, narratives, and interactive displays.

Transdisciplinary Learning

It is noteworthy to also mention transdisciplinary methods in education, as a few authors wrote specifically about this pedagogical practice. Similar to interdisciplinary learning, transdisciplinary learning spans across and among disciplines. However, transdisciplinary learning is a complex technique that enables connections across various disciplines while exploring a relevant concept, issue, or problem at an in-depth level (Jao & Radakovic, 2017; Hunter-Doniger & Sydow, 2016). While implementing a transdisciplinary method of learning, subjects are well-defined but intentionally interconnected, allowing for a holistic learning experience. As such, children can apply what they are learning across the curriculum simultaneously while developing understanding at a deeper level.

Silos in Education

On a farm, the design of a silo is meant to keep grains isolated from other grains and contaminants until it is ready to be used or sold. In traditional schools, subjects are, more times than not, taught in metaphoric silos. In these conventional curricula, disciplines are taught at a specific time, for a predetermined amount of time, and they are not supposed to mix with other disciplines to maintain focus and clarity. Sometimes, there is even a specific room designated for a particular discipline's intellectual stimulation to be carried out, such as an art room or music room. Most public school experiences in the United States are based on silos (Byrne & Mullally, 2016; Taylor & Taylor, 2017). School schedules usually have a separate book for each class subject. It is seldom, if ever, that students are assigned a book that crosses over between disciplines. However, in the real world, everything is intermingled. No subject is actually experienced in a vacuum, all experiences are influenced by others, and all knowledge is based upon a foundation of information found elsewhere (Hunter-Doniger, 2018). This argument can be extended to careers as well. For example, scientists utilize math, charts, diagrams, reading, writing, and sketching to comprehend the full scope of what they are studying. In turn, Broadway actors' skill sets involve reading, dancing, singing, science, math, and language skills. There is not a single job that does not utilize multiple disciplines. The concept of STEAM education breaks down the silo walls and blurs the lines of the traditional curriculum. STEAM permeates throughout the curriculum with multiple disciplines at the same time to provide a more true-to-life experience for the learner. The purpose of this book is to demolish the walls of the silos. From the rubble, the readers can build a stronger, more interactive curriculum based on 21st-century learning.

Value of the Arts in and as Education

Visual and performing arts education are time-honored, rigorous methods of learning that remain important for the skills students can develop throughout their educational experiences (Baxter, 2014; Hetland & Winner, 2000). Researchers contend that the arts are, and have constantly been, fundamentally important to education (Hetland & Winner, 2000). The arts provide motivation for students, allowing them to imagine future possibilities while creating a desire to explore, provide a space for autonomous learning, respect multiple perspectives, and persist in investigations (Hetland et al., 2013). As such, the configuration of this book is based around the fundamental notion that the arts are valued in and as education.

The Structure of This Book

This book unites the ideology of STEAM education in 21 chapters, divided into six sections. Section I is an introduction to STEAM and the environments that are conductive for interdisciplinary learning. The remaining five sections adhere to the STEAM acronym: Section II, Science; Section III, Technology; Section IV, Engineering/Design; Section V, The Arts (Performing Arts), and Section VI, Math. The sections contain two to four chapters. Each chapter explores the interdisciplinarity of the STEAM subjects. Individual chapters investigate how these disciplines can coalesce enhancing learning, enrich pedagogical practices, or provide examples of best practices when implementing STEAM. Below are synopses of each chapter.

Section I: Conducive Environments for STEAM Education

Art Infusion: Ideal Conditions for STEAM
Tracey Hunter-Doniger

With the rise in interest in STEAM education, this article presents the art-infused school as an environment that provides ideal conditions for embedding STEAM education. Art is an inseparable fiber of the curriculum in an art-infused school for sustainable STEAM education because the curriculum acknowledges the rigor of the arts and encourages creativity and innovation.

STEAM Team: A Cross-Curricular Adventure
Pamelia D. Valentine

Science and art teachers collaborated to create a cross-curricular lesson for 4th graders called "Seeing Color; Using Color," using a color and light lab to teach about the visual light spectrum in science class while the art teacher taught about pigment color. These lessons led to further collaboration with 7th- and 8th-grade students, where they created a STEAM garden as a science lesson and learned about botanical drawing in art. These activities ultimately led to the design and installation of water features and garden structures utilizing both the science and art lessons.

Section II: Science

What if We Crank It Up a Notch?
Samantha Melvin

Designed for 4th and 5th graders, this lesson utilized LCD microscopes to build observation skills, leading to collaboration installations exploring art and science. The goal of the lesson was to strengthen skills for visual literacy and expressions through nuances in design. Students developed a heightened awareness of textures, patterns, and structures, and they integrated these observations into their individual works of art.

A Model for High School STEAM Activities: Science and Visual Art
Pam Stephens

This chapter focuses on how a high school art program can seamlessly meet the challenges of the industrial revolution. The author offers a model for planning, implementing, and measuring learning outcomes of STEAM activities. She explains that what is significant to quality STEAM activities is treating all content areas as equals; that is, no subject is treated as a handmaiden to another. The best art activities are those that move away from linear thinking to embrace the wholeness of STEAM.

The Process of Building an Art Installation With Plastic Waste
Tina Hirsig

This chapter focuses on a school's collaboration with an environmental artist. The school-wide K–12 project was designed to bring to light plastics in the ocean, which is one of the largest threats to the ocean and marine life. The students collected plastics and created a mobile art design that symbolized the manifesto of the school. This STEAM lesson allowed students to create a work of art that raised awareness for this global problem.

Culturally Relevant STEAM
Tracey Hunter-Doniger, Courtney Howard, Rénard Harris, and Cynthia Hall

The authors contend that along with proper art-infusion techniques, nonarts teachers need to be taught how to engage their students in culturally relevant teaching. This chapter discusses a professional development course that included storytelling to connect to students' cultures, making STEAM lessons more meaningful.

Introduction

Section III: Technology

I Am Here Too! Career and Technical Education
Digital Arts & Design Cluster and STEAM Integration
Indira Bailey

This chapter discusses the significance of CTE Digital Art & Design program in a vocational–technical high school environment. The author describes a graphic designer's role in the Commercial Illustration II class that she taught to promote real experiences using STEAM. Highlighted is one student's problem-solving process, creativity, mathematics, drawing skills, and technology in creating a Moroccan travel poster. The author provides strategies for STEAM education and suggestions for how traditional art educators can incorporate the design and engineering field into their classrooms.

Art-Based Makerspaces: *Making* the Connection to STEAM
Melissa Negreiros

This chapter describes the result of a passion project, commonly known as the Genius Hour, in which time was set aside for 3rd- and 4th-grade students to explore their passions and ideas, solve problems, and generate products. The art teacher introduced the students to issues caused by plastic pollution and its impact on the environment, then demonstrated artwork that could be created from it. The students collected plastic trash from their neighborhoods and used it to create unique pieces of art. Students were engaged in solving real-world problems while creating authentic art.

Digital Technology in the Art Room: Breakfast Cereal Box Design
Rachel Wintemberg

Developing skills in design technology and visual arts was the goal of this high school project. Each student was required to invent an original breakfast cereal and imaginary food company and design a mascot and logo with Photoshop and Illustrator. As they created their cereal boxes, the students learned to create 3D letters, photograph food, and create games on the back of the boxes—a combination of art and design.

Virtual Reality Art Education
Jeremy Blair

This chapter discusses the development of engaging virtual reality experiences for students at elementary and secondary schools. The students were able to critically reflect on virtual reality capabilities in the art classroom. Throughout the chapter, the author presents the foundations of virtual reality and shares the processes, discoveries, and barriers of three K–12 educators enrolled in the yearlong professional development program during the 2018–2019 school year.

Section IV: Engineering/Design

Engineering Joy: Toying With Process in Expanded Media Arts
Sean Justice

This chapter describes a hybrid art, engineering, and technology activity in a digital methods course in an art education program, in which preteaching students explored the intersections between art and engineering and technology. During the toy-remixing exercise, students learned the lesson of the upside-down object. Toy remixing begins with a product and becomes a process; learning the process is the lesson that makes students think and learn.

Building Forts at Recess: When Student-Initiated Creativity Becomes STEAM Learning
David Rufo

In a student-initiated fort-building activity for 4th- and 5th-grade students, the author explores multiple concepts the students used throughout the activity. These include scientific concepts as students explored the outdoors searching for building materials, developing new technologies as students found efficient methods and tools for the building process, using engineering skills as they constructed the forts, utilizing art-based thinking to design the interior and exterior of the forts, and employing mathematics to estimate the appropriate size and shape of each fort.

Engineering Intersections of STEAM: Maker-Centered Learning to Support Teachers' Engineering Confidence and Connections Between Design Processes
Shaunna Smith

This chapter focuses on a 15-week MEd Education Technology program open to practicing teachers of all content areas and all grade levels. The goals for the course included engaging in and reflecting on intersections of STEAM content and design processes through diverse materials, tools, and contexts. The key theme of the course was for teachers to reflect on the design process while encouraging students to document their designs and artifacts they created each week, as well as engage in discussions and critiques of other students' craftsmanship.

How Might We Make This Work? Using Design Thinking to Engineer Kinetic Sculptures in the Art Room
Kristin Vanderlip Taylor

This chapter discusses a kinetic sculpture lesson with 6th-, 7th-, and 8th-grade students. The objectives of this lesson were for the students to collaboratively utilize the design process, experiment with materials, and present their findings to one another after they had designed and built their own kinetic sculptures. These three-dimensional movable works of art required equal focus on visual arts, engineering, and science concepts to ensure the sculptures met visual standards as well as effectively move based on engineering and the forces enacted upon them.

Section V: Art (Performing Arts)

COVID-19 Leads to Powerful STEAM Lessons in Music
Rodney Harshbarger

This chapter discusses a project that combines science and music in a virtual lesson for 3rd-grade students. The object of the project was for each student to design and build a musical instrument resembling a guitar or cello. Students learned music terms, such as "sound," "sound waves," "pitch," "vibration," and "tone"; they also learned science terms, such as "energy," "medium," "frequency," and "wavelength." The students used household objects to create their individual instruments, which they used to perform for the virtual classroom.

When the "A" Stands for Dance: Transdisciplinary STEAM Education That Dances to Connect Disciplines
Alison E. Leonard

This collaborative project involving dance, virtual reality, computer science, and digital production arts was incorporated into the classrooms of 5th- through 8th-grade students. It involved an interactive dance-centered curriculum and a virtual platform to support computer programming education. The connections between dance, math, chemistry, geometry, the life cycle, and transformation of energy were utilized to explore new concepts.

"But What About the Eyeballs?": Devised Theatre as Interdisciplinary Knowledge-Generation Tool
Vivian Appler and Emily Pears

Appropriate for K–12, this multidisciplinary theatre lesson revolved around devised theatre, which is created through methods of movement, text, and other generation techniques. The context is viewed through the eyes of a 10-year old, who offers a unique perspective on the play that was performed, *That Which We Call a Rose*.

Section VI: Mathematics

Connecting Mathematics to Verbal–Visual Art
Punya Mishra and Danah Henriksen

Distorting visual letterforms and writing words to express mathematical symmetries is an example of engaging with math learning in this interdisciplinary lesson. This high school lesson encouraged STEAM education and allowed students to work individually or collectively. As the lesson progressed, students grappled with the task of exploring the perceptual flexibility of shape perception and pattern formation through creative visual wordplay.

Guitar Makers on the Border: Bilingual Elementary Students Learning Math by Designing and Building Guitars
Daniel A. Tillman and Song A. An

Once per week, a class of bilingual 3rd-grade students participated in guitar-making activities. These activities were intended to provide an engaging, real-world context for math concepts the students were learning in math, so that language barriers would become less detrimental to their learning. Just as the students had to solve geometrical problems by determining the placement and number of strings on their guitars, they undertook other math experiences to connect and solve math and math-themed problems during the activity.

Providing a Compass for STEAM With M.C. Escher and Tessellations
Melody Weintraub

Designed for 7th-grade art students, this lesson began with a study of tessellations and the mathematical processes they used to make similar designs with applications of this skill to make art. The students learned the importance of accurate measurement and application of geometric principles to the creation of art.

Imagination, Color Theory, and Symmetry
Nancy Walkup

This chapter brings the complex concepts of color theory and mathematical symmetry to an early childhood level. The author explains the connections to STEAM in a way young children can comprehend, helping them retain the information through hands-on learning and experimentation.

The authors presented in this book each share a unique perspective and expertise of STEAM education. By redefining the methods used in teaching, and by blasting the walls of the silos, this book blurs the lines of the curriculum, permitting interdisciplinarity of the subjects. We recognize that while the authors provided insight into STEAM education, its methods, and pedagogical practices, this book only provides a small sample of the possibilities and experiences STEAM education offers. Our intent is for readers, whether they are arts educators, nonarts classroom teachers, researchers, academics, or administrators, will use the information and perspectives found in this book to provide a foundation of STEAM experiences to children across the globe.

This book speaks directly to the interdisciplinarity of the arts in STEAM education. Often, STEAM references comprise lesson plans that superficially add the arts. The significance of this book is that it provides scholarly research and best practice with the arts as the foundational discipline. This book compiles existing arguments in STEAM education literature, such as students are more engaged with the arts are included (Daugherty, 2013), the arts can be used to help inform other subjects like science, and that STEAM can give a deeper perspective on social issues (Guyotte et al., 2014). It also relies on the expertise of the in-service art educator to discuss best practices and connections for the STEAM subjects. The breadth and depth of this book is unique because it will embrace the knowledge and perspectives from scholars and practitioners alike to reach a broader audience for real-world applications.

References

Arts in Basic Curriculum. (2005). *An arts infusion continuum*. https://www.abcinstitutesc.org/wp-content/uploads/2016/09/4.1_Documents_Arts-Infusion-Continuum.pdf

Baxter, K. (2014). A convergence of three: The reflexive capacity of art practice, curriculum design, and pedagogy. *Art Education, 67*(6), 28–34. https://doi.org/10.1080/00043125.2014.11519295

Byrne, E. P., & Mullally, G. (2016). Seeing beyond silos: Transdisciplinary approaches to education as a means of addressing sustainability issues. In W. L. Filho & S. Nesbit (Eds.), *New developments in engineering education for sustainable development* (pp. 23–34). Springer. https://doi.org/10.1007/978-3-319-32933-8

Daugherty, M. K. (2013). The prospect of an "A" in STEM education. *Journal of STEM Education, 14*(2), 10–15.

Eisner, E. (1997). *Educating artistic vision*. National Art Education Association.

Eisner, E. W. (2002). *The arts and the creation of mind*. Yale University Press.

Guyotte, K. W., Sochacka, N. W., Constantino, T. E., Walther, J., & Kellam, N. N. (2014). STEAM as social practice: Cultivating creativity in transdisciplinary spaces. *Art Education, 67*(6), 12–19. https://doi.org/10.1080/00043125.2014.11519293

Hartle, L. C., Pinciotti, P., & Gorton, R. L. (2015). ArtsIN: Arts Integration and Infusion framework. *Early Childhood Education Journal, 43*(4), 289–298. https://doi.org/10.1007/s10643-014-0636-7

Hetland, L. (2013). Connecting creativity to understanding. *Educational Leadership, 70*(5), 65–70.

Hetland, L., & Winner, E. (2000). The arts and academic achievement: What the evidence shows. *Journal of Aesthetic Education, 102*(5), 3–6. https://doi.org/10.1080/10632910109600008

Hetland, L., Winner, E., Veenema, S., & Sheridan, K. M. (2013). *Studio thinking 2: The real benefits of visual arts education*. Teachers College Press.

Hunter-Doniger, T. (2018). *Creative arts in education: Experiencing the arts* (2nd ed.). Kendall Hunt.

Hunter-Doniger, T. (2019). STEAM education afterschool and summer learning. *STEAM Journal, 4*(1), Article 12. https://scholarship.claremont.edu/steam/vol4/iss1/12

Hunter-Doniger, T. (2021). Early childhood STEAM: The joy of creativity, autonomy, and play. *Art Education, 74*(4), 22–27. https://doi.org/10.1080/00043125.2021.1905419

Hunter-Doniger, T. (2022). Creativity, autonomy, and play: Key factors to child-centred approaches and STEAM. *ChildLinks*, (3), 16–20. https://knowledge.barnardos.ie/bitstream/handle/20.500.13085/863/childlinks_issue_3_2022_0725.pdf?sequence=3

Hunter-Doniger, T., & Sydow, L. (2016). A journey from STEM to STEAM: A middle school case study. *Clearing House, 89*(4–5), 159–166. https://doi.org/10.1080/00098655.2016.1170461

Jao, L., & Radakovic, N. (Eds.). (2017). *Transdisciplinarity in mathematics education: Blurring disciplinary boundaries*. Springer International. https://doi.org/10.1007/978-3-319-63624-5

Johnson, C. C. (2012). Implementation of STEM education policy: Challenges, progress, and lessons learned. *School Science and Mathematics, 112*(1), 45–55. https://doi.org/10.1111/j.1949-8594.2011.00110.x

Lowenfeld, V. (1957). *Creative and mental growth* (3rd ed.). Macmillan.

National Art Education Association. (2022, March). *Position statement on STEAM education*. (Original work published 2014). https://www.arteducators.org/advocacy-policy/articles/552-naea-position-statement-on-steam-education

Peterson, T. K. (Ed.). (2013). *Expanding minds and opportunities: Leveraging the power of afterschool and summer learning for student success*. Collaborative Communications Group.

Riley, S. M. (2012). *STEAM point: A guide to integrating science, technology, engineering, the arts, and mathematics through the Common Core*. CreateSpace.

Sandberg, A., & Ärlemalm-Hagsér, E. (2011). The Swedish national curriculum: Play and learning with fundamental values in focus. *Australasian Journal of Early Childhood, 36*(1), 44–50. https://doi.org/10.1177/183693911103600108

Sousa, D. A., & Pilecki, T. (2013). *From STEM to STEAM: Using brain-compatible strategies to integrate the arts*. Corwin.

Taylor, E., & Taylor, P. C. (2017). Breaking down enlightenment silos: From STEM to ST^{2}EAM education, and beyond. In L. A. Bryan & K. G. Tobin (Eds.), *13 questions: Reframing education's conversation: Science* (pp. 455–472). Peter Lang. https://doi.org/10.3726/b11305

Vygotsky, L. S. (1974). *The psychology of art*. MIT Press.

Wells, N. M. (2000). At home with nature: Effects of "greenness" on children's cognitive functioning. *Environment and Behavior, 32*(6), 775–795. https://doi.org/10.1177/00139160021972793

SECTION I
Conducive Environments for STEAM Education

This section provides methods, strategies, and environments that are conducive to STEAM education. Each chapter discusses how teachers can take advantage of the interdisciplinary nature of STEAM. The authors in this section illuminate the pedagogical environments where STEAM can thrive. These chapters embrace STEAM education and its interdisciplinary characteristics, delivering authentic examples of how STEAM can be implemented in schools. The chapters lay a potential foundational structure of how a sustainable program could be put in place by revealing what researchers and in-service teachers have found to be integral to the STEAM learning process.

Art Infusion: Ideal Conditions for STEAM

Tracey Hunter-Doniger

> " *Life is a great tapestry. The individual is only an insignificant thread in an immense and miraculous pattern.*
>
> —Albert Einstein

Visual art in an art-infused school is the foundational fiber of the woven tapestry of education. The arts can metaphorically be the weft through which nonart disciplines are woven (Brown, 2007; Efland, 2002). Each interlacing thread creates an intricate yet resilient configuration that is not only aesthetic but also functional. The art-infused classroom creates an educational environment that embraces visual arts as an essential equal to all disciplines through a wide variety of approaches. This environment provides the ideal conditions for science, technology, engineering, art, and math (STEAM) education to be embedded within a curriculum. STEAM education is a viable pedagogical approach to achieving positive student outcomes, such as engagement, comprehension, and retention of skills and content (Wolf et al., 2007). In response to the trend in STEAM education, the National Art Education Association (NAEA, 2014/2022) established four criteria for STEAM education: valuing all STEAM disciplines equally, implementing a wide variety of approaches, encouraging creativity and innovation, and acknowledging the rigor found in visual art (Hunter-Doniger, 2020). These criteria serve to ensure that the arts and artistic ways of thinking have equal value as the STEM subjects. Artistic ways of thinking and visual arts content are fundamental and valuable components of high-quality STEAM education (Guyotte et al., 2014; Wynn & Harris, 2012). The benefits of STEAM include increased interest and engagement in STEM subjects and connectivity with artistic behaviors (Baxter, 2014; Hetland et al., 2013; Winner & Cooper, 2000). Indeed, in 2015 the president of the United States verified this when he signed into law the Every Student Succeeds Act, providing new opportunities for arts education, including STEAM (U.S. Department of Education, 2015). According to research, students learn better when the arts are a central part of their curriculum (Baxter, 2014; Hetland et al., 2013; Winner & Cooper, 2000). Yet for the model of a STEAM education to be successful, it must be embedded into a school that not only acknowledges the rigor in the arts but also encourages creativity and innovation. Although claims for a causal link between art and student academic achievement have provided no evidence, further investigation is needed to determine what happens when art is the central focus of education (Bequette & Bequette, 2012; Winner & Cooper, 2000).

Hart Hall Art Infused Magnet School (HHA), a pseudonym chosen for the purposes of this paper, was not a STEAM school, but its interconnection to the arts allowed for a seamless transition to a STEAM program. This chapter first defines art infusion and provides an overview of HHA and the STEAM program in which it participated. It then explores how this school offered ideal conditions for STEAM development. Finally, the chapter discusses how replicating these conditions can benefit schools considering a STEAM education.

Definitions and Benefits of Art Infusion

No consensus for a definition of art infusion exists, yet similarities are evident among the various definitions presented (Baxter, 2014; Hartle et al., 2014). Drawing upon these similarities, in this chapter, *art infusion* is defined as a model empowering the arts in education by employing three strategies: (1) all disciplines are regarded equally in pedagogy, content, and assessment; (2) collaboration exists between art and generalist educators; and (3) students are encouraged to delve deeper into subjects through art.

Art infusion depends on a strong and equal collaborative effort between the art and nonart teachers to provide a dynamic shift in how academic subjects are presented and received by students (Hartle et al., 2014). This type of teaching allows for a deeper understanding of both art and nonart subjects (Rubin, 2017). Art infusion places the arts on equal ground with all disciplines in order to enhance the learning of each and is realized through equal assessments of the arts and nonart material. *Equal assessment* refers to the practice of evaluating the art standards as rigorously as the nonart standards through assessments such as quizzes, rubrics, and written artist statements, which demonstrate understanding as well as self-evaluation. Art and generalist teachers must maintain meaningful and ongoing collaboration to provide art-infused lessons. Working in an environment where the arts are valued enhances teachers' professionalism, efficacy, flexibility, energy, openness, and content knowledge (Vitulli et al., 2013). As teachers learn new strategies, gain confidence, and become more knowledgeable, they become more qualified within their profession. Consequently, their students would benefit from a higher quality education where their individual needs are met, and they are motivated to learn.

Art infusion allows students to do more than just memorize content; it encourages them to search for it, find it, make their own meaning out of it, and apply this newfound knowledge in ways that interest them (Hunter-Doniger, 2015). When the art-infused classroom is operating successfully, lessons are student centered as they construct their own knowledge; thus, students have multiple ways of reaching their potential, providing each child with the necessary skills, tools, and strategies for success (Friend & Bursuck, 2012). The successful implementation of art infusion takes place in an environment where students' diverse needs are met in a single classroom via tasks of varying, flexible grouping, different levels of scaffolding, and differentiated evaluation. Infusing the arts into schools gets students questioning, reflecting, problem solving, and thinking more critically (Walker et al., 2011). Similarly, to maintain a successful STEAM education, students must be proficient in creative problem solving facilitated by a strong visual arts education (NAEA, 2014/2022). In this way, art infusion naturally shares some of the basic ideas and principles of STEAM education, thereby benefiting both art and nonart subject areas as the arts and artistic pedagogies are in place for the STEM subjects to be woven among them.

Overview of HHA

As a researcher from a nearby university, I was told of HHA's success and decided to investigate. I have since been embedded in this school for 3 years and have logged 420+ hours. To understand how the school functions, I interviewed the principal and sought out teachers to define specific benefits and challenges of teaching at this school.

HHA began its journey more than 10 years ago with educators passionate about the arts in education. These educators formulated a plan for a school that mandated both the curriculum and teachers would have an ongoing commitment to the arts. Enrollment was to be determined by lottery rather than auditions to ensure that the student body would be representative of the school district population's socioeconomic and ethnic/racial composition. The success of this school is demonstrated through the applicants each year, with nearly 500 students requesting one of the approximately 50 student openings annually. In addition, HHA continually scores above the state average on statewide standardized testing, and it has received multiple awards in art education.

These achievements could arguably be a direct result of embracing an art-infused curriculum. Evidence for this argument is that schools in the same district with the same demographics rate in the top 30% to 50% of the state, while HHA rates in the top 10% (South Carolina Department of Education, n.d.). Among these comparable schools, the variable factor is that HHA incorporates the arts into all aspects of the learning environment throughout the school day. While other factors could be attributed to the success of HHA, it is undeniable that the arts play an important role. All students attend weekly curricular classes in each of the four arts areas (visual arts, music, dance, and theatre) and participate in one of two school musical performances each year. Not only has HHA scored consistently among the top schools in the state for standardized testing for the past 7 years, it has also received recognition with national and state awards for excellence, such as the National Blue Ribbon award, the Kennedy Center's Creative Ticket Award, and the Governor's Award for outstanding achievement to the arts.

Yet such excellence does come at a price. According to the teachers I interviewed, being a teacher at HHA is demanding. One teacher commented, "Teachers not only have to learn their own standards, they have to learn the arts and arts teachers have to learn six levels of all subject [sic]. It means lots of extra work and lots of cooperation between teachers." Another teacher mentioned that scheduling is always contentious because there has to be a lot of give and take when all subject areas are given equal time; she stated, "ELA does not necessarily rule as in other schools."

Through my hours of observations, I found that at HHA the arts are not used as a showpiece or a prop to engage children in learning; rather, they are valued and assessed in tandem with the nonart subjects. My observations and interviews confirmed that arts teachers are viewed not only as equal educators, but also as leaders in providing a dynamic learning environment through the arts. Because of its superior art and academic achievement, I chose HHA for the STEAM Project research.

The STEAM Project

During the 2014 spring semester, the HHA kindergarten classes participated in the STEAM Project, educational research focused on oceanography by infusing visual arts, math, and engineering into the curriculum. During the 3-month STEAM Project, students became familiar with correlations among the disciplines through STEAM lessons. Using 10 lessons that I developed, I introduced kindergarteners to the ecology of the ocean through art techniques while simultaneously teaching them about math and science, culminating in a field trip to a public beach at the Atlantic Ocean. There students became researchers, collecting data by sorting and classifying found objects; they then together became artists by using the found objects to create works of art. Figure 1 depicts the art lesson on radial design and patterns in math using materials found in the ocean. As evidenced through teacher, parent, and student surveys, this experiment in STEAM was well received, and in the 2015 spring semester, a second STEAM Project was launched. Collaborating with the art

Figure 1. A radial design visual arts lesson infusing math, science, and design for the STEAM Project.

and kindergarten teachers, the second STEAM Project was themed around flora and fauna and the art of Andy Goldsworthy. Similar to the first STEAM Project, kindergarten students were taught lessons in class, then used that knowledge when recording species in their field sketchbooks. This included creating observational paintings, gathering materials in the forest to create works of art, and digitally photographing them, similar to the work of Goldsworthy, a natural landscape artist (see Figure 2). As the STEAM Projects progressed, it became evident that certain unique qualities of this school were essential and brought to the forefront as viable conditions for STEAM: (1) taking time to value the arts, (2) ensuring 100% buy-in for the arts, (3) encouraging collaboration between the arts and nonarts, and (4) reinforcing the rigor of the arts through community partners. These conditions are described in the following sections.

Taking Time to Value the Arts

A false divide between the art and nonart subjects was established more than a century ago (Daugherty, 2013). In order for a STEAM educational program to be received well, the walls of this divide must be broken. In an art-infused school, the walls of this facade are not only broken; a solid structure of art and academic excellence is built from the rubble. This sort of progressive thinking takes time—time for planning, time for students to complete work, and time for assessment. For example, HHA's (n.d.) vision statement is

Figure 2. *Bird's Nest.* A Goldsworthy-inspired student made a nature sculpture and took digital images of the process.

"to continuously advance as an exemplary model of arts infusion dedicated to artistic and academic excellence." This does not happen overnight. HHA has discovered that art and generalist teachers need to have a common planning time to design unique lessons that draw all areas of the curriculum together. Once a week after students leave, various grade levels meet with the arts teachers for an hour to collaborate on designing lessons. These work sessions are intense; there is no time for idle conversation, and teachers walk in the door ready to work. These lessons are then effectively and cooperatively taught as a team during a designated art-infusion time. The art-infused lessons are in addition to the regular art schedule.

Time is one of the biggest challenges for teachers. One teacher said that, although students are given more opportunities in art, they might not have enough time for many in-depth projects that could be carried out over several weeks, especially for 3rd- through 5th-grade students. Another teacher commented that, in addition to the time given to plan and execute art lessons, much time is given to assessing the arts: "There is no time for fluff." This dedication and commitment to the arts allowed HHA to transition to a STEAM program more easily. Teachers desiring to ensure significant achievement by using a STEAM curriculum rely on having the time to plan, infuse, and implement the arts on a consistent basis.

Ensuring 100% Buy-In to the Arts

The HHA's (n.d.) mission is "to provide dynamic learning with quality arts experiences as an essential component of the curriculum." To bring this mission to fruition, everyone must buy in to this philosophy 100%, including teachers, parents, students, and administrators. This does not come easily given the pressure to succeed on standardized tests. Daugherty (2013) contended that schools sometimes view art as a luxury, and a sense of elitism may exist when clinging to the idea that art should be practiced exclusively by the privileged. As I observed, at HHA, art is not seen as a luxury or an elite privilege; it is part of the interwoven makeup of the school and is accessible to all. During one interview, the principal stated that 100% buy-in is a necessity for the school's overall success. The arts are an integral component of the daily environment and school culture and, with extensive art infusion and 100% buy-in, HHA provided the ideal conditions for STEAM education with a positive mindset ready for curricular crossover.

Encouraging Collaboration Between the Arts and Nonarts

An effective component of art infusion is collaboration, which encourages creativity and innovation for both teachers and students. Art infusion involves networking between art and generalist teachers (Smilan & Miraglia, 2009). Collaboration is key because it allows for everyone involved to share ideas and experiences relevant to art infusion, resulting in enhanced lessons and shared knowledge. Collaboration helps relieve some of the pressure of developing lessons in isolation, thereby providing an atmosphere of creativity and innovation for teachers. At HHA, this typically results in team-taught art-infusion lessons, making it easier to catch students before they fall through the cracks simply because there are so many different individuals paying attention to student learning outcomes (Vitulli et al., 2013). I observed a lesson collaboratively taught with the art and generalist teacher. The teachers took turns explaining the lesson and assisting students as they explored how to construct the most durable structure and why certain materials work better than others (Figures 3 and 4). During this lesson, it would be difficult for an outsider to identify the art teacher from the generalist teacher. Regarding such collaboration, one teacher explained that

> teachers have to be willing to give up some of what they want to teach in order to make the school work. It takes a special kind of teacher—one who is creative, cooperative, and organized enough to balance everything the school brings with it.

Through these collaborative efforts, HHA teachers have become better prepared to implement creative lessons, providing students with an environment that exemplifies STEAM and maximizes student potential.

STEAM Education: An Interdisciplinary Look at Art in the Curriculum

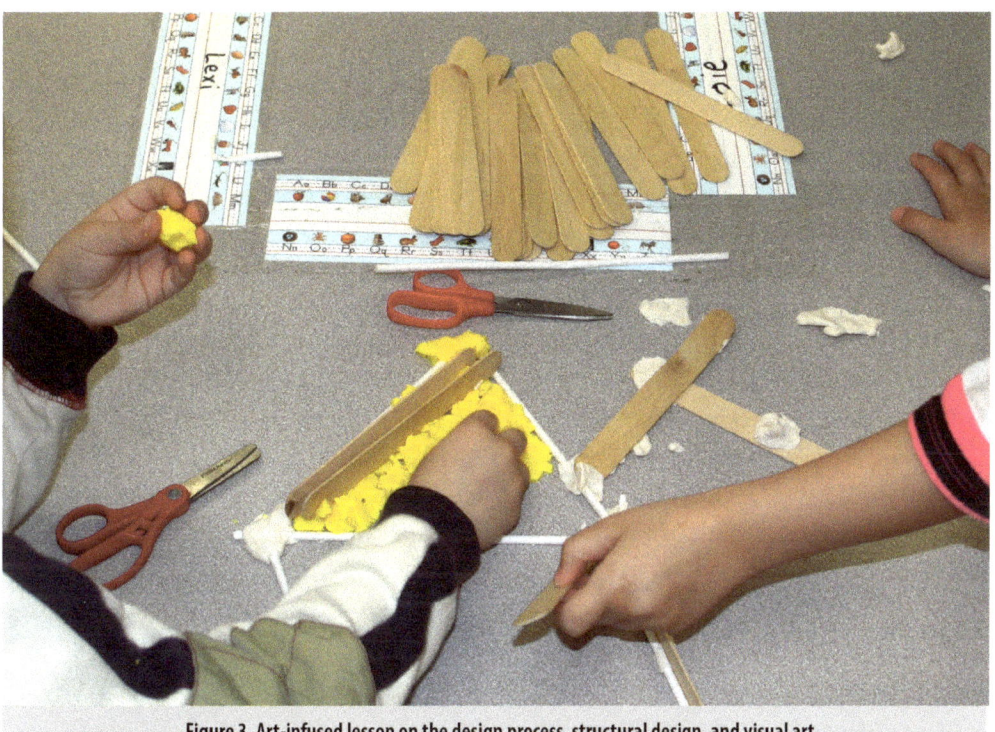

Figure 3. Art-infused lesson on the design process, structural design, and visual art.

Figure 4. Art-infused engineering lesson planned by the art teacher and kindergarten generalist teacher.

Reinforcing the Rigor in the Arts Through Community Partnerships

Rigor is defined as creating an environment in which each student is expected to learn at high levels and demonstrates learning at high levels (Blackburn, 2008). HHA reinforces the rigor found in visual arts through partnerships within the community. One example demonstrating rigor in the arts is the school's artist-in-residence program, which was designed specifically for each grade level to explore various art careers with local artists who come to the school for a 2-week period. These projects have included ceramic self-portraits, playwriting, and drumming. The children replicate the technique, craftsmanship, and high skill level needed for these careers as they learn the rigor of artists' expertise. Another example of reinforcing rigor through community partnerships is HHA's first induction into STEAM through the partnerships in the previously described STEAM Projects. During these projects, multilayered and rigorous lessons challenged students to explore art through STEM subjects and vice versa. Because HHA has been conditioned to sustain community partnerships through artists-in-residence and local universities, the rigor found in the arts is bolstered, creating a prime environment for STEAM.

Reflection of Art Infusion and STEAM

Art-infused schools like HHA provide the ideal environmental conditions, including a reciprocal dynamic, in which STEM subjects can embrace a STEAM curriculum. These conditions are not unique to HHA and can be found in most art-infused schools providing a ready-made platform for instituting a STEAM program. In this chapter, I have identified four essential components of successful STEAM instructional approaches: (1) taking time to value the arts, (2) cultivating 100% buy-in into the arts, (3) encouraging collaboration between discipline areas, and (4) reinforcing the rigor of the arts through community partnerships. Although each school's conditions differ, replicating these conditions can benefit schools considering a STEAM curriculum. When considering STEAM education, schools should look to art-infused schools as the model for the ideal conditions for success. Working toward the daily practice of these teaching approaches will create the right conditions for embracing STEAM education. Such pedagogies encourage a view of the arts that will put it on par with other academic subject areas.

Moving forward, art-infused schools should be further investigated to define school scheduling and assessment strategies that could also benefit STEAM education. The findings have the potential to reveal substantial evidence for transitioning to the artistic mindset needed for STEAM. Just like a Neolithic tapestry, art is part of the fiber of an art-infused education that cannot be separated. STEAM education brings to light the notion that the arts have always—and will continue to be—fundamental to student learning.

Author's Note: Permission for all images were obtained through signed IRB consent.

Publication Note: This was originally published in Art Education *as Hunter-Doniger, T. (2018). Art infusion: Ideal conditions for STEAM.* Art Education, 71(2), 22–27. *Permission to reprint was granted from Taylor and Francis.*

Tracey Hunter-Doniger *is an associate professor and the department chair of teacher education at the College of Charleston in South Carolina. She specializes in arts in education. She began her career as a public school teacher, a role in which she served for 15 years. Her central research focuses on STEAM education, art infusion, and forest schools.*

References

Baxter, K. (2014). A convergence of three: The reflexive capacity of art practice, curriculum design, and pedagogy. *Art Education*, *67*(6), 28–34. https://doi.org/10.1080/00043125.2014.11519295

Bequette, J. W., & Bequette, M. B. (2012). A place for art and design education in the STEM conversation. *Art Education*, *65*(2), 40–47. https://doi.org/10.1080/00043125.2012.11519167

Blackburn, B. R. (2008). *Rigor is not a four letter word*. Eye on Education.

Brown, S. L. (2007). An arts-integrated approach for elementary level students. *Childhood Education*, *83*(3), 172–174.

Daugherty, M. K. (2013). The prospect of an "A" in STEM education. *Journal of STEM Education*, *14*(2), 10–15.

Efland, E. D. (2002). *Art and cognition: Integrating the visual arts in the curriculum*. Teachers College Press.

Friend, M., & Bursuck, W. D. (2012). *Including students with special needs: A practical guide for classroom teachers*. Pearson Education.

Guyotte, K. W., Sochacka, N. W., Constantino, T. E., Walther, J., & Kellam, N. N. (2014). STEAM as social practice: Cultivating creativity in transdisciplinary spaces. *Art Education*, *67*(6), 12–19. https://doi.org/10.1080/00043125.2014.11519293

Hart Hall Art Infused Magnet School. (n.d.). *Mission, vision, core values, & goals*. https://www.bcsdschools.net/o/hha/page/vision-mission-core-values-goals

Hartle, L. C., Pinciotti, P., & Gorton, R. L. (2014). ArtsIN: Arts Integration and Infusion framework. *Early Childhood Education Journal*, *43*(4), 289–298. https://doi.org/10.1007/s10643-014-0636-7

Hetland, L., Winner, E., Veenema, S., & Sheridan, K. M. (2013). *Studio thinking 2: The real benefits of visual arts education*. Teachers College Press.

Hunter-Doniger, T. (2015). An artist-in-residence: Teaching with a sense of urgency. *International Journal of Education Through Art*, *11*(2), 229–243. https://doi.org/10.1386/eta.11.2.229_1

Hunter-Doniger, T. (2020). The A^2 Curriculum ARTvocacy and Autonomy: Giving a voice to the next generation. *Art Education*, *73*(4), 37–43. https://doi.org/10.1080/00043125.2020.1746160

National Art Education Association. (2022, March). *Position statement on STEAM education*. (Original work published 2014). https://www.arteducators.org/advocacy-policy/articles/552-naea-position-statement-on-steam-education

Rubin, C. M. (2017, December 6). The global search for education: More arts please. *The Blog*. HuffPost. http://www.huffingtonpost.com/c-m-rubin/the-global-search-for-edu_9_b_932670.html

Smilan, C., & Miraglia, K. M. (2009). Art teachers as leaders of authentic art integration. *Art Education*, *62*(6), 39–45. https://doi.org/10.1080/00043125.2009.11519044

South Carolina Department of Education. (n.d.). *Report cards*. Retrieved September 1, 2017, from http://ed.sc.gov/data/report-cards

U.S. Department of Education. (2015). *Every Student Succeeds Act of 2015, Pub. L. No. 114-95*. http://www.help.senate.gov/imo/media/doc/ESSA FINAL Conference Report.pdf

References continued

Vitulli, P., Santoli, S. P., & Fresne, J. (2013). Arts in education: Professional development integrating the arts and collaborating with schools and community. *International Journal of Pedagogies and Learning, 8*(1), 45–52. https://doi.org/10.5172/ijpl.2013.8.1.45

Walker, E., Tabone, C., & Weltsek, G. (2011). When achievement data meet drama and arts integration. *Language Arts, 88*(5), 365–372.

Winner, E., & Cooper, M. (2000). Mute those claims, no evidence (yet) for a causal link between art and student and academic achievement. *Journal of Aesthetic Education, 34*(3/4), 11–75. https://doi.org/10.2307/3333637

Wolf, D. P., Bransom, J., & Denson, K. (2007). *More than measuring: Program evaluation as an opportunity to build the capacity of communities.* Big Thought.

Wynn, T., & Harris, J. (2012). Toward a STEM + arts curriculum: Creating the teacher team. *Art Education, 65*(5), 42–47. https://doi.org/10.1080/00043125.2012.11519191

STEAM TEAM:
A Cross-Curricular Adventure

Pamelia D. Valentine

In a galaxy far, far away.… Well, actually, in a rural school district in the State of Washington, 25 miles from the capital, Olympia, there is a town named Shelton. Within the town limits, there is a school system that has two science teachers and one art teacher, who were very interested in the cross-curricular connections between science, technology, engineering, art, and math (STEAM). The 800 junior high students, 1,680 high school students, and 4th graders from the five elementary schools in the Shelton School District have profited from this collegial alliance by the creation of a STEAM program that is now district-wide. Throughout this chapter, I use metaphors from the Star Wars series to lightheartedly explain this adventure.

The 4th-grade students visited and rotated through the classrooms of the CTE teachers and were led through a lesson by the high school students who were taking the class. In my jewelry class, the students made copper bracelets from large-gauge copper wire. The wearable metals and jewelry design students taught the entire lesson, from safety in the jewelry studio to completion of the project. There were six 4th-grade students who worked with six teams of high school students. We had a different group every Friday and taught 30 students how to make copper bracelets. These same students rotated through our high school foods, biomedical, carpentry, agricultural and environmental science, and welding classes.

The benefit of introducing 4th-grade students to this model at an early age is that they are primed and ready to understand how the subjects they study now and in their future educational journeys all have cross-curricular overlap, so learning in one area automatically transfers to another area. This helps them understand how their lives and interests can all work together to enhance their learning. By the time the students get to 8th grade, they have a foundational vocabulary, and they are prepared to take their learning to the X-Wing Fighter stage.

Where Did This Originate?

But where did the interest in these cross-curricular connections spring from, one might reasonably posit? The STEM education revolution can be traced back to American biologist Judith Ramaley, who first used the acronym STEM when she was assistant director of the education and human resources directorate at the National Science Foundation from 2001 to 2004. The acronym had previously been SMET, for science, mathematics, engineering, and technology; Ramaley rearranged the words to form the STEM acronym in 2001 (National Science Foundation, n.d.). The first explicit mention of STEM—using the acronym—seems to be in 2005. Representative Vernon Ehlers, a Republican from Michigan, and Representative Mark Udall, a Democrat from Colorado, had set up the STEM Caucus in Congress (Chute, 2009).

The official founder of the STEAM initiative is undoubtedly Georgette Yakman, who, in addition to raising the idea of adding the arts to the STEM acronym, has conducted research and practicum since 2006 based on researching the formal way subjects work together and correspond to the global socioeconomic world (Yakman, 2008). Her work formed the basis for the integrative approach to arts inclusion with the traditional STEM subjects.

In 2009, President Obama announced the Educate to Innovate initiative. He further endorsed STEM in his State of the Union address on January 25, 2011. He thus ignited a movement to teach students 21st-century skills to become more competitive with other nations in the fields of STEM and called for the recruitment of 100,000 new STEM teachers as well as the reauthorization of the Secondary Education Act. On December 15, 2015, President Obama signed the Every Student Succeeds Act into law. Millions of dollars in funding from public and private sectors have since flooded in for teacher training, grants, research, and school programs that promote STEM. In the past decade, U.S. schools have seen an increase in math and science course offerings, higher expectations for testing, and an evolution of project-based learning using STEM as a framework for exploration.

Literature Review

STEM did not end with this presidential push. Neuhauser's 2015 article in the *U.S. News and World Report* cites several studies that showed that racial and gender gaps actually *increased* with the advent of STEM programs. There is evidence to substantiate that STEM schools aren't producing amazing results. One study compared non-STEM and STEM schools in Florida and North Carolina and found no evidence demonstrating higher scores for students in STEM schools (Hansen, 2014). So if the goal was to improve math skills, that just didn't happen—or at least, it was not tracked back to the STEM classes. Racial and gender gaps have continued to increase, possibly because the STEM programs did not include as much diversity as they should have. There was also no stated art component, which may have given students the opportunity to connect the learning through illustrating and designing how STEM applied to their own lives. Without the component of authentic application, students may not have been able to apply their learning to real life. "It's not revelatory to say that the arts can engage kids. But that engagement can also be leveraged to boost academic growth and improve discipline seems like a secret that really needs to be revealed" (Nobori, 2012, para. 3). This certainly is a secret, in my mind, that needs to be revealed and acted upon.

In tracking the inclusion of the arts into the STEM paradigm, it is undeniable that much of the movement has been headed up by John Maeda, president of the Rhode Island School of Design (RISD), who began his endorsement of including the arts in STEM as early as 2008 and spoke in 2016 at Concordia on this topic. He posits that the arts (including liberal arts, fine arts, music, design thinking, and language arts) are critical components to innovation, and that the concept is not about giving equal or more time to STEM or arts, but to incorporate, where appropriate, the artistic and design-related skills and thinking processes to student learning in STEM. Maeda was instrumental in creating the STEM to STEAM movement during his time at RISD, and his main argument for including the arts was that design thinking and creativity are essential ingredients for innovation.

This is the crux of why it is so important to include the arts as we work to stimulate that innovation in our students. Student designers have to think, plan, and execute their ideas in supportive but autonomous environments. The artist isn't just completing a lesson and "jumping through the hoops" but actually taking real-world risks and solving problems in sophisticated ways. Every time that happens, student growth is maximized, and the benefits become internalized. This is REAL learning at a Jedi Master level!

Babette Allina (2018), the director of government and corporate relations at RISD, states that there are unlimited real-world applications in art and design that provide new models for creative problem solving and interdisciplinary learning. Discussions about including visual arts in cross-collaborative efforts to engage and enhance learning are strengthened by this sort of advocacy, and this research bolsters the arts' inclusion and continued efforts to encourage the application of a shared curriculum.

According to Segarra et al. (2018):

> STEAM has shown great potential for making science (and science professions) accessible and relatable to students. STEAM learning is especially effective when students are cast in the role of artist and scientist rather than in that of audience. A successful template for STEAM-for-accessibility has been to first facilitate students' scientific participation or discovery, and then facilitate the students' reflection on their scientific experience through the creation of visual art—often a drawing or painting. (p. 2)

This research and information didn't actually cause an epiphany, but it was so exciting to me that I immediately began sharing it with all my fellow teachers! The science teachers were very receptive to this research and wanted to see if the arts could increase engagement with *their* students. This interest and desire to work together spawned a new approach that coherently connected student learning, and thus, the Shelton School District STEAM Team was born.

Our Curriculum Connections

As with any research, there should be a connection to the curriculum for it to be valuable to students. Through STEAM, students were able to make connections to color and light, working with scale, and experimenting with proportion.

Color and Light

In our exploration of STEAM education concepts, we compared the lessons we were already teaching separately and discovered many natural connections between our subject areas. This led to the creation of our first cross-curricular lesson: "Seeing Color; Using Color." In this lesson, the science teachers used a color and light lab to teach about the visual light spectrum while I, the art teacher, taught about pigment color. We teach this lesson concurrently with the students who are all taking science as well as the students who have chosen art as an elective class.

The lesson focuses on the comparison and use of color in both the visible light spectrum and in pigment usage. The science students who have not chosen art as their elective class get visual arts exposure in their science classes while the science students who *have* chosen art as their elective receive the lesson in both science and art classes. Sometimes this discovery of the connection between science and art leads to students signing up for art classes for the very first time. Teaching interconnected lessons mirrors real-life experiences, in that we all learn more efficiently when we understand that learning does not occur in a vacuum of bits and pieces but as a broad collection of facts and reason that creates a complete picture.

Working With Scale

As we maxed into warp speed to seal the alliance, we discovered that our subjects both use math to calculate scale! Scale is really important in art and architecture, and I had developed a unit of study in which my students created scaled houses and researched architectural styles common to our community. In science classes, the students were studying energy efficiency and the effects of global warming. Their project required them to build efficient housing for penguins to save them from a dangerous climate.

When we combined these lessons, our students built housing for the penguins based on their favorite and most efficient architectural styles. They used the architecture lessons and scale building they learned in art class along with information about heat convection and conduction to make the most efficient houses for their little ice-cube penguins.

Working With Proportion

Much like Han Solo, our enthusiasm translated into action, so we tackled the shared topic of proportion! We knew that kids enjoyed friendly competition, and we loved the idea of having them use prior knowledge to solve problems before actual instruction. In that spirit, we created two contests that used proportion as the main focus of the competition. The science classes created and launched paper rockets that students built with no prior instruction, while the art students created and raced sailboats before they learned about how proportion might affect the efficiency of the vessels.

This led to amazing discoveries! One group designed and built a beautiful rocket with huge asymmetrical fins—it crashed within 2 feet of takeoff. Sailboats with giant sails sunk gloriously when the "wind" was turned on. The crashes and soggy ships led to immediate understanding and appreciation for the concept of proportion in student projects going forward.

Change Is Inevitable

Just as our STEAM Team was getting used to facilitating cross-curricular lessons and beginning to incorporate technology and engineering principles into our lessons, we got news of changes to the district grade configurations at the junior high school level. Our shared planning time and professional learning groups that occurred twice a month at our junior high school had fueled our ability to collaborate and had given us the opportunity to develop this curriculum. But now things would have to change.

Instead of having our Grade 8–9 configuration, these students would move to a brand new high school building, and the 7th grade would come up to form a new junior high grade band. The school where we had all been working together for nearly 2 decades would be a 7–8 junior high and the high school would service Grades 9–12. It was as though we had been abruptly transferred to the planet of Hoth! Adaptations had to be made quickly in order to preserve our STEAM Alliance.

We decided that our best route would be to focus our instruction on a framework of career technical education (CTE). The journey to that new realm began with intense training and classes for all of us. The increased budget gained by taking this path was only part of our reasoning for pursuing it. The increased flexibility for our students and the opportunity to continue our collaboration was the main driver. We were excited to learn that students could earn occupational credits by taking CTE classes, and they could join nationwide clubs and participate in competitions and learning outside of school that would build them up as individuals and could set them up for career certifications before graduating from high school.

Luckily, we didn't have to go to Dagobah to be trained, because our local community college agreed to do CTE classes for our school district. We completed our classes to qualify as CTE educators in 1 year of great transformation. I moved to the new high school, and all my art classes became CTE focused. My science colleagues gained their CTE certifications, and a new adventure unfolded before us as we rose to embrace the changes that teaching CTE classes would bring.

We had to write frameworks to comply with the CTE curriculum while still teaching the standards in our subjects. We were required to create our own professional advisory committees to help us with the career components, and we needed to join or develop a club for our students to participate in an extracurricular activity. We ultimately decided to focus our efforts on the SkillsUSA model for our club because we felt it offered the most advantages for our students and emphasized industries that focused on making and creating. We also began to work with new colleagues outside our original group of three educators, including robotics teachers at the junior high and high school and environmental science teachers at the high school.

Our curriculum underwent many changes as we developed our new approach. The science teachers stayed at the junior high school and worked with the 7th–8th graders to create a STEAM garden; I focused my drawing classes on botanical drawing from nature featuring the work of Elizabeth Blackwell, Arthur Harry Church, Lee Adams, and Janice Glimn-Lacy; we used the STEAM garden 2–3 days a week for observational drawing. The science teachers started a composting program, while the CTE high school art classes created logo designs to use on the compost containers.

The garden was collaboratively designed by the high school art students and built by the junior high science students. Students used STEAM to measure, research, design, build, and create this garden, which sits between our two schools and is accessible to our shared classes. We created the STEAM Team entirely on our own, and we sustain our teaching practice by doing frequent presentations in our district, at school board meetings, at our state arts conference, and at regional as well as national conferences. We believe in the power of STEAM because it has made our students more inquisitive and engaged than they were before we put this group together. Now students in the 7th and 8th grades are drawing the plants they have grown in their garden! The high school students are using online plant identification applications to expound upon the plants they have seen on hikes and around their own homes.

Composting has become a regular part of what our students do at home and at school. Many of our shared students recognized that they were creating their own cross-curricular connections, and they have shared that those connections led to better problem-solving skills and an improved growth mindset. They take pride in their accomplishments and enthusiastically lead garden tours in their very own STEAM garden.

As our adventure has continuously unfolded, the high school CTE sculpture classes created scale models of water features and garden sculptures for the STEAM garden. They drew and built small models of their proposed water features, then presented their work to partner pairs in the high school class, and we sent the drawings and models to the junior high for the science students to select the design they liked the best.

The STEAM Team promoted and participated in the district-wide CTE introduction to the 4th graders in the Shelton School District. Students attended an all-day training session, where they worked with high school students in the STEAM garden and learned how STEAM subjects complement one another in a cross-curricular approach. Students had introductions to environmental science, they did a food lab, they did a project with our technology teacher, and they came to the art room to make jewelry with information after learning about the conductivity, melting point, and metallurgical aspects of copper. They sent notes of thanks to our classes, and it truly made an impact on them. They will not soon forget these activities, and we look forward to their participation next year. May the adventures and force of the STEAM Team always be with us!

Pamelia D. Valentine is a 21-year veteran teacher, the district STEAM leader, and a presenter of teaching and learning at the NAEA National Convention (2012–2019). Valentine is National Board Certified (Early Adolescent and Young Adult Visual Arts, 2006), renewed (2015), and certified in CTE (2016) Business Management, Entrepreneurship, and Commercial Art.

References

Allina, B. (2018). The development of STEAM educational policy to promote student creativity and social empowerment. *Arts Education Policy Review*, *119*(2), 77–87. https://doi.org/10.1080/10632913.2017.1296392

Chute, E. (2009, February 10). STEM education is branching out. *Pittsburgh Post-Gazette*. https://www.post-gazette.com/news/education/2009/02/10/STEM-education-is-branching-out/stories/200902100165

Every Student Succeeds Act, 20 U.S.C. § 4642 (2015).

Hansen, M. (2014). Characteristics of schools successful in STEM: Evidence from two states' longitudinal data. *Journal of Educational Research*, *107*(5), 374–391. https://doi.org/10.1080/00220671.2013.823364

National Science Foundation. (n.d.). *History*. https://new.nsf.gov/about/history

Neuhauser, A. (2015, June 29). 2015 STEM index shows gender, racial gaps widen. *US News & World Report*. https://www.usnews.com/news/stem-index/articles/2015/06/29/gender-racial-gaps-widen-in-stem-fields

Nobori, M. (2012, August 29). *How the arts unlock the door to learning*. Edutopia. https://www.edutopia.org/stw-arts-integration-reform-overview

Obama, B. (2011). State of the Union 2011: Winning the future. *The White House*. https://obamawhitehouse.archives.gov/state-of-the-union-2011

Segarra, V. A., Natalizio, B., Falkenberg, C. V., Pulford, S., & Holmes, R. M. (2018). STEAM: Using the arts to train well-rounded and creative scientists. *Journal of Microbiology & Biology Education*, *19*(1). https://doi.org/10.1128/jmbe.v19i1.1360

Yakman, G. (2008, February 21–23). *STEAM education: An overview of creating a model of integrative education* [Conference presentation]. Pupils' Attitudes Towards Technology (PATT-19) Conference: Research on Technology, Innovation, Design & Engineering Teaching, Salt Lake City, Utah, USA.

SECTION II
Science

Scientists are known to be creative, as are artists. The common ideas, concepts, and methods are similar, as the chapters in this section demonstrate. In the chapter "What if We Crank It Up a Notch?," the author encourages interdisciplinary learning by allowing students to observe textures, patterns, and structures for visual literacy through the lens of an LCD microscope. "A Model for High School STEAM Activities: Science and Visual Art" focuses on how a high school art program can seamlessly meet the challenges of the industrial revolution. The chapter "The Process of Building an Art Installation With Plastic Waste" focuses on a school's collaboration with an environmental artist. Bringing an often-overlooked perspective to STEAM, "Culturally Relevant STEAM" utilizes storytelling as a way to make learning science relevant to students of color. Each chapter contributes firsthand experiences and scholarly investigation to interdisciplinary STEAM learning.

What if We Crank It Up a Notch?

Samantha Melvin

The Sounds of Discovery

The "oohs" and "aahs" were coming from all parts of the art classroom. Students were standing in small groups at tables, observing through microscopes, looking together at specimens. Their excitement was palpable. I felt a tug on my arm. A student came up to say, "Can you believe that a fly's legs are so hairy?" As students explored the different slides of specimens in the kits, they also recorded their observations in their research journals. They were laughing, talking, and excitedly switching specimen slides to discover new details under the lens. This aspect of developing their skills at looking, at observing nuances in color, texture, shape, and composition were naturally components of art class, yet they are also instrumental in scientific studies. Engaging students at the elementary level in interdisciplinary connections between art and science was at the core of learning in this unit. By fluidly moving between what they observe as artists and what they observe as scientists, the line between the two is blurred.

This chapter will investigate the implementation of LCD microscopes in an elementary art classroom to build observational skills in the first phase of student learning, leading to collaborative installations exploring art and science. The unit strengthens skills for visual literacy and expression through which nuances in design are perceived and shared. It teaches students to see! Students develop a heightened awareness of textures, patterns, and structures, integrating these observations into their individual works of art, which are then displayed in collaborative installations in the community.

This project addresses needs by engaging students in activities from across the curriculum, reinforcing skills in observation, expression, interpretation, and reflection. By "cranking up" the magnification of specimens in our environment, the observations informed 4th graders' motifs for their embossed foil work. Fifth-grade students created textured clay pots with lids that served as simple machines: synthesizing lessons of inclined planes and wedges into sculptural form to create a unique Rube Goldberg–inspired multilevel track for marbles. By implementing artistic problem solving and creative vision through collaborative effort, their work celebrated the exploration of art in science and of science in art!

Rendering Visual Possibilities

In *Educating Artistic Vision*, Elliot Eisner (1997) explored how artistic learning occurs in children. There are several factors at play, which include the following:

- Maintaining the ability to perceive the natural environment.

- Being able to imagine visual possibilities in the mind's eye.

- Managing materials so the medium is the vehicle through which expression can happen.

- Inventing schemas that will transform medium from an original image, idea, or feeling (Eisner, 1997).

Children, when given the opportunity, have the capacity to develop visual codes for their observations, transferring the image in their mind to 2D or 3D form. In turn, by associating verbiage to these renderings, students develop the capacity to describe what they see, sharing the experience with others. The learning is imbued with aesthetic knowing (Stewart & Walker, 2005) in which sensory experiences in metal and clay reflect the scientific observations through a lens. In this way, art and science are curriculum partners, allowing them to "contribute their own distinctive richness and complexity to the learning process as a whole" (Burton et al., 1999, p. 45; see also Stewart & Walker, 2005). Jointly, they foster aesthetic awareness.

Additionally, there is the component of "attentive living" (Gude, 2007, p. 10). The excitement of discovering new worlds through the lens of a microscope provides a visceral experience of awe at the natural world. Then we look closer! What comes next is the synthesis of such discoveries into other aspects of our learning, especially the creative. This process is also about the teacher relinquishing control over the product. There is a quality of the unknown, or as Olivia Gude frames it, a "not knowing" (2007, p. 14) for both the teacher and the student, which takes the scientific specimen on a journey through different lenses: that of a student–scientist, representing analytically what they see, and that of the student–artist, which is left to the imagination. The notion of playful, creative interpretation applies. The product is not guided by the teacher sample. Instead, it is spurred by the child's own divergent thinking, informed by observation, curiosity, and artistic exploration. Play is an important aspect here. Learning should be fun. The art classroom studio as a playground for learning opens up possibilities to exploration, experimentation, and collaboration, building a sense of mastery, creativity, and self-confidence (Resnick, 2018) as part of the learning experience.

By removing the silos of the different disciplines of art and science, problem solving and analytic and creative thinking merge, interconnecting and transferring concepts, much like how Leonardo da Vinci applied his thinking through practical experience. The seven principles derived from da Vinci's work guided our learning:

Curiosita - An insatiably curious approach to life and an unrelenting quest for continuous learning.

Dimostrazione - A commitment to test knowledge through experience, persistence, and a willingness to learn from mistakes.

Sensazione - The continual refinement of the senses, especially sight, as the means to enliven experience.

Sfumato - (literally "Going up in Smoke") A willingness to embrace ambiguity, paradox, and uncertainty.

Arte/Scienza - The development of the balance between science and art, logic and imagination. "Whole-brain" thinking.

Corporalita - The cultivation of grace, ambidexterity, fitness, and poise.

Connessione - A recognition of and appreciation for the interconnectedness of all things and phenomena. Systems thinking. (Gelb, 1998, pp. 2–4)

Da Vinci's journals displayed his process. His investigations were a way for him to find questions about the world around him. They serve as a springboard for an inquiry-based approach while also demonstrating how to make thinking visible in research journals. How does nature influence art? And further, how can nature influence design, like on machines?

Simple machines are also a component of elementary science standards. They provide an opportunity for students to study the effects of force, motion, and energy. The unit includes the work of Rube Goldberg, the cartoonist whose drawings have inspired playful and extensive simple machine contraptions. Even the band OK Go had a go with simple machines! Design and systems thinking tells us that our first iterations may be failures (American Association of the Advancement of Science, 1993), so we need to test our ideas and be flexible with the outcomes: "Students should become increasingly comfortable with developing ideas and analyzing the product: 'Does it work?'; 'Could I make it work better?'; 'Could I have used better materials?'" (ch. 3, sec. B). In the process, habits of mind are nurtured, which fit both the scientific and artistic realms (American Association for the Advancement of Science, 1990; Hetland et al., 2007). Artists develop craft, persist with the exploration of ideas, find ways to express them, and playfully test those ideas, despite the possibility of failure as part of the studio process. For scientists, similar dispositions exist, exhibited by da Vinci's *Dimostrazione*.

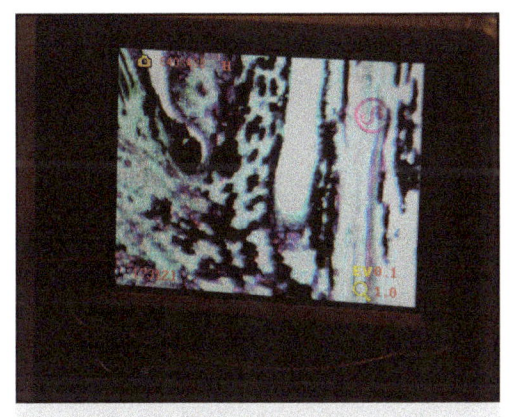

STEAM Education: An Interdisciplinary Look at Art in the Curriculum

Figure 1. WhatIfSpecimen.jpg. Microscopic view of a specimen. Photo by author.

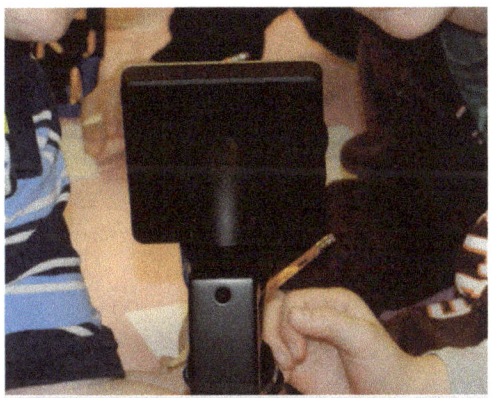

Figure 2. WhatIfMicroscope.jpg. Students viewing the specimens collaboratively. Photo by author.

Individual and Collaborative Work

In efforts to engage students in collaborative projects, some students lose the opportunity to showcase their individual ability within the context of group work. Often, it is the students for whom school is a struggle, whose abilities may not stand out like those of other students. What I have attempted to showcase is a means to give each student a voice, exhibited through their own work, through preliminary studies in their journals and individual works of art, encouraging conversations with others around the learning, followed by cumulative, collaborative installations in which all students participate together. Students shine individually and collectively. This is a fantastic opportunity to raise esteem in our more challenged students, providing a safe context for showcasing their work alongside the work of other-abled students. Everyone contributes (see Figures 1 and 2). Everyone exhibits. And ultimately, each artist has work to take home once the installation is disassembled, as seen in Figures 3–5.

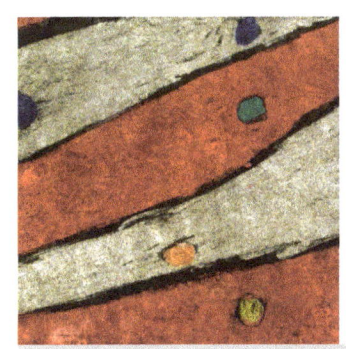

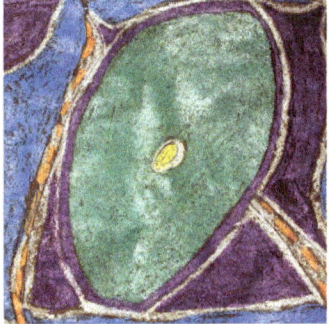

Figures 3–5. *What If Abstraction* student work. Photo by author.

Under the Lens

Funded through a generous grant from Crayola and the National Association of Elementary School Principals, the LCD microscopes and loupes arrived in the art classroom early in the fall semester. This facilitated implementation of the unit for 4th and 5th graders. Lessons in art coincided with lessons in science. Both grade levels started with making careful observations and documenting their findings in the research journals, referencing work by Maria Sibylla Merian, 17th-century Swiss naturalist and scientific illustrator. Evolutions of their drawings informed future work. Each drawing was labeled with the name of the specimen and its visual characteristics. We played with words by using analogy to describe what we saw (Ruef, 1992). Students worked in table teams of three to four students, collaboratively viewing the LCD screen on each microscope. Students gathered a minimum of eight documented observations in their research journals of onion skin, fly legs, butterfly tongues, and bee wings, among others. We did a gallery walk each day to view the variety of observational drawings. After 2 days of microscopic focus, we moved the microscopes and loupes to a smaller station in the art classroom so that students could do independent research as needed.

Fourth-grade students developed one of the observation drawings for the first phase of their artmaking, in which they magnified that drawing to fit a 9-by-12 inch piece of paper. Using construction paper, crayons, and watered-down black tempera paint for a resist

Figure 6. WhatIfAssembling.png. Assembling the metal quilt as a collaborative process. Photo by author.

process based on batik, students created abstract works inspired by scientific observations. This particular process was selected to give students the opportunity to play with color, while also highlighting the patterns in the specimens magnified as abstract compositions.

Students then proceeded to select one of the drawings they had done in their journals to draw on a 4-by-4 inch piece of newsprint, selecting different parts of the design for positive and negative spaces. This was used to trace onto a foil square for a textural design effect, embossing the surfaces with metal tools. The process took two to three class periods to complete. At the beginning of each class, we viewed short segments via Art21 featuring different artists, for example: El Anatsui, whose monumental textural wall installations informed our construction, and Do Ho Suh, who addressed collaboration as part of his process. Indeed, Janine Antoni's work, *Moor*, served as a conversation starter around accepting different individuals' contributions for the richness of the stories in the final work.

As each piece was completed, they were laid next to each other as a grid, which echoed DaVinci's *Connessione* or systems-thinking process. Students used a hole punch on the corners to assemble the works together as a quilt (Figure 6). Students worked together as each one finished their work to assure that the finished collaborative work was balanced. A large dowel was attached at the top to allow the works to hang (Figure 7).

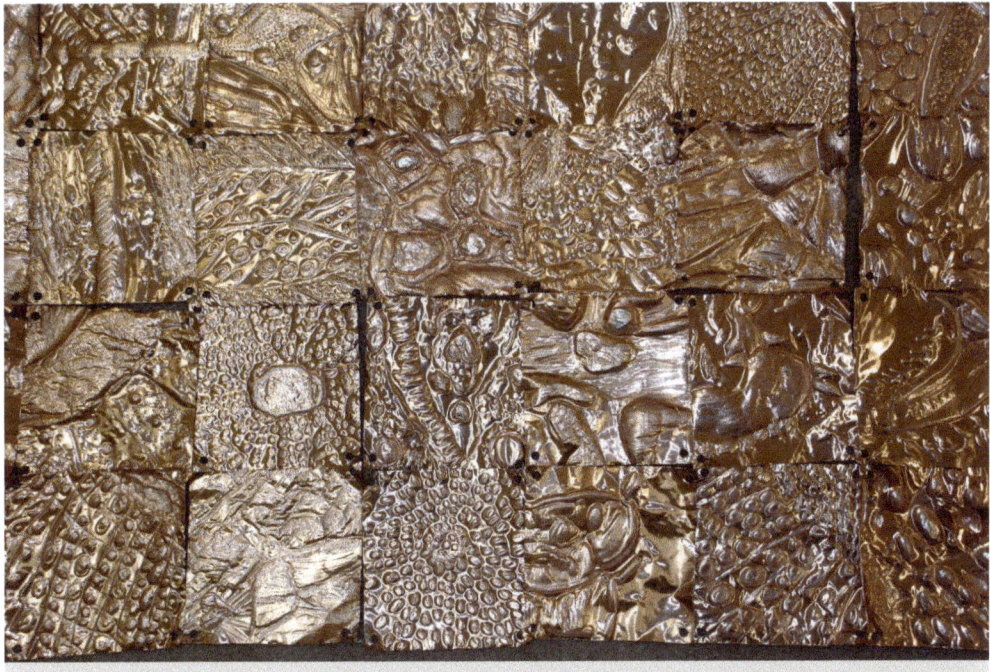

Figure 7. WhatIfGrid.jpg. The grid-like pattern on view. Photo by author.

Meanwhile, 5th graders learned about and tested simple machines to apply those principles to the path of the marble on their sculpture. Utilizing a marble works kit (Figure 8), as well as simple machines from our school's science laboratory, they explored aspects of inclined planes, ramps, and screws to determine a balanced design for their clay work. They gathered their research in the journals, drawing their ideas, then testing them with the kits.

Students viewed work by artists who use machines in their art. Tim Hawkinson, for example, has implemented many engineering components in his work. He "tinkers with everyday materials to build surprising mechanical artwork: 'I guess it comes from early on in childhood, a fascination with moving parts and sort of the magical'" (Art21, 2003, para. 1). The Museum of Modern Art has resources, which were available for the students on rotation at a research station. Additionally, students gathered important science facts from their 5th-grade science teacher, which they contributed to our Science in Art wall (Table 1), which included:

Figure 8. WhatIfExploration.jpg. Students' construction of a simple machine for marbles. Photo by author.

Table 1. Science in Art Wall	
Energy	The ability to do work.
Force	A push or pull.
Relationships	A force that causes a moving object to slow down or prevents a stationary object from moving.
Resistance Force	A force that causes a moving object to slow down or prevents a stationary object from moving.
Machines	A machine converts the force provided from an input energy into motion that changes the magnitude or direction of that force. This motion against a resistive force is the work done by the machine.
	• Makes something easier to do but will take you longer or require you to cover more distance while doing it. • All machines must overcome resistance forces. • Gravity is a force pulling down on every atom of an object. • Inertia – Newton's First Law – Object's tendency to keep doing what it's doing. • Friction – Force that resists the motion of a solid object that is in contact with another object or material. • Is problematic/resists motion, causes heating, wears things down, and wastes energy. • Is beneficial/necessary for writing, driving, etc.
Complex Machines	Two or more simple machines combined to perform a function.

Fifth-grade students selected one of their observational drawings to transform into 3D for the surface texture of the clay bowl. The bowl was used as the support for the simple machine top, allowing the marbles to travel from one sculpture to the next in the final installation, as a play on form and function.

Confluency of the Disciplines

As both 4th- and 5th-grade students' work evolved, there was a notable shift in the perception of what fit in which discipline. Students were connecting concepts fluidly from art and science as they discussed surface texture, design, construction, forms, patterns, observations, and prototypes. As contemporary artists, they were exploring ways to express ideas about nature and science in their art (Figure 9). Much like da Vinci, their work and conversations addressed the arts and the sciences, finding ways to discuss ideas and find questions about what they were learning. Interdisciplinary approaches were in full swing!

Figure 9. WhatIfResearch.jpg. Students use a variety of sources for their research on how artists express ideas about nature. Photo by author.

Students saw the practicality of planning designs, exploring ideas, testing, and improving even in view of failure, as they saw this as a need for an adjustment in art as in science. Students had channeled my art class slogan—"Turn your mistake into a masterpiece!"—into a motto for their work in any discipline. Failure is just part of the process of taking risks (American Association for the Advancement of Science, 1993).

Additionally, students were willing to take risks collaboratively, building and testing their ideas with others. Resnick (2018) refers to this as the Creative Learning Spiral, in which students imagine, create, play, share, reflect, imagine, and so on, as an engine for creative thinking. When Resnick studied this phenomenon, he was watching kindergarteners interact, fluidly exchanging ideas and building on them without fear. This was the intent for our studio classroom experience, where students in 4th and 5th grades would revisit their natural creative flow and implement it playfully with connections to art and science, refining their abilities as creative thinkers. The "what if" sculpture shown in Figure 10 demonstrates their critical thinking.

What Did We Learn?

For one thing, we learned about flexibility—not only from the malleable metal that was part of our 4th-grade artwork, but also from the bounce of marbles across the art classroom floor. We had to allow extra time for the learning to actually take place, where each student had the opportunity to experience the construction of simple machines, testing ideas, and making observations. We learned with clay sculptures (fragile), bouncing marbles (hard), and cement floors (hard) that there may be casualties. Fortunately, as the works in both 4th and 5th grade were completed, students photographed them before the group installation. For the final installation of the simple machine sculptures, wooden blocks, paper towel tubes, Lego stands, and the students' imagination were implemented to get the marbles to travel from one simple machine to another, building complex machines out of art. There were lots of exclamations of surprise and laughter from all around the studio.

Figure 10. WhatIf5thSculpture.jpg. An example of a 5th grader's simple machine sculpture. Photo by author.

Further, my own collaboration with professional colleagues was essential. As the students' guide, my understanding of simple and complex machines needed to account for the correct vocabulary in order to facilitate an interdisciplinary flow to our process. Likewise, 4th- and 5th-grade teachers addressed visual aspects of the students' observations with greater intensity, as these were essential for the transfer into their hands-on art projects. We met regularly in preparation of the grant application. Then as part of our ongoing review, we met and discussed student learning and how we could adjust the teaching in our respective classrooms to simultaneously teach concepts and accommodate each learner.

This process reflects the Reggio Emilia approach, where ongoing dialogue between students and teachers, is an essential component of creating a rich learning environment. The classroom is the third teacher (Gandini et al., 2015). The use of microscopes and other science instruments is also common practice. Students pursue creative investigations based on their own curiosity and wonder, supported by their teachers and the classroom space.

Art does not exist in a vacuum. Nor does any other subject. Artists throughout time have been inspired by words, by science, and by history, and this project serves to demonstrate how interdisciplinary approaches are a vital link to creative, critical, and whole thinking across disciplines. This project shares how through collaborative processes, students can broaden their experience to create individual works of art that connect with others' work and ideas. While we teach artistic processes and techniques, we can teach students to view the world around them as inspiration for their work, infused by scientific knowledge in the process.

Author's Note: This unit would not have been possible without the generous support of Crayola and the National Association of Elementary School Principals through the Champion Creatively Alive Children Grant Program. The funds provided a sustainable unit that has been implemented year to year with different students. https://www.crayola.com/for-educators/ccac-landing.aspx

> *Samantha Melvin was named the 2012 National Elementary Art Educator of the Year by the National Art Education Association. She believes every individual is an artist and a thinker. Her teaching philosophy is to create a platform for artistic expression and develop patrons of the arts through research-based, tactile, and interdisciplinary investigations of art education practices with the whole child in mind.*

References

American Association for the Advancement of Science. (1990). *Science for all Americans*, Project 2061. Oxford University Press.

American Association for the Advancement of Science. (1993). *Benchmarks for science literacy*, Project 2061. Oxford University Press.

Art21. (2003, September 17). Tim Hawkinson in "Time" (Season 2) [Web series episode]. In *Art in the twenty-first century*. https://art21.org/watch/art-in-the-twenty-first-century/s2/tim-hawkinson-in-time-segment

Burton, J., Horowitz, R., & Abeles, H. (1999). *Learning in and through the arts: Curriculum implications*. Center for Arts Education Research, Teachers College, Columbia University. https://artsedge.kennedy-center.org/champions/pdfs/Learning.pdf

Eisner, E. (1997). *Educating artistic vision*. National Art Education Association.

Gandini, L., Hill, L., Cadwell, L., & Schwall, C. (2015). *In the spirit of the studio: Learning from the atelier of Reggio Emilia* (2nd ed.). Teachers College Press.

Gelb, M. J. (1998). *How to think like Leonardo da Vinci: Seven steps to genius every day*. Delacorte Press.

Gude, O. (2007). The principles of possibility: Considerations for a 21st-century art & culture curriculum. *Art Education, 60*(1), 6–17. https://doi.org/10.1080/00043125.2007.11651621

Hetland, L., Winner, E., Veenema, S., & Sheridan, K. M. (2007). Studio thinking: *The real benefits of visual arts education*. Teachers College Press.

Resnick, M. (2018). *Lifelong kindergarten: Cultivating creativity through projects, passion, peers, and play*. MIT Press. https://doi.org/10.7551/mitpress/11017.001.0001

Ruef, K. (1992). *The private eye: Looking / thinking by analogy*. Private Eye Project.

Stewart, M., & Walker, S. (2005). *Rethinking curriculum in art*. Davis.

Resources

Crystal Productions, collection of art posters: *Renaissance*, as well as Leonardo da Vinci

Do-Ho Suh, Art21, https://art21.org/watch/art-in-the-twenty-first-century/s2/do-ho-suh-in-stories-segment

El Anatsui, Art21, https://art21.org/artist/el-anatsui

Ferrin Contemporary ceramics, sculpture, paintings, and photography, http://www.ferringallery.com

Inventors' Workshop from Discovery Education, https://www.discoveryeducation.com/community/workshop

Leonardo da Vinci: Leonardo Interactive Museum, https://leonardointeractivemuseum.com/en

Museum of Modern Art: MoMA Learning about designs and simple machines, https://www.moma.org/learn/moma_learning/themes/design/simple-machines

Museum of Science website: Mysterious Machinery, https://www.mos.org/leonardo/activities/inventions-quiz

National Museum of Women in the Arts, Maria Sibylla Merian, https://nmwa.org/art/artists/maria-sibylla-merian

OK Go, "This Too Shall Pass" Rube Goldberg Machine "Official" video, https://www.youtube.com/watch?v=qybUFnY7Y8w

Ruef, K., 1992. *The Private Eye, 5X Looking/Thinking by Analogy - A Guide to Developing The Interdisciplinary Mind*. Seattle: The Private Eye Project.

Rube Goldberg website, http://rubegoldberg.com

Texas Education Agency: Texas Essential Skills and Knowledge (Curriculum Standards), https://tea.texas.gov/academics/curriculum-standards

Tim Hawkinson, Art21, https://art21.org/artist/tim-hawkinson

Visionary Inventions, PBS resources, https://www.livebinders.com/play/play?id=852923

A Model for High School STEAM Activities: Science and Visual Art

Pam Stephens

Why Now?

A paraphrased statement attributed to Leonardo da Vinci voices an extraordinarily modern, insightful, and forward-thinking perspective: "Study the science of art. Study the art of science. Develop your senses—especially learn how to see. Realize that everything connects to everything else" (Roche et al., 2018, p. 3). This remarkable philosophical observation, likely reworded from da Vinci's many notebooks, serves as a guidepost for contemporary art education practice; a practice that encourages flexible thinking, envisioning the unknown, creative problem solving, and finding links between and among divergent subjects. Implementing these processes contributes to students' future success in an information-rich global society.

Fast forward to the 20th century. In 1984, futurist author Alvin Toffler correctly forecasted that "a knowledge-based economy would eclipse the post-industrial age, shifting focus from manufacturing and labour to information and data" (as cited in Subramanian, 2016, para. 5). Toffler's prediction rings true as we regularly assume without question our consumption of technology—especially the Internet, computers, and software—in our daily lives. Today we are amid what is being proclaimed as the fourth industrial revolution, otherwise known as Industrial Revolution 4.0. Like prior industrial revolutions, technological advances are changing the world, its economies, and ways of living. Schwab contends that this current industrial revolution is "characterized by a range of new technologies that are fusing the physical, digital and biological worlds, impacting all disciplines, economies and industries, and even challenging ideas about what it means to be human" (2015, para. 3).

Complex problems, such as those we see in Industrial Revolution 4.0, require inventive ways of responding. Instead of staying in the comfort zone of curricular content specialization, we should consider working in collaboration across disciplines. Zafeirakopoulos and van der Bijl-Brouwer found that "transdisciplinary innovation is impossible without collaboration" (2018, Discussion section, para. 6). Working as a collective to address intellectual endeavors develops a learning community that fosters high-quality learning outcomes.

Incumbent upon K–12 and postsecondary instructors is to prepare our students for what Wiggins labeled "future usefulness" in the workforce (2011, p. 32). Since many jobs or roles that our students will someday fill are not yet in existence, how do we coach them toward this usefulness? One way is teaching in and through the arts while meaningfully bridging with other content areas such as science, technology, engineering, and mathematics; that is, STEAM. The arts and arts educators are uniquely positioned to take on the difficult but exciting task of preparing tomorrow's careers.

This chapter focuses on an Arizona high school art program that seamlessly meets the challenges of Industrial Revolution 4.0 and offers a model for planning, implementing, and measuring learning outcomes of STEAM activities. Findings based upon this model are also reported.

School Setting

Pinnacle High School (PHS), located in Paradise Valley, Arizona, is a part of the Paradise Valley Unified School District (PVUSD). A large campus with a student population of approximately 2,600, the PHS student population closely mirrors the population of the city, with 22% identifying as ethnic/racial minority and 9% of students economically marginalized (USA School Info, n.d.).

Notably, PVUSD places great value on the arts, as evidenced by visual arts programs at the elementary, middle, and high school levels. At the secondary level, PVUSD curriculum is intended to prepare students to enter college or university or continued vocational training, as well as partake in productive citizenship (PVSchools, n.d.). High school students are required to successfully complete a minimum of one unit of career and technical or fine arts studies. Students may choose to take six units of electives, which can include fine arts.

Kelsey Greenland is one of three full-time art educators at PHS. In addition, three career and technical education teachers provide courses in photography, animation, and graphic design. As a highly qualified art educator, Greenland is passionate about teaching art. Her 2D art program covers art foundations, drawing, advanced art, advanced placement, and open studio. In testimony to the quality of the PHS art program, students have won multiple awards, including the 2020 Gold Key for Scholastic Art and Writing.

The activity referenced in the remainder of this chapter was developed by Greenland and demonstrates a real-life connection between art and science. In the activity, students had the opportunity to apply their prior knowledge of art media and the scientific method as they experimented and documented how alcohol inks can be made from natural materials, such as fruits and vegetables (Greenland, 2020, see Figure 1).

Figure 1. Variety of alcohol inks made from fruits and vegetables.

Planning: Finding Memorable Connections

Significant to quality STEAM activities is that all content areas are treated as equals; that is, no subject is treated as a handmaiden to another. Brenner explains that the concept of

> transdisciplinarity… has the task of seeing what all disciplines have in common, what lies in, through and beyond them. What they have in common is a basis for "making sense" of a part of human knowledge and hopefully providing a path to a unified understanding of it. (2011, para. 4)

Science educator Anne Jolly (2014) further suggests that "we shape STEAM programs by exploring opportunities where art naturally fits in the STEM arena" (para. 17).

Accepting these lesson planning recommendations helps ensure rigorous, memorable learning activities. To determine commonalities between or among art and STEM content, proceed to the national academic standards. Because the goal of Greenland's art–science activity involved inquiry-based learning, several standards were applicable. She chose for her students to "synthesize and relate knowledge and personal experiences to make art" (National Core Art Standards, 2014, Connecting section) and to "evaluate or refine a technological solution that reduces impacts of human activities on natural systems" (Next Generation Science Standards, HS-ESS3-4 section).

Measuring Learning

After comparing standards and finding an expedient point of convergence, a sensible next step is to write a measurable objective to effectively direct teaching and learning. An example of a measurable objective for this art–science activity might be the following:

> After students demonstrate an understanding of the various steps involved with the scientific method, each student will create an effective and accurate visual representation that includes rational hypotheses, clearly shows collected data and observations, provides accurate analysis of the data, and draws a factual conclusion based upon evidence.

Figure 2. Example of ink made from spinach and the end product of the inquiry.

This objective explicitly allows for depth of knowledge to be measured. For example, student work that meets expectations would follow the objectives' criteria as stated. Student work that exceeds expectations would go beyond the stated criteria to be original or unique and include elaboration. Student work not meeting expectations would ignore criteria.

Implementing: Activity Sequence

Consider measurable objectives, such as the example provided, as bread crumbs to an activity sequence. While each of the steps mentioned in the objective must be covered in the activity sequence, the best activities go beyond those steps to include questioning strategies that encourage students to dig a little deeper (see Figure 2). The following four strategies, when added to activity sequences, provide a method for engaging students, encourage risk taking, and prompt deeper investigations of a chosen topic.

- Link to the "right now" in student lives. What in students' recent memory serves to advance understanding of the concepts to be taught?

- Value what students already know. Include open-ended questions that honor prior knowledge. Go a step further to ask what students don't know or what they need to know to identify connections.

- Foster elaboration of ideas whether in oral, written, or visual communication.

- Include a reflection that allows time to consider performance and outcomes. What went right? What went wrong? What did you learn? How can you use this knowledge in the future?

Outcomes

Possibly the best markers of quality learning outcomes are products and statements made by students. For this art–science activity, students created a graphic organizer that itemizes each step of the scientific method as they experimented to create vivid colors of ink. To further exemplify the experiment's outcome, the resultant ink was used on the graphic organizer to visually demonstrate the intensity of pigment.

Recall that the proposed measurable objective included criteria to measure depth of learning. In the following example, a student predicted an outcome based upon prior knowledge, completed the experiment, reflected upon the outcome, and forecasted how the experiment informs future applications—all examples of critical thinking and exceeding expectations.

> Hypothesis: The ink from this material will have a low intensity of greenness. The ink will not come out as the same color as the material.... Conclusion: I would recommend this material to be used [as] ink. My initial hypothesis was partially correct: the ink was not the same color as the spinach, but it had a brighter intensity of greenness than expected.... In the future, I will try using objects/materials with more green pigment. (Kiera F., as cited in Greenland, 2020, p. 22, Figure 3)

Student comments were gathered at the conclusion of the activity. These comments further underscore the importance of experiential learning. "I learned that the color of the plant/object is not always the color of the ink" and "Ink can be made from many different things, but not everything makes vivid colors."

Findings: The Charge for Art Educators

Preparing students for usefulness in the 21st-century workplace is a significant responsibility placed before today's educators—a charge that art teachers in STEAM environments are well equipped to address. Rather than preparing students for a specific job, the visual arts traded in concepts that readily address the disparate and sometimes ambiguous workforce needs of Industrial Revolution 4.0. Marr (2020) supports this assertion and states that "problem-solvers in the future will have to look beyond what first feels like

STEAM Education: An Interdisciplinary Look at Art in the Curriculum

Figure 3. Sample of work made with ink from nature.

a limitation and approach challenges with inquiry, wonder, and innovation. These are skills that the arts exercise" (para. 10). Art–science activities such as the activity focused upon in this chapter illustrate the characteristics Marr mentions (see Figure 3).

Our students are the winners if we keep in mind the interdisciplinary nature of the visual arts while planning lessons, units of study, or entire programs. The best art activities are those that move away from linear thinking to embrace the wholeness of STEAM. This approach prompts curiosity, encourages flexible thinking, crisscrosses between and among similar and dissimilar concepts, contributes to development of problem-solving and critical-thinking skills, offers real-world learning experiences, and honors variable ways of knowing (among other implicit and explicit skills). The 21st century is full of challenges. Students in STEAM programs are prepared to meet those challenges head-on.

Pam Stephens, *professor of art education at Northern Arizona University (NAU), began her teaching career in Texas public schools. Today she heads the art education program at NAU. Stephens has published books, animated videos, and other art resources for students and teachers. She maintains active membership with state and national art education associations.*

References

Brenner, J. (2011, September 1). *The transdisciplinary logic of transdisciplinarity*. Metanexus Institute. http://www.metanexus.net/essay/transdisciplinary-logic-transdisciplinarity

Greenland, K. (2020, March). Critical (th)inking. *SchoolArts, 119*(7), 19–22.

Jolly, A. (2014, November 18). STEM vs STEAM: Do the arts belong? *Education Week*. https://www.edweek.org/tm/articles/2014/11/18/ctq-jolly-stem-vs-steam.html

Marr, B. (2020, January 15). We need STEAM, not STEM education to prepare our kids for the 4th industrial revolution. *Forbes*. https://www.forbes.com/sites/bernardmarr/2020/01/15/we-need-steam-not-stem-education-to-prepare-our-kids-for-the-4th-industrial-revolution/#208a1c0155fb

National Core Arts Standards. (2014). *Connecting*. https://www.nationalartsstandards.org

Next Generation Science Standards. (2016). *Earth and human activity*. https://www.nextgenscience.org/pe/hs-ess3-4-earth-and-human-activity

PVSchools. (n.d.). *High school (9-12) curriculum*. https://www.pvschools.net/academics/curriculum/high-school-curriculum

Roche, R. A. P., Farina, F. R., & Commins, S. (2018). *Why science needs art: From historical to modern day perspectives*. Routledge. https://doi.org/10.4324/9781315660745

Schwab, K. (2015, December 12). The fourth industrial revolution: What it means and how to respond. *Foreign Affairs*. https://www.foreignaffairs.com/articles/2015-12-12/fourth-industrial-revolution

Subramanian, C. (2016, July 1). *Alvin Toffler: What he got right—and wrong*. BBC. https://www.bbc.com/news/world-us-canada-36675260

USA School Info. (n.d.). *Paradise Valley High School in Phoenix, Arizona*. http://www.usaschoolinfo.com/school/paradise-valley-high-school-phoenix-arizona.3794/school-information

Wiggins, G. (2011). A diploma worth having. *Educational Leadership, 68*(6), 28–33.

Zafeirakopoulos, M., & van der Bijl-Brouwer, M. (2018, August). Exploring the transdisciplinary learning experiences of innovation professionals. Technology *Innovation Management Review, 8*(8), 50–59. http://doi.org/10.22215/timreview/1178

The Process of Building an Art Installation With Plastic Waste

Tina Hirsig

> *The majority of the work I've been doing over the past decade has been centered around exploring plastic debris as a viable art material. We think of plastic as disposable when it is precisely the opposite, so I extract it from its problematic destructive fate and utilize its potential to become a source for enjoyable reflection.*
>
> —Aurora Robson, environmental artist

The Process of Building an Art Installation With Plastic Waste

Human-made debris, including plastic, is one of the largest threats to the ocean and marine life (Johnson, 2019). Plastics in particular have caused a lot of damage, including from wildlife ingesting plastics by accident or by mistaking the plastic as food (UNEP, 2011). Tiny fragments of plastic, which are called microplastics, are also a danger. These microscopic bits are formed from the breaking down of larger pieces from the sun's radiation and waves (van Sebille et al., 2015). Sea creatures then ingest the microplastics, which do not completely break down and make their way through the marine food web (Johnson, 2019). There is an urgency to this global environmental issue, and some artists have taken up the charge to educate people on this topic and advocate for the removal of single-use plastics. One such environmental artist is Aurora Robson.

The Artist: Aurora Robson

Aurora Robson's artwork uses materials that would otherwise be disposed of in landfills. She intercepts the waste stream to build sculptures for interior and exteriors. Her work extends far beyond her own practice and into communities as she develops partnerships with schools and businesses to educate about plastic pollution. For more information about Robson and her community action work, see her website at http://www.aurorarobson.com. Figure 1 is taken from Robson's website and demonstrates some of her work.

Figure 1. Aurora Robson in her studio.

The Inspiration: Robson Exhibit at the Halsey Institute of Contemporary Art

In the fall of 2019, Ashley Hall took a field trip to Aurora Robson's art exhibition at the Halsey Institute of Contemporary Art at the College of Charleston, which sparked curiosity among the students and faculty about plastic pollution. Ashley Hall is an all-girls school in Charleston, South Carolina, along the East Coast of the United States. The proximity to the Atlantic Ocean made this school perfectly situated to engage in conversations about ocean conservation. The students were intrigued by Robson's art installation as it gracefully hung from the ceiling like a wave in the ocean filled with creatures and plants (see Figure 2). The most fascinating aspect about her artwork for the children was that it was built from discarded single-use plastic consumer products. After having excellent conversations with our students about what to do with plastic waste while viewing the exhibit, we reached out to Robson to see if she would come to the Ashley Hall campus to work with our students. Our thought was to develop an interdisciplinary experience for educating about single-use plastic in our environment. Robson eagerly agreed to be an artist-in-residence, knowing her mission for educating about plastic waste in our environment directly related to Ashley Hall's mission for environmental stewardship. What started as an inquiry by the students into the art materials used in her work, an all-school adventure blossomed into a permanent installation on campus.

Figure 2. Ashley Hall 5th and 6th graders visit Aurora Robson's installation at the Halsey Institute of Contemporary Art. Robson suggested they view the installation as if they were looking up from the bottom of the ocean and the artwork was floating in the water above.

The School: Ashley Hall

Ashley Hall is an independent school for girls, serving kindergarten through 12th-grade students, with a coeducational preschool in Charleston, South Carolina. Ashley Hall has maintained its original mission: "to produce educated women who are independent, ethically responsible, and prepared to meet the challenges of society with confidence" (n.d., para. 1) since its founding by Mary Vardrine McBee in 1909. This mission is realized in all aspects of campus, from our traditions to our innovative curricula and teaching philosophy. It inspires both faculty and students to engage in a vitally enriching educational community. The school is broken down into four divisions: the Early Education Center (ages 2–5), the Lower School (ages 5–10), the Intermediate Program (ages 10–13), and the Upper School (ages 13–18). Every student on campus took part in this art installation.

The Problem: Plastic Waste

During science lab, the students in grades kindergarten through 6th grade (Lower School) had engaging conversations about plastic pollution. Teachers led them in a discussion regarding the statistics stating that as of 2015, approximately 6,300 metric tons of plastic waste had been generated, around 9% of which was recycled, 12% was incinerated, and 79% was accumulated in landfills or the natural environment (Geyer et al., 2017). The students were astonished at how little plastic was being recycled. They began to wonder where plastic comes from, how it has become so pervasive in our consumer life, and what steps can be taken to advocate for products using less plastic in packaging.

Upon further discussions, the teachers shared that the vast majority of monomers used to make plastics are derived from fossil hydrocarbons. In sum, this means that the molecules that are bonded together to form a polymer (monomers) are made from ethylene and propylene, which are found in fuel oil. Further, the students were surprised to find that most of the commonly used plastics we use today are not biodegradable. As a result, the plastics accumulate rather than decompose in landfills or the natural environment (Barnes et al., 2009). With this understanding, the students began to see the importance of rethinking plastic as an art material rather than waste. During our workshop with Robson, she made connections to the problems associated with plastic and taught the Lower School students that part of her process of artmaking is, as she stated, intercepting the waste stream by reimagining this material.

The Process: Designing an Art Installation

The faculty and students began the artmaking process with an essential question: What do we do with plastic waste? In the art studio we explored more of Robson's work and viewed other installation artists, such as Sayaka Ganz and Ruth Peche, who also pondered the same question. In the main building of the Lower School is an indoor courtyard. It was decided that this vast open common space would be the location of the art installation. Each group of students sat in the space, talked in small groups, sketched, dreamed of the possibilities, and wrote notes on ideas and configurations. Using Robson's installations as a model, they were encouraged to think big and incorporate other areas of the curriculum.

The lesson was interdisciplinary. Students had conversations joining their visual arts knowledge with their science and sustainability knowledge to suggest what statement we wanted our collaborative artwork to make. Many conversations centered around the health of our oceans and the animals that live in them. Living near the ocean, many students enjoy this outdoor resource regularly with their families. During school hours the students explored ways to be good stewards of the ocean, such as through environmental partnerships in our city like the South Carolina Aquarium and Charleston Waterkeeper.

After the initial brainstorming session, students illustrated their ideas on paper and submitted them for teacher review (see Figure 3). Finding a common thread of the ocean, the faculty combined many of the children's designs into one final plan that also encompassed the Ashley Hall character traits, which we call *Hallmarks*. At Ashley Hall, we teach these Hallmarks alongside the academic and artistic curriculum. The seven Hallmarks are that the Ashley Hall students are (1) compassionate, (2) purposeful, (3) creative, (4) discerning, (5) intelligent, (6) collaborative, and (7) worldly (Ashley Hall, n.d., para. 2). Because of the importance of the Hallmarks, the students felt it was essential that their sculpture reflected these character traits alongside an ocean theme. Figure 4 is a schematic demonstrating how the artwork would be created and the meaning behind it as each strand directly corresponds to one of the seven Ashley Hall Character Traits.

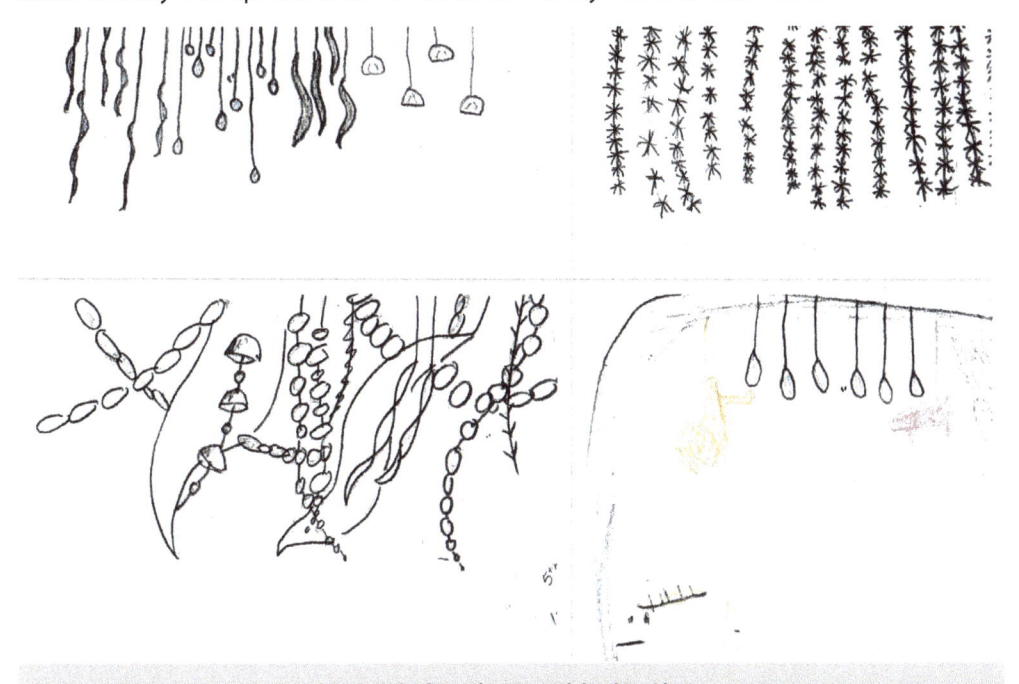

Figure 3. Students planning and sketching ideas.

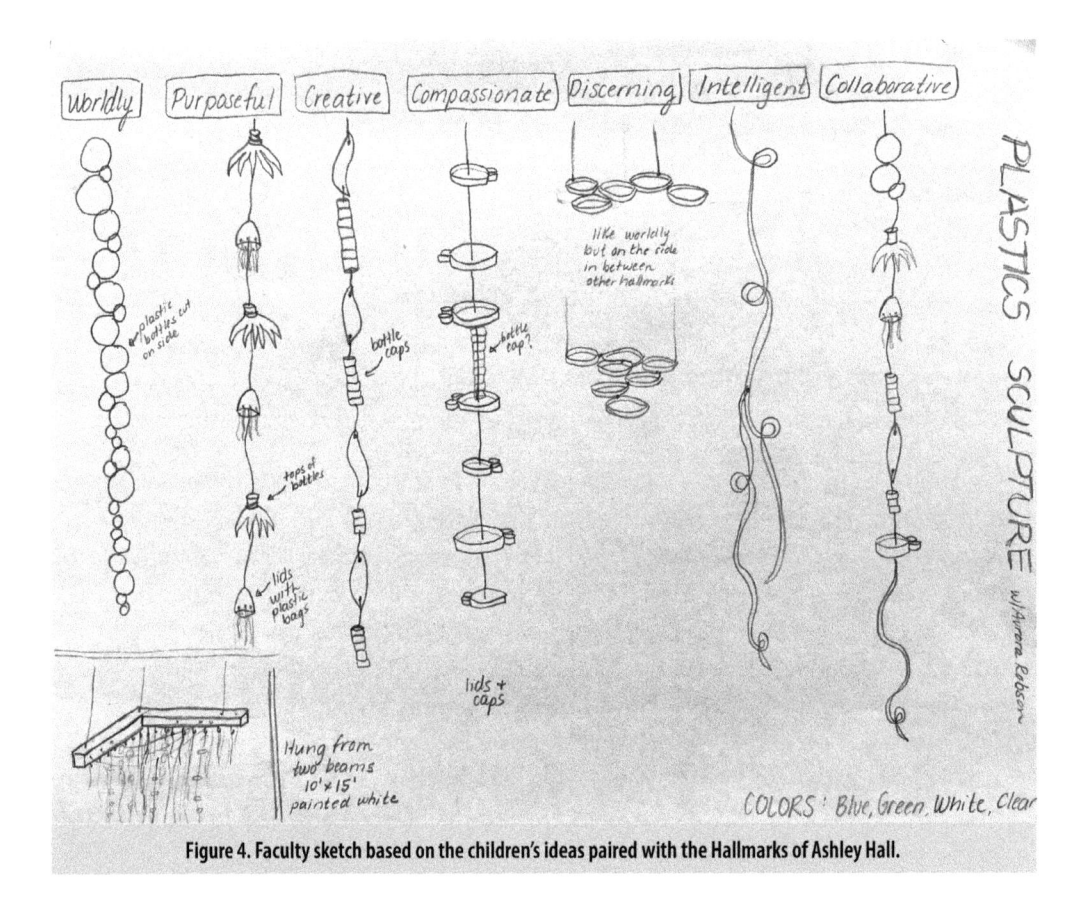

Figure 4. Faculty sketch based on the children's ideas paired with the Hallmarks of Ashley Hall.

The Connection: Family Participation and Cross-Division Work

We sent a letter to all Ashley Hall families explaining the sculpture. We had hoped to create a collective involvement for the purpose of choosing this medium. Students brought single-use plastics from their homes and collected them in display tanks in the school common areas. Several families visited during the process to see what their children were talking about. Plastics were also collected from campus, but because of our efforts to minimize plastic use, we did not have enough usable material on campus alone and therefore needed family assistance. In the collection and cleaning process, we learned important details about the different features of the plastics and their longevity on the planet. Robson taught us that many of these plastics will take hundreds of years to decompose. If we turn that material into something that will stand the test of time (like artwork) instead, perhaps we can begin to see this material in a new light.

The excitement grew on campus, and the Upper School students and faculty stepped in to help. The physics students studied the design developed by the Lower School students and tested out materials they thought would work. Materials that were tested by the physics students were single-use plastic, packing peanuts, straws, magazines, paper, and painted paper to study color design. These students created a small prototype of what would become the larger piece of art and discussed the details of the upcoming building process with the younger children. As a reference, the prototype was hung in the courtyard while the full-size sculpture was being created. Eventually, some of these prototype pieces were incorporated into the final installation. We found that during the construction the prototype was an excellent reference point so everyone could visualize where the project was headed.

While constructing the sculpture, the energy around solving our essential question, *What do we do with plastic waste?*, was ever present. For instance, during weekly swimming instruction, the swim teacher simulated plastic waste in the ocean by bombarding the pool with some of our collected plastics (see Figure 5). The students had to swim through the debris and contemplate what life is like for our ocean creatures. The librarians also showed the Lower School students how to locate primary resources and research our essential question. The students wrote nonfictional brochures through a variety of digital platforms to share with our campus community. Additionally, Lower School and Upper School science classes learned what efforts are in place to reduce plastic in our environment locally. These groups visited the recycle center, waste treatment plant, and the South Carolina Aquarium to dig deeper into our essential question. Visual arts classes explored a variety of artists working with plastics as an art material. Plastics became an essential part across

Figure 5. Students swim with collected debris to build empathy for our sea creatures.

Figure 6. Adding color to the plastics and the building of the installation under the guidance of Robson.

the curriculum. As a result, the sculpture and the inclusive lessons became the center in the Lower School and upper School students, as they explored this material to express their authentic voice and ideas.

The Process: Building an Art Installation

For 3 wonderful days, the courtyard was turned into a collaborative artist workshop. The students had their hands in every aspect of this artwork from cleaning the materials, to constructing each intricate part of the artwork, to using a variety of tools, and to the painting and hanging the final product (see Figure 6). Tables were set up according to each Ashley Hall Hallmark–themed piece with directions, supplies, and information about the project. Classes rotated to work in hour-long shifts constructing the installation. Pieces were laid out on the floor or hung on long wires as they were completed.

Robson worked one-on-one and in small groups mentoring students on how to create with plastic as a sculpture material. She gave advice on how to safely cut, tie, drill, and join plastic elements together with rivets. Typically in society, girls are not invited to learn how to use power tools, but our students had an immersive experience in developing applicable skills from a fellow female artist. This experience directly relates back to our mission of "preparing women to meet the challenges of society with confidence" (Ashley Hall, n.d., para. 1). From fixing something in their own home to potentially engineering at a construction site, the students were empowered to move forward knowing that they can build with their hands.

Adding Single-Use Plastic to the Studio

Providing plastic as a sculptural material to students was inexpensive and was easily used in the project. Included in Table 1 is a list of supplies we used to explore the potential of this art material. No heavy adhesives were necessary. We found that rivets, screws, nuts and bolts, and knots easily held this lightweight material together. An important factor in using this material was that cleaning the plastic was key to a successful building process. We soaked the plastic in one part Citra Solv and 10 parts water, which removed the labels and contaminants. We then rinsed the plastics with biodegradable dish soap to degrease the Citra Solv residue. Once the plastics were properly cleaned and aired out, they were ready for construction.

Table 1. Tools Used for the Building Process

• Drills (electric and manual hand crank)	• Gloves (some plastic edges are sharp when cut)
• Rivets and rivet gun	• Single-use plastic items (thinner plastic is easier to cut)
• Heavy-duty snips and scissors	
• X-Acto knife	• OPTIONAL: Paint specifically designed to adhere to plastics
• Hole punch	• OPTIONAL: Airbrush tools and compressor to spray large-scale projects
• Fishing line (for hanging; many local parks have recycling programs that collect old fishing line)	
• Reusable zip ties (for hanging, attaching, or process work)	

The Process of Building an Art Installation With Plastic Waste

Figure 7. Robson helped hang the final touches in the courtyard.

Conclusion

Artist Aurora Robson taught the students of Ashley Hall that plastic is a global problem, and art is a global language that can speak to solutions of this large problem. The sculpture that hangs in our courtyard today serves as a reminder that our choices matter, and solutions are around us for plastic waste—which Robson simply calls "displaced abundance" (see Figure 7). Working on this project brought a real-world problem to our doorstep. But it didn't just sit there. We had important conversations and did something about it with our creative hands and our promise to be good stewards to our planet. We pledged to cultivate the seven virtues of compassion, intelligence, worldliness, creativity, collaboration, purposefulness, and discernment for the health of our planet; all for the purpose of producing young women who have both the will and the ability to be independent, ethical, and confident. Our students learned that big, complicated problems are worth tackling through a variety of academic and creative lenses. We have the power to change the future. Robson left us with the following inspirational words: "I see creative stewardship as a future positive way of artmaking that provides elements of creative problem solving and present-day relevance to any studio practice."

Acknowledgment

I would like to acknowledge the dedication and hard work of my colleagues who worked in collaboration to make this idea become reality: Beth McCarty (Lower School science teacher), Erin Libaire (Lower School literacy coordinator), Elizabeth Flowers (2nd-grade teacher), and Lillian Apple (Upper School physics teacher).

> **Tina Hirsig** *is a faculty member at Ashley Hall School, an all-girls school in Charleston, South Carolina. She teaches K–6 visual arts and serves as the visual arts department chair. Her passion for the environment informs not only her teaching but also her active studio practice. She also practices a Teaching for Artistic Behavior (TAB) model of learning in her art room.*

References

Ashley Hall. (n.d.). Our mission. https://www.ashleyhall.org/about

Barnes, D. K. A., Galgani, F., Thompson, R. C., & Barlaz, M. (2009). Accumulation and fragmentation of plastic debris in global environments. *Philosophical Transactions of the Royal Society B: Biological Sciences, 364*(1526), 1985–1998. https://doi.org/10.1098/rstb.2008.0205

Geyer, R., Jambeck, J. R., & Law, K. L. (2017). Production, use, and fate of all plastics ever made. *Science Advances, 3*(7), Article e1700782. https://doi.org/10.1126/sciadv.1700782

Johnson, R. B. (2019). The plastic ocean: An art educator's interpretation [Master's thesis, Georgia State University]. https://scholarworks.gsu.edu/art_design_theses/250

United Nations Environment Program. (2011). *UNEP Year Book 2011: Emerging issues in our global environment.*

van Sebille, E., Wilcox, C., Lebreton, L., Maximenko, N., Hardesty, B. D., van Franeker, J. A., Eriksen, M., Siegel, D., Galgani, F., & Law, K. L. (2015). A global inventory of small floating plastic debris. *Environmental Research Letters, 10*(12), Article 124006. https://doi.org/10.1088/1748-9326/10/12/124006

Culturally Relevant STEAM

Tracey Hunter-Doniger • Courtney A. Howard • Rénard Harris • Cyndi Hall

> *When we think of humane and liberating classrooms in which every learner is recognized and sustained in his or her struggle to learn that we can perceive the insufficiency of bureaucratized, uncaring schools. And it may be only then that we… choose to repair or renew.* (Greene, 1995, p.5)

Creative activity as a human right is giving all students the right to create from their own minds, which are shaped from their values and customs, and an invitation to share without judgment and comparison to a culture that is not their own. Over the past 33 years, since the report *A Nation at Risk* (National Commission on Excellence in Education, 1983) demanded educational reform to prevent schools in the United States from falling behind other countries, legislation like No Child Left Behind (NCLB) in 2002 was passed, leaving in its wake a widening achievement gap (Ladson-Billings, 2006). According to bell hooks (1984), being oppressed is the absence of choices, and students were beginning to lose choices in the arts to make room for test prep during the NCLB era. To counteract inequalities done to underserved populations, the U.S. Department of Education (DOE) designed an initiative called the Science, Technology, Engineering and Math: Education for Global Leadership, to make STEM subjects a priority (DOE, 2010). Sparked by the estimated dramatic increase in STEM jobs in the future, this initiative was designed to recruit and retain 100,000 excellent STEM teachers between 2010 and 2020, including underrepresented groups like women, Hispanics, and African Americans (DOE, 2010). Then, President Barack Obama stated, "Leadership tomorrow depends on how we educate our students today—especially in science, technology, engineering and math" (as cited in DOE, 2010, p. 1). This has encouraged creative and innovative ways of engaging students with the STEM subjects, which, in turn, created the science, technology, engineering, art and math (STEAM) movement by adding the "A" for art to STEM.

Currently, STEAM education is on the rise (Taljaard, 2016). As more and more schools are adopting a STEAM model, professional development is needed. Nonarts educators need to learn how to infuse the arts into the STEM subjects and vice versa, but we contend that is not where the preparation should end, especially in schools with underserved populations. Teachers need to understand that STEAM education must be presented in a way that makes the lessons culturally relevant to the students. This is imperative to assist in closing the achievement gap. Culturally relevant teaching (CRT) as a specific pedagogy allows the cultural references, ideas, and experiences of students to be an important part of the learning process (Ladson-Billings, 1995b). CRT encourages each student to explore subjects through their own personal lens. CRT teaches through the students' values, customs, experiences, and accomplishments.

When invited to explore artistically, students can access their imaginations, pushing the boundaries of their own cultural identity into a space that is unfamiliar. This model acknowledges that culture is fundamental to learning, and in order for learning to be meaningful, the central facets of culture should be embraced—not just as a passing fad but with deeper meaning that gets to the core of who students are and encompasses from where they came. In doing so, CRT provides equitable access to education. Ladson-Billings (2009) argued that effective teachers believe that all children are capable of excellence and build upon students' strengths, create relationships with parents, and act more as coaches rather than authoritarians. Another study examined culturally responsive teaching and found that teachers who are most effective first learn about their students, then teach through themselves (Gay, 2010). But how can we demonstrate the significance of knowing while validating the imaginative path students take when exploring the sciences? Teaching each subject separately isolates curriculum and prevents students from making essential connections. Separatism of any kind supports marginalization of those reluctant to cope with the knowledge and creative works accessible to others (hooks, 1994). Kokkotas et al. (2010) reminded us that the foundation of science exploration is a blend of curiosity, imagination, and wonder. Therefore, what we need to do is eliminate the separation of types of knowledge and combine them into a cohesive collaboration of knowing.

Making STEAM Culturally Relevant

In the spring of 2016, the assistant dean of our college brought a team of faculty members together with the intent of creating an innovative multimodal approach to teaching STEAM as a professional development course. This team was brought together to plan a 6-hour pathway that was to be offered at the Next Steps Institute conference, organized by the South Carolina Afterschool Alliance, Smithsonian Science Education Center, and South Carolina's Coalition for Mathematics and Science. This conference targeted educators from across the country. Once the conference proposal was accepted, the team began meeting in earnest to plan the details of the professional development. The team met and in robust consultation, created a unique approach to STEAM through CRT and storytelling. Each faculty member, an expert in their respective field of study, enthusiastically devised a method of teaching STEAM that is contradictory to traditional educational pedagogical practices. Together this team provided an arsenal of informational expertise in STEM,

Culturally Relevant STEAM

the arts, and CRT. The dynamics of this group were undeniable. When they met, within moments vigorous conversation erupted with rapid-fire questions and comments: "What if we tell a story about bullying but make it relevant to the underserved children of our city?" "Great, I can illustrate it in a comic book, using an app I just found." "Yes, and I'll provide another version using stop motion." "But where is the science or math?" "Well, we could use the time of day and the placement of the sun as part of the story." "Yes, and the shadow could be a character in the story that is long in the morning, and small at noon." Before long, a unique approach to STEAM was created through CRT and storytelling. The storytelling was the hook that provided the personal element that the students could relate to and make connections (Gay, 2010). This innovative professional development approach had five segments: (1) storytelling examples, (2) infusion of the arts into STEM, (3) technology, (4) CRT and storytelling, and (5) participant work time and showcase. The professional

Figures 1–3. (Above) Still frames from the stop motion animation.

Figures 4 and 5. (Left and Below) Samples of the comic book.

development was designed in a way that unpacked the process by introducing techniques, procedures, methods, and pedagogies using the arts; exploring STEM subjects in a creative way; and considering how CRT practices can be applied.

Session 1: This session began with the oral telling of an original story, *The Squashing*, followed by two renditions of the same story using stop motion animation (Figures 1–3) and a comic book (Figures 4–5). All three versions had the common curricular focus of a 4th-grade science standard explaining sun position throughout the day casting shadows of different lengths. *The Squashing* was created from an actual recounting of a child getting bullied throughout the day. The shadow in the story was the child's moral support that all but disappears during the noon hour because the sun is directly overhead. However, the protagonist of the story is vindicated when he realizes that after school, the sun will be lower in the sky and his moral support (shadow) will be there at the end of the day to help him triumph over the bully. This is an example of how lessons can be created to encourage students to visualize and see themselves inside the narrative or the content (Acuff et al., 2012). The session participants then discussed how they can work toward changing the power dynamics in their classrooms by using a student-centered approach (Buffington, 2014). In this case, the student-centered approach was artmaking. Lee (2012) reminded us that artmaking experiences can facilitate students' exploration of race and/or cultural diversity. Maintaining this information provides teachers with learning opportunities on ways to make content relatable to students' lives and experiences (Lee, 2012). While some session participants jumped right in, others balked at the idea of leading an artistic lesson. By the end of Session 1, however, all participants were fully engaged. This session presented the necessary steps to create each lesson while demonstrating how to achieve the end product as students both learn about shadows and become empowered as storytellers. Additionally, the nonarts educators discovered three avenues they could use that were engaging, produced quality results, and relinquished the power of learning to the students, thus allowing them to relate a story of their life to a science standard through the arts (Figure 6).

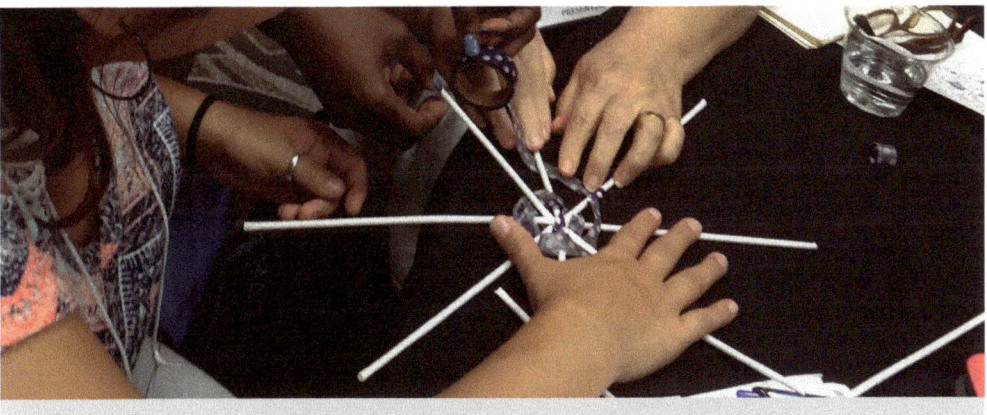

Figure 6. Project-based learning: engineering and artistic designs to cultural issues.

Session 2: With the playful title of *STEAM-a-licious*, this segment was designed to make infusing the arts a reassuring experience for nonarts people. This 3-hour long session included a variety of lessons presented in rapid-fire succession to keep the energy, engagement, and feelings of success high. The participants discussed what they considered to be the key factors to STEAM success. They began to understand that when teachers embrace STEAM education, the construction of knowledge becomes an intertextual process through which art is experienced in conjunction with other disciplines within the curriculum (J. A. Taylor et al., 2015). After the discussion, the STEAM-a-licious session embarked on hands-on activities that included the power of doodling and notetaking, musical math, theatrical geology charades, and tableaus. Teachers should create venues for students to reflect and reexamine ideas and possibilities through their everyday lives (Martinez, 2012). To that end, a project-based learning (PBL) lesson combining engineering and the arts was conducted. Participants were first taught the five-step design process (ask, imagine, plan, create, and improve). Then, we *asked* the participants to put themselves in the place of their students and discuss an issue that was culturally and locally problematic in their school or community. Topics such as bullying, homelessness, and providing food for families during the weekend embodied the concerns and discussions. Participants were asked to *imagine* a solution, no matter how far-fetched it may be, and then *plan* their design. Once they had a plan in place, the participants were given limited supplies to *create* their solution. After their designs were constructed, each group reported out their problem, their solution, and how they could *improve* their prototype (Figure 7). CRT demands more than raising awareness about other cultures; students need to be encouraged to make a change (Martinez, 2012). This lesson put the teachers in the place of the students to imagine how they could respond to an overarching issue that affects them by creating a solution. This session helped the participants feel empowered and engaged in the process, while still respecting the rigor that is involved in the arts, not just as a prop, but as a legitimate discipline.

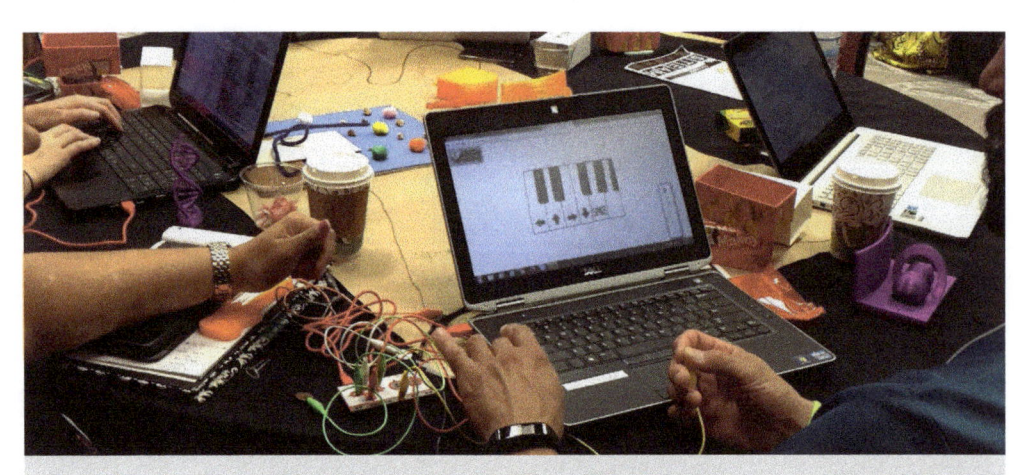

Figure 7. Programming practice for storytelling presentations.

Session 3: This hands-on session provided access to a 3D printer and circuit gadgets connected to the computer to create animation and sounds. The participants were taught how to program circuits into a computer, making inanimate objects interactive. They were given time to become comfortable with programming before being divided into groups. Each group was to tell a story with relevance to their students because CRT needs to have "elements of the students' culture and life experiences in their implementation of curriculum and instruction" (S. V. Taylor & Sobel, 2011, p. 16). The session was designed to help teachers become comfortable with a constantly changing medium and exhibit how technologies can be applied across disciplines.

Session 4: Participants were encouraged to explore the possibilities of acknowledging cultural differences, challenging routine teaching practices, and validating students in the classroom through CRT. This session emphasized that teachers must understand that culture comes from ways of doing and ways of being over a long period of time, and that being creative is part of culture and a basic human right. Each group created a "gingerbread child." They all started out looking the same, but after all the details were added, such as culture, socioeconomic status, geographical location, and family background, the cutouts all took on different traits (Figure 8). The cutout was a physical representation of how all students come to school with a variety of experiences, and the message that the cookie-cutter mentality of teaching cannot work with a diverse population. Each "gingerbread child" was actually a composite of characteristics familiar to members of the group, and became the hypothetical students that needed to be able to relate to the story shared during the final presentation.

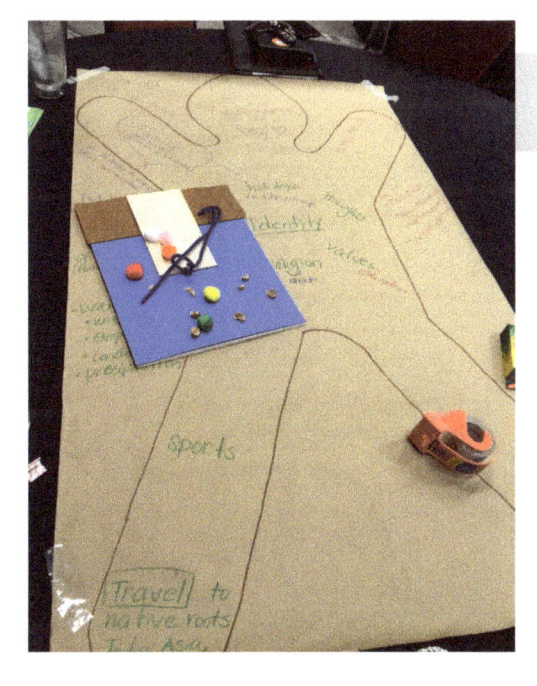

Figure 8. Cultural exploration of the students, the "gingerbread child."

Session 5: This was a final work session for participants to actively apply the skills, content knowledge, and pedagogies they learned, culminating in a showcase of their own STEAM lessons through culturally relevant storytelling. Facing the era of globalization, culturally responsive teachers must recognize that students' home cultures are inevitably influenced by global forces (Lai, 2012). The presentations were impressive, as they touched on topics deeply important to the culture of the students in each group.

For instance, one group from a Native American reservation in Arizona presented a story/lesson on ecology and the environment. This story was told from a child's point of view, and it positioned the grandfather as central to their culture. The group created a stop motion animation using cut paper and telling a story of heritage. The theme of the story was how modernization and surrounding city encroachments impede the survival of that culture's "great hunt" tradition. Another group related its lesson to students who are culturally connected to India. The lesson had a game component that taught children respect for environmental issues as they cleaned the Ganges River. These presentations provided entry points to the narrative for the teachers and their diverse student populations so that all parties could have a stake in the metanarrative (Acuff et al., 2012). Through these sample lessons, the participants gave relevant examples of how culture was evident. This can be translated to the experiences, schools, and media important to students, leading to their engagement with examples germane to their cultures and connected to both content and their lives (Buffington, 2014). The overall professional development illuminated the notion that teachers need to recognize that students learn in different ways and have different cultural experiences, and that they—the teachers—need to respond to those differences (Lee, 2012).

Closing

Culturally relevant pedagogy rests on three criteria or propositions: (1) Students must experience academic success; (b) students must develop and/or maintain cultural competence; and (c) students must develop a critical consciousness through which they challenge the status quo of the current social order. (Ladson-Billings, 1995a, p. 160)

This workshop adhered to Ladson-Billings's framework as it (1) provided educators several models to embolden children in constructing academic knowledge through artmaking and storytelling, (2) gave students the voice or the cultural competence to approach standards in ways that make the information relevant, and (3) used artmaking as a means for students to have the opportunity to develop a sociopolitical consciousness and evoke change, as in the PBL lesson's devised solutions.

In a Eurocentric world, it is easy to forget that not everyone derives from a Eurocultural background. With the rise of STEAM teaching in schools across the country, teachers have to consider how to engage their students. Respecting the students' cultures provides grounding and a solid foundation to begin. As a teacher, one must find students' cultural roots and respect them, because that is how you demonstrate to your students that they, too, bring value to the classroom. It demonstrates that they are important contributors to the process. In doing this, the students, in turn, have buy-in and want to delve deeper. Art shapes the understanding of the past and present, including social issues, equity, community, and identity; the students then can make inferences about the world around them (J. A. Taylor et al., 2015). Until the classroom feels like home, the students will continue to struggle. Workshops like this can teach nonart educators to embrace CRT and the arts, empowering both students and teachers. CRT allows students to have a voice—we just need to start listening.

Publishing Note: This chapter was previously published in Art Education *as Hunter-Doniger, T., Harris, R., Howard, C., Harris, R., & Hall, C. (2017). Culturally relevant STEAM. Art Education, 71(1), 46–52. Permission to reprint was granted by Taylor & Francis.*

Tracey Hunter-Doniger *is an associate professor specializing in arts in education, and the department chair of teacher education at the College of Charleston. She began her career as a public school teacher, which she did for 15 years. Her central research focus is art infusion, forest schools, and STEAM education.*

Courtney A. Howard *is the chief diversity officer and vice president for diversity, equity, and inclusion at the College of Charleston. She has taught science methods courses, served as associate dean, and directed a center for educational partnerships.*

Rénard Harris *is an associate professor of management in the School of Business at the College of Charleston. He has taught methods courses in social studies and has a research line that focuses on culture and storytelling.*

Cynthia Hall *has taught geology at the College of Charleston. She is currently a support scientist for NASA. She has taught several classes regarding infusing art and science through STEAM education.*

References

Acuff, J. B., Hirak, B., & Nangah, M. (2012). Dismantling a master narrative: Using culturally responsive pedagogy to teach the history of art education. *Art Education*, *65*(5), 6–10. https://doi.org/10.1080/00043125.2012.11519186

Buffington, M. L. (2014). Power play: Rethinking roles in the art classroom. *Art Education*, *67*(4), 6–12. https://doi.org/10.1080/00043125.2014.11519277

Gay, G. (2010). *Culturally responsive teaching: Theory, research, and practice* (2nd ed.). Teachers College Press.

Greene, M. (1995). *Releasing the imagination: Essays on education, the arts, and social change*. Jossey-Bass.

hooks, b. (1984). *Feminist theory: From margin to center*. South End Press.

hooks, b. (1994). *Teaching to transgress: Education as the practice of freedom*. Routledge. https://doi.org/10.4324/9780203700280

Kokkotas, P., Rizaki, A., & Malamitsa, K. (2010). Storytelling as a strategy for understanding concepts of electricity and electromagnetism. *Interchange*, *41*(4), 379–405. https://doi.org/10.1007/s10780-010-9137-9

Ladson-Billings, G. (1995a). But that's just good teaching! The case for culturally relevant pedagogy. *Theory Into Practice*, *34*(3), 159–165. https://www.jstor.org/stable/1476635

Ladson-Billings, G. (1995b). Toward a theory of culturally relevant pedagogy. *American Educational Research Journal*, *32*(3), 465–491. https://doi.org/10.3102/00028312032003465

Ladson-Billings, G. (2006). From the achievement gap to the education debt: Understanding achievement in U.S. schools. *Educational Researcher*, *35*(7), 3–12. https://doi.org/10.3102/0013189x035007003

Ladson-Billings, G. (2009). *The dreamkeepers: Successful teachers of African American children*. Wiley.

Lai, A. (2012). Culturally responsive art education in a global era. *Art Education*, *65*(5), 18–23. https://doi.org/10.1080/00043125.2012.11519188

Lee, N. (2012). Culturally responsive teaching for 21st-century art education: Examining race in a studio art experience. *Art Education*, *65*(5), 48–53. https://doi.org/10.1080/00043125.2012.11519192

Martinez, U. (2012). Cultur(ally) jammed: Culture jams as a form of culturally responsive teaching. *Art Education*, *65*(5), 12–17. https://doi.org/10.1080/00043125.2012.11519187

National Commission on Excellence in Education. (1983, April). *A nation at risk: The imperative for educational reform*. U.S. Department of Education. https://edreform.com/wp-content/uploads/2013/02/A_Nation_At_Risk_1983.pdf

Taljaard, J. (2016). A review of multi-sensory technologies in a science, technology, engineering, arts and mathematics (STEAM) classroom. *Journal of Learning Design*, *9*(2), 46–55. https://doi.org/10.5204/jld.v9i2.274

Taylor, J. A., Iroha, O., & Valdez, V. (2015). Culturally responsive teaching with visual art in the social studies. *Councilor*, *76*(1), Article 3. https://thekeep.eiu.edu/the_councilor/vol76/iss1/3

Taylor, S. V., & Sobel, D. M. (2011). *Culturally responsive pedagogy: Teaching like our students' lives matter*. Emerald. https://doi.org/10.1163/9781780520315

U.S. Department of Education. (2010). *Science, technology, engineering and math: Education for global leadership*. https://www.ed.gov/sites/default/files/stem-overview.pdf

SECTION III
Technology

Section III provides a wide spectrum of options for STEAM education through technology. "I Am Here Too! Career and Technical Education Digital Arts & Design Cluster and STEAM Integration" is a chapter that highlights STEAM careers that embrace art and technology within the digital arts. The chapter "Art-Based Makerspaces: Making the Connection to STEAM" hones in on makerspaces, as well as how to take advantage of the space for an optimal STEAM environment. "Digital Technology in the Art Room: Breakfast Cereal Box Design" is an exciting example of STEAM, visual arts, and technology. Lastly, "Virtual Reality Art Education" is a chapter that taps into the world of virtual reality and how it is relevant to current pedagogical strategies found in some schools today.

I Am Here Too!

Career and Technical Education Digital Arts & Design Cluster and STEAM Integration

Indira Bailey

When you sit down to read a magazine or a restaurant menu, have you ever wondered who created it, who the artist is, or what training they received? Many people think of an artist as a person who creates sculptures and paintings, to name a few. The term "starving artist" is usually in people's minds when they think of an artist. The belief of wearing a beret while holding a paintbrush trickles down to high school students, who may want to pursue an art career. This contrasts with artists who use science, technology, engineering, arts, and mathematics (STEAM) in their creative artistic practice (Gettings, 2016). The career and technical education (CTE) digital arts and design cluster offers an array of disciplines integrating STEAM that often go unnoticed.

STEAM is being recognized as a significant component in the 21st-century K–12 classroom to cultivate creativity, curriculum development, instruction, and assessment (Gettings, 2016; Gross & Gross, 2016; Herro et al., 2017; Liao, 2016). Many art educators in the K–12 sector are highlighting the aspects of STEAM by focusing on the various ways Leonardo da Vinci used creativity in his inventions and art (Gettings, 2016; Rolling, 2016). As the art education field is becoming familiar with STEAM's benefits, the CTE Digital Arts & Design cluster in vocational–technical high schools have already integrated STEAM into their curriculum.

For 15 years, I taught Commercial Illustration courses in the Digital Arts & Design cluster at a vocational–technical high school in New Jersey. The Digital Art & Design cluster offers high school students a career pathway using STEAM in graphic design, illustration, computer graphics, animation, web design, and advertising majors. The CTE program's uniqueness is that the student selects a cluster as a career choice rather than an elective. Students enter the program for 3 consecutive years and must fulfill 360 hours of training per school year.

As a CTE art educator, I found myself alone in many art education venues. I listened as other art educators tried to understand STEAM and how they could apply it to their curriculum. I realized that the voice of CTE art educators was missing in the discussion of K–12 art education. This chapter will discuss the significance of CTE Digital Art & Design program in a vocational–technical high school environment. I will then describe a graphic designer's role in the Commercial Illustration II class I taught to promote real-life experiences using STEAM. I highlight one student's problem-solving process, creativity, mathematics, drawing skills, and technology in creating a Moroccan travel poster. Last, I suggest strategies for traditional art educators to incorporate the design field into their classrooms.

What Is Career and Technical Education?

CTE programs provide workplace-readiness skills for real-world experiences and career future employment at an early age (Yağci & Çevik, 2017). Many education policy makers and leaders neglect CTE exposure to students based on a negative reputation (Petrilli & Zeehandelaar Shaw, 2016). For example, when I taught at a vocational–technical high school, people assumed I worked at juvenile detention, an alternative high school, or with students who lack the academic skills to enter higher education (Petrilli & Zeehandelaar Shaw, 2016). Far from the negative stereotypes of attending a vocational–technical high school, a CTE program is not the "shop" class for high school students not interested in higher education. CTE offers various career clusters that include STEAM, illustration techniques, package design, environmental design, animation, computer graphics, magazine design, and more.

U.S. Department of Education (2019) data on CTE programs mention that art, audiovisual technology, and communication are some of the "most prevalent career clusters in the nation's high schools" (para. 3). The report further states that STEM in CTE is a critical subject to the U.S. economy. The Perkins Collaborative Resource Network national initiative, Pathways to STEM Apprenticeship for High School Career and Technical Education Students (Perkins, 2018), explains that the purpose of awarding funds to CTE programs is to create apprenticeships opportunities in STEM fields. The "A" in STEAM is a significant factor toward a career pathway in the digital arts to help high school students transition into the real world.

STEAM in the CTE Environment

Even though some scholars question the definition of STEAM and its integration into the classroom, the National Art Education Association (NAEA) acknowledges the importance of STEAM to infuse art and design concepts, principles, and techniques into instructional learning (Katz-Buonincontro, 2018; Liao, 2016). The Digital Arts & Design curriculum exposes students with visual communications using technology. Scholars have recognized that STEAM could consider design, computer graphics, and other design education disciplines as a learning approach to problem solving (Herro et al., 2017). However, there is a gap in CTE that does not discuss STEAM's impact in vocational-education high schools. The Digital Arts & Design cluster in CTE programs is designed to provide the space to incorporate STEAM.

Commercial Illustrations as STEAM

The Commercial Illustration curriculum I designed is meant to prepare students to enter the job market on an entry-level basis or to continue their education in a postsecondary school. Most art teachers in a traditional school setting do not have the resources or time to facilitate STEAM projects (Roberts & Schnepp, 2020). The Perkins funding provided resources such as state-of-the-art Apple computers, Adobe Suite, and studio art materials for infusing STEAM. The CTE environment also has block scheduling and fewer students than an elective art class. For example, I taught two classes a day for a 2-hour block schedule; in each block, there were two grade levels. The morning block consisted of freshmen and sophomores. The afternoon block consisted of juniors and seniors. Both the morning and afternoon classrooms ranged from 16 to 18 students in each block. I had the opportunity, time, and resources to help students develop portfolios that demonstrated their style and ability, essential for future employment or postsecondary education.

The Bureau of Labor Statistics (2020) explains that a graphic designer's duties include meeting with clients or art directors to determine a project's scope, using digital or hand-drawn illustration, editing photos, designing layout and typefaces, and using various software programs to create a design. More importantly, a graphic designer creates images to deliver a message and present design concepts to the client that will best market, promote, and sell the product.

There are six essential qualities of a graphic designer the Bureau of Labor Statistics (2020) highlight, which are the following:

- **Analytical skills.** Graphic designers must perceive their work from a consumer point of view to ensure the designs convey the client's message.
- **Artistic ability.** Graphic designers must be able to create designs that are artistically interesting and appealing to clients and consumers. They produce rough illustrations of design ideas, either by hand sketching or by using computer programs.
- **Communication skills.** Graphic designers must communicate with clients, customers, and other designers to ensure their designs accurately and effectively convey information.
- **Computer skills.** Most graphic designers use specialized graphic design software to prepare their designs.
- **Creativity.** Graphic designers must be able to think of new approaches to communicating ideas to consumers. They develop unique designs that convey clients' messages.
- **Time-management skills.** Graphic designers often work simultaneously on multiple projects.

In the next section, I will describe how I incorporated the six qualities of a graphic designer and STEAM in a lesson to promote tourism. I will show a student's examples of the process of thinking as a graphic designer to prepare them for the real world.

Moroccan Travel Poster Project

I created the Moroccan travel poster project in alignment with the Bureau of Labor Statistics qualities of a graphic designer. This project allowed the 11th-grade Commercial Art II students to work as graphic designers. The students created a Moroccan travel poster over 10 days on a 90-minute block schedule. Students had been in the class for 2 years and had already learned the fundamentals of studio art practice in previous assignments. The purpose of the Moroccan travel poster was to teach students the functions of a graphic designer advertising a country to promote tourism and better the economy. The goal was to help students demonstrate their understanding of visual concepts, problem solving, layout design, typography, and computer graphics skills.

My Fulbright-Hays Fellowship inspired the Moroccan travel poster project to Morocco in 2011. I spent 6 weeks in Morocco studying the culture and the arts. My goal was to learn about the geometric designs and vegetal patterns in *zillij* mosaic tiles. In Morocco, I took Arabic language and calligraphy lessons. I traveled throughout the country, learning about Moroccan culture, food, music, religion, ethnicities, and art. To motivate the students, they watched a documentary I created about Morocco. I was able to give firsthand details about the Moroccan culture. In Figure 1, I am in Ouarzazate in a clay pottery studio demonstrating making a clay saucer on the wheel. I shared my experiences, which raised the curiosity of the students to ask questions about Morocco. Based on the information I provided to the students, they were responsible for researching Moroccan culture on their own to prepare their design.

Figure 1. Indira Bailey in Morocco.

Communicating Visually Through Graphic Design

I divided the Moroccan travel poster project into six sections. In the first section, students brainstormed by making a list of thoughts and ideas about Morocco. To help motivate them, I played Moroccan music and showed pictures. I asked the students to make a list of what they knew about this African country. Students researched key attractions about Morocco, collected pictorial references, and determined the demographics.

In the second section, students used analytical skills and creativity to design several thumbnail sketches that focused on attracting Morocco tourism. They included a design layout, typography, and the principles and elements of design. Each student presented their thumbnail sketches as graphic designers to their clients (the students) in the third section. They communicated how each thumbnail sketch included the images, color schemes, and typography that best represented Morocco. As a group, the students helped each other decide on which thumbnail sketch was the most effective way to advertise and promote tourism in Morocco. The fourth section was based on the class's feedback, where students selected one thumbnail and created a rough draft. The students presented their rough drafts to their clients (the other students) to see a larger and clearer layout.

Figure 2. Student drawing images onto canvas.

Figure 3. Student's final sketch on canvas.

STEAM Education: An Interdisciplinary Look at Art in the Curriculum

The students made revisions to their rough draft in the fifth section to the clients (students) for final approval; they then transferred their sketch on to the canvas (Figure 2). The student in Figure 2 demonstrates her artistic ability and creativity by drawing three tagine pots. To further communicate the Moroccan culture, in Figure 3, she puts a belly dancer, a mosque, and the Sahara Desert on each tagine pot. This student incorporated traditional colors, shapes, and repetitive patterns of the zillij tile styles (Figure 4). From her research, she continued to incorporate Moroccan colors and images in her design (Figure 5). In demonstrating problem-solving skills to encourage tourism to Morocco, the student's research helped her create three different cultural destinations of Morocco.

Figure 4. Student's artwork: beginning sketch and painting.

Figure 5. Student's artwork in progress.

Figure 6. Student's final painting completed.

–71–

In the sixth section, the student scanned her artwork into the computer after she completed the painting (Figure 6). Using Adobe Photoshop, she then created the layout for the travel poster and looked at several fonts to decide which one would best represent the culture and not interfere with the artwork (Figure 7). At the end of the lesson, all of the students displayed their artwork and critiqued each other on how effective their posters advertised and promoted tourism for Morocco.

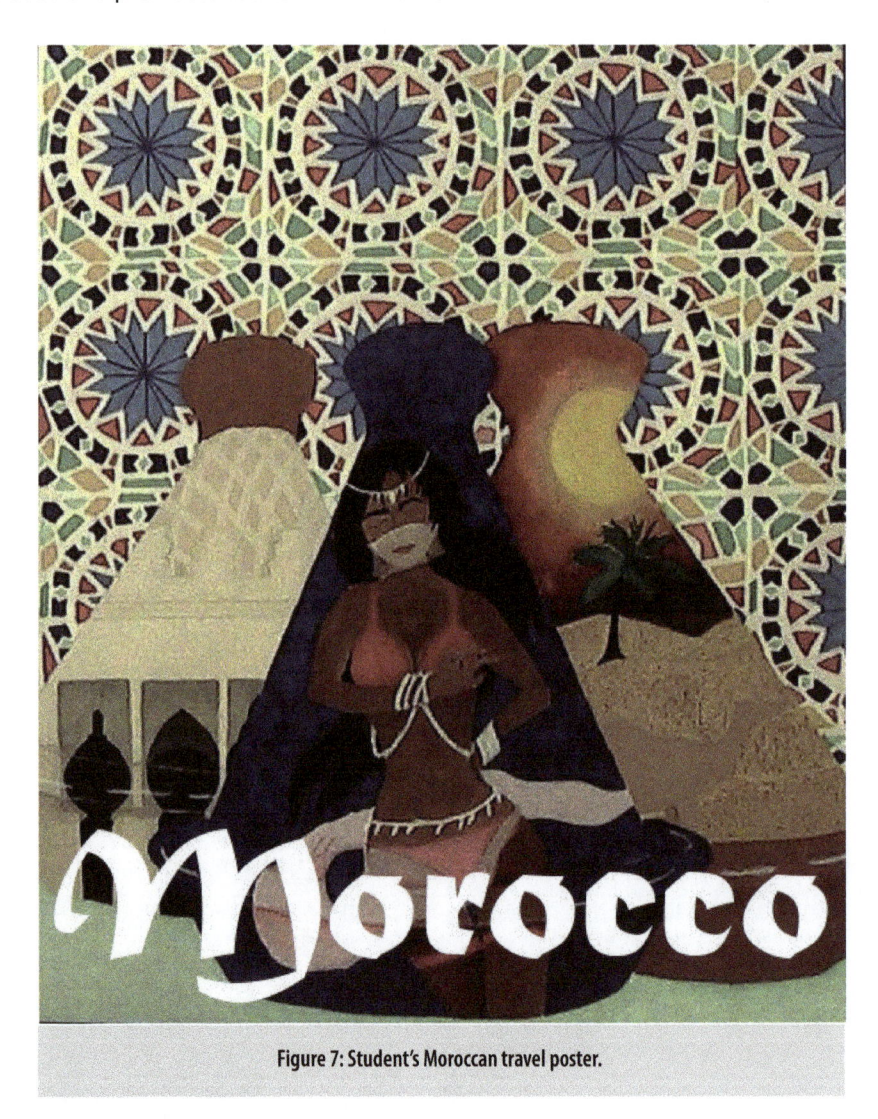

Figure 7: Student's Moroccan travel poster.

The Benefits of STEAM in CTE

The Moroccan travel poster project provided students the experience of working as graphic designers and taking feedback from their peers as clients. Each student took their role as a graphic designer seriously, as the project challenged them to listen and communicate with each other. For some students, accepting feedback was difficult because they did not understand why they had to change their layout or revise their design. Many students questioned why they had to create many thumbnail sketches and not select the one they liked the best. They learned that being a graphic designer is not the same as being a studio artist, where you paint what you feel. Being a graphic designer is a job, and the job is to promote an event or product for a client. The Moroccan travel poster project allowed them to experience the skills they need to become successful graphic designers. As a result, the students infused their creativity and artistic skills with technology and created Moroccan travel posters. Each student's travel poster illustrated a different destination or cultural component of Morocco. The student's example in the figures is an example of how students took the time to research, collaborate, and critique each other to present new approaches that effectively conveyed their message. Students demonstrated the six qualities of a graphic designer, from hand-drawn thumbnail sketches to the finished product using Adobe Photoshop.

I learned from this lesson that STEAM in a CTE Digital Arts & Design cluster is a way for students to learn real hands-on experiences, creativity, and advertising through art and technology. The CTE environment is a platform to incorporate STEAM in the classroom because of the career-readiness pathway established in vocational–technical education.

The field of art education could benefit from observing a CTE Digital Arts & Design curriculum because there are many similarities between CTE and traditional high school art classrooms. According to Sarabeth Berk (2016), "For students to be successful in the workplace, they need to explicitly learn design skills and habits, and that means design needs to exist across the curriculum in art and non-art classrooms" (p. 16). Berk further states that art educators do not need to teach students to become designers; however, they should introduce problem-solving fundamentals. I understand that the CTE environment is different from the traditional art classroom, with block scheduling, fewer students, and funding. However, I create suggestions for the art educator who wants to incorporate STEAM into their curriculum.

Strategies to Incorporate STEAM in the Art Classroom

It is time for art education to recognize and include the CTE digital art programs in vocational-education high school as a significant educational path for students. The CTE Digital Arts & Design clusters are an extension of art education, yet they are rarely discussed. The benefits students receive from learning creative techniques and technology offer them artistic skills and a career. At the beginning of the chapter, I raised the question of looking at a magazine or restaurant menu and questioning the artist. Art educators have to look beyond studio art as the only form of aesthetics and look at the arts industry as a whole.

The digital arts have made significant contributions to the art world, which is rarely acknowledged. More importantly, we want students to use their artistic skills to create, explore, experiment, and design. I recommend three strategies based on my teaching experience for art teachers in a traditional art environment.

The first strategy is for art educators to familiarize themselves with the digital art field. Introduce students to careers in graphic design, illustration, animation, advertising, industrial design, and multimedia design. Many high school students are unaware that these are art careers where they can still combine their love of art with technology and design. Some art educators would need professional development in design to create a curriculum to introduce to their students. In other words, adding the "A" to STEM is not painting an object without a purpose.

The second strategy is for the institution to provide and encourage preservice art educators to enroll in digital art courses. This exposure could help future art teachers understand and prepare lessons that include technology before entering the classroom. Some teachers may be intimidated by learning technology and design when not introduced early in their careers.

The third strategy is for art educators to invite graphic designers and illustrators into the classroom and take their students to the artists' studio. Several organizations focus on art and design; the Society of Illustrators (https://societyillustrators.org) has a museum, lecture series, and exhibitions. The Professional Association for Design (https://www.aiga.org) provides types of design practice and downloadable lesson plans with handouts, a glossary, and a rubric. The Graphic Artists Guild (https://graphicartistsguild.org) is a community of graphic design and illustrators. They provide curriculum-development materials for teachers that can introduce art and technology into the classroom.

These are three suggested strategies and resources and are not a fixed list of ways to incorporate STEAM into the curricula. Our task as art educators is to introduce students to all aspects of art and design. Gettings (2016) emphasized that by adding STEAM into the curriculum, you engage students in real-world problems, allowing them to use artistic thinking, experiment with different materials, and demonstrate artistic design aesthetics.

Acknowledging CTE in Art Education

The Digital Arts & Design cluster in CTE programs is a significant component of STEAM. It is imperative to address the gap between art education in a traditional classroom and CTE programs. There is much to learn from both sides of art education, as the goals in teaching art to students are similar. The CTE program holds a strong connection to STEAM and allows students to connect to real-world experiences. STEAM projects are more than STEM alone (Roberts & Schnepp, 2020). By offering courses such as graphic design, illustration, web design, video production, and more, CTE has established a curriculum platform that includes critical thinking, creativity, communication, and computer and design skills. If the CTE Digital Arts & Design cluster was acknowledged fully by art education, then we could work together to offer more for students who wish to obtain a career in the arts. By acknowledging the art programs in CTE and how they connect to STEAM, we can guide students to all facets of art, including technology, and not just the art stereotypes.

Note: All artworks in this chapter have received permission for publication.

> **Indira Bailey** taught CTE art and digital design at a high school in New Jersey for 15 years. She is the finalist for 2012 New Jersey Teacher of the Year. Bailey received the Elliot Eisner Research Award from NAEA. She is an assistant professor of Art Education at Claflin University in South Carolina.

References

Berk, S. (2016). Designing for the future of education requires design education. *Art Education*, *69*(6), 16–20. https://doi.org/10.1080/00043125.2016.1224844

Bureau of Labor Statistics. (2020). What graphic designers do. In *Occupational outlook handbook*. U.S. Department of Labor. Retrieved October 25, 2020, from https://www.bls.gov/ooh/arts-and-design/graphic-designers.htm

Gettings, M. (2016). Putting it all together: STEAM, PBL, scientific method, and the Studio Habits of Mind. *Art Education*, *69*(4), 10–11. https://doi.org/10.1080/00043125.2016.1176472

Gross, K., & Gross, S. (2016). Transformation: Constructivism, design thinking, and elementary STEAM. *Art Education*, *69*(6), 36–43. https://doi.org/10.1080/00043125.2016.1224869

Herro, D., Quigley, C., Andrews, J., & Delacruz, G. (2017). Co-measure: Developing an assessment for student collaboration in STEAM activities. *International Journal of STEM Education*, *4*(26). https://doi.org/10.1186/s40594-017-0094-z

Katz-Buonincontro, J. (2018). Gathering STE(A)M: Policy, curricular, and programmatic developments in arts-based science, technology, engineering, and mathematics education: Introduction to the special issue of *Arts Education Policy Review*: STEAM focus. *Arts Education Policy Review*, *119*(2), 73–76. https://doi.org/10.1080/10632913.2017.1407979

Liao, C. (2016). From interdisciplinary to transdisciplinary: An arts-integrated approach to STEAM education. *Art Education*, *69*(6), 44–49. https://doi.org/10.1080/00043125.2016.1224873

Perkins Collaborative Resource Network. (2018). *Work-based learning*. U.S. Department of Education Office of Career, Technical, and Adult Education, Division of Academic and Technical Education. https://cte.ed.gov/initiatives/work-based-learning

Petrilli, M. J., & Zeehandelaar Shaw, D. (2016, April 8). *How career and technical education in high school improves student outcomes*. Thomas B. Fordham Institute. https://fordhaminstitute.org/national/commentary/how-career-and-technical-education-high-school-improves-student-outcomes

Roberts, T., & Schnepp, J. (2020). Building problem-solving skills through STEAM. *Technology and Engineering Teacher*, *79*(8), 8–13.

Rolling, J. H. (2016). Reinventing the STEAM engine for art + design education [Editorial]. *Art Education*, *69*(4), 4–7. https://doi.org/10.1080/00043125.2016.1176848

U.S. Department of Education. (2019, September 27). *U.S. Department of Education releases interactive data story on career and technical education in high school* [Press release]. https://www.einnews.com/pr_news/497650879/u-s-department-of-education-releases-interactive-data-story-on-career-and-technical-education-in-high-school

Yağci, A., & Çevik, M. (2017). Predictions of academic achievements of vocational and technical high school students with artificial neural networks in science courses (physics, chemistry and biology) in Turkey and measures to be taken for their failures. *SHS Web of Conferences*, *37*, Article 01057. https://doi.org/10.1051/shsconf/20173701057

Art-Based Makerspaces:
Making the Connection to STEAM

Melissa Negreiros

"**My** kid won't stop picking up trash!" one parent exclaimed when I encountered her in the hallway of the elementary school where I taught a group of 3rd and 4th graders during a program called Passion Project each morning. Her child, along with his classmates, had become obsessed with solving the problem of plastic pollution in our oceans. Picking up trash was only the beginning of their journey, which led to beautiful artwork, engaging with a practicing artist, and advocating with a shared passion for saving the world's oceans.

In the current age of mobile devices and digital media, young people are spending more time consuming digital media than ever before (Rideout & Robb, 2019). While these powerful digital devices offer unprecedented opportunities for today's youth to create digital content (Peppler, 2010), young people devote very little time to creating authentic digital artifacts. Instead, most of their time is spent consuming entertainment media, including videos, social media, games, and music (Rideout & Robb, 2019). Thomas (2016) explained that it is essential to provide all students with opportunities to use new technologies as tools to engage in creative and productive learning. These opportunities enable them to become creators of digital content, not simply consumers. The push for science, technology, engineering, the arts, and math (STEAM) and maker education provides fertile ground for engaging students as creators of multimodal and multimedia content.

STEAM education and the maker movement can equally partner with art and design to create, share, and make connections providing reciprocal benefits to all disciplines (Patton & Knochel, 2017). *Making*, in this sense, can be seen as a gateway to deeper engagement in science, technology, engineering, arts, and mathematics (Dougherty, 2012b). Situating creativity and design as transcending disciplinary lines furthers the notion of STEAM education as an interdisciplinary space.

In this chapter, I explore the potential of creating art-based makerspaces for STEAM. In the first section, I review the maker movement, its constructionist roots, and its connection to making in art education. In the next section, I share a STEAM project situated in an art-based makerspace. This project exemplifies the promise of combining traditional studio practices with maker practices to innovate and offer solutions to real-world problems. Finally, I discuss implications for bringing these practices to the art room.

Literature Review

In this section, I outline the literature relevant to creating art-based makerspaces for STEAM. Specifically, I present constructionism as the theoretical framework for positioning making in art education. I also explore the maker movement, the evolution of makerspaces, and the role of making in art education.

Constructionism

Educators and researchers have been talking for decades about the role of *making* in learning. Seymour Papert's theory of constructionism unites Piaget's framing of the learner as knowledge constructor with Dewey's processes of learning through hands-on, experiential, and inquiry-based activities (as cited in Groff, 2014). Constructionism posits that learning occurs by constructing knowledge through the act of making something shareable (Papert & Harel, 1991). Because constructionism is the theory of learning that serves as the foundation for making in education, Papert is credited as "the father of the maker movement" (Martinez & Stager, 2013, p. 17). The maker movement and STEAM education provide one avenue for the meaningful integration of technology in arts education.

While this theoretical lens has propelled an ample amount of research on making in education, problem-based learning, and learning with technology (Groff, 2014), it is largely absent in research on the arts and arts education (Halverson & Sheridan, 2014; Peppler, 2010). Halverson & Sheridan (2014) argue "that art making is fundamentally a representational domain and therefore resonates with a constructionist perspective on learning" (p. 498). Peppler (2010) echoes the stance that constructionism serves the goals and aims of art education. This is a relevant frame from which to view making in art education because the act of making is central to the arts.

Maker Movement

Every few decades, educational trends change (Blikstein, 2013). This reality is reflected in the rise of the maker movement. Spurred by increasingly accessible and affordable digital technologies and fabrication tools, virtual communities (Dougherty, 2013), and the do-it-yourself ethos (Sweeny, 2017), amateurs worldwide are engaged passionately with hands-on activities that go beyond being a consumer (Dougherty, 2012a). Indeed, the maker movement is characterized by hands-on, playful engagement with new technologies and digital tools to create, design, or innovate something new or learn a new skill and share it with the larger community (Dougherty, 2012a; Halverson & Sheridan, 2014; Sweeny, 2017). In short, the maker movement emphasizes the creation of digital and physical artifacts to innovate and solve problems utilizing both high-tech and low-tech materials.

Dougherty (2013) broadly describes the maker mindset as a "growth mindset that encourages students to believe they can learn to do anything" (p. 10). Martin (2015) goes into more detail, describing the maker mindset as playful, growth- and asset-oriented, failure positive, and collaborative. Makers believe that given time, effort, and materials, they can learn any skill and how to make anything they can imagine. They look at failure as an indication that more effort is needed, and they collaborate as they share ideas, projects, and expertise. The maker movement complements the aims of STEAM and art education by combining the traditional physical acts of construction with digital media to make a sharable artifact.

Makerspaces

Having a designated place in schools to make things creates new opportunities for all students, cultivates practices of making, and gives students access to tools and materials they might not have otherwise (Dougherty, 2012b). These spaces provide students with a place to safely make, build, and share their creations (Blikstein, 2013). Physical spaces for *making* are crucial for both art education and the maker movement (Sweeny, 2017). The act of *making* is central for art education, and makerspaces emerge as a natural progression (Lu, 2005). Makerspaces provide a setting for people to explore, share, and learn how to use a range of fabrication tools and techniques, a practice also found in art studios such as ceramics, printmaking, and darkrooms (Patton & Knochel, 2017). The primary difference between making in art studios and makerspaces is that makerspaces are characterized by combining tools and techniques from a variety of fields, while the majority of studio practices derive from ways of making that are traditional to the field (Sweeny, 2017). Taken together, the maker practices present in makerspaces and art studio practices offer a space where all disciplines converge to serve student problem solving and innovation.

Making in Art

The rise of the maker movement provides an opportunity for art educators to redefine the role of art education and challenges them to evaluate their ideas about what art is, who makes art, how and where art is taught, and who teaches art (Manifold, 2017). It is important to remember that while media and methods have evolved with the times, making art remains central to art education (Sweeny, 2017). In their evaluations, art educators may find that maker practices and artmaking practices tend toward ways of making that are similar. New technologies in this context, including digital fabrication tools, physical computing components, and programming languages, serve as additional tools that have entered the palette for artists (Peppler, 2010). Blikstein (2013) argued,

> The real power of any technology is not in the technique itself or in the allure it generates, but in the new ways of personal expression it enables, the new forms of human interaction it facilitates, and the powerful ideas it makes accessible to children. (p. 17)

The integration of new technologies characteristic of the maker movement, combined with historical traditions and practices, offer a view of what a maker's approach to arts education may look like.

Methods: Art, STEAM, and Making

In the spring of 2018, my coteacher, Rosie, and I initiated a guided Passion Project with our group of 3rd and 4th graders at a STEAM school in the southeastern United States. "Guided Passion Projects" were our version of initiating the students into the concept of what is commonly referred to as "Genius Hour." Genius Hour was a time set aside during the school day for students to explore their passions. As stated on the school's website:

> Passion Projects create a culture among students and teachers that allows for free exploration of passions, failure, and experimentation. Students are encouraged to take risks within a safe, nurturing environment. During this time, students explore ideas, solve problems, generate products, peer review, and make their learning public. This time provides opportunities for students to solidify both content skills as well as those soft skills necessary towards a productive work life after the educational path ends. (PSE STEAM Instructional Program, n.d., para. 1).

We began the spring semester with a new group of students, who were selected via lottery. In order to help students gain skills and cultivate a maker mindset, we decided to conduct a guided project prior to students undertaking their own projects. Reflective of the vision for STEAM education, the school strives to engage students in real-world problems through an interdisciplinary approach to learning focused on STEAM disciplines. This vision helped us select the problem of plastic pollution in our oceans. This problem was local, relevant, and timely because the school is in a coastal community, where evidence of plastic pollution serves as a daily reminder of the greater, global problem. The project was organized into three phases: (1) identify the question or problem, (2) research, and (3) solutions. The goals of the project were for students to:

- Gain inspiration from artists' work to enhance the urgency of the issue while demonstrating the power of art for effective communication.
- Engage in the cyclical process of research, problem solving, creating and innovating, and design involved in a meaningful passion project.
- Utilize the visual artmaking process to communicate and advocate for the problem at hand.
- Develop and cultivate a maker mindset and maker skills.
- Develop a global perspective by focusing on real-world, global issues.
- Leverage technology as a tool for learning, creating, and communicating.
- Make, do, learn, and/or teach something that contributes to solving the problem.
- Make learning public.

Art-Based Makerspaces: Making the Connection to STEAM

> By the year 2050, there will be more plastic in the ocean than fish.

Figure 1. Presentation slide depicting Mandy Barker's artwork with facts about plastic pollution.

To introduce the problem, we displayed Mandy Barker's artwork (see Figure 1 for an example) with facts about the effects of plastic pollution. Mandy Barker is a photographer and activist who communicates about the plastic pollution problem through her artwork. She creates her beautiful images using plastic debris from oceans around the world and works with scientists to include facts about plastic pollution in the captions of her work. She explains that the contrast between the beautiful images and difficult-to-hear facts help her effectively communicate with viewers (IKEA Sverige, 2016).

After viewing a series of facts and images, the students responded to a "What's the Problem?" Padlet, a virtual pinboard, and included hashtags with their emotional responses. To make the problem more local, we displayed an image of the storm drain in the school parking lot (see Figure 2) and asked, "How does plastic end up in the ocean? Could our plastic end up in the ocean? Does anyone recognize this?"

The students immediately recognized the storm drain in the school's parking lot. We then displayed an aerial photograph of the school (see Figure 3)—a great reminder of the school's proximity to the Wando River, which feeds the Atlantic Ocean.

We prompted, "What kind of trash do you think would end up in the Wando River if it were to rain today?" Several students called out ideas, including plastic bottles and candy wrappers. One student suggested taking a walk to the parking lot to see for ourselves.

STEAM Education: An Interdisciplinary Look at Art in the Curriculum

Figure 2. Slide of storm drain in school parking lot with prompting questions.

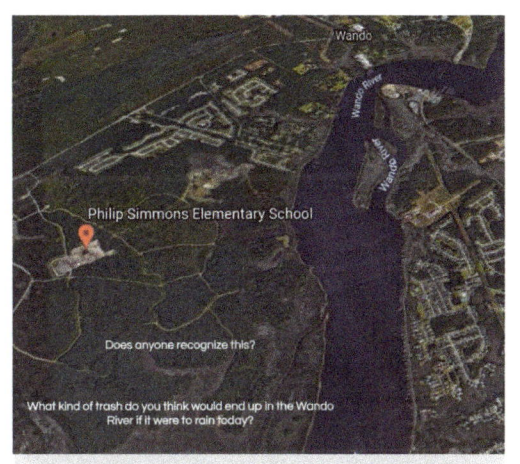

Figure 3. Slide of aerial image of the school's proximity to the Wando River with prompting questions.

Once outside, the students began collecting the trash that littered the grounds. They were horrified that they were able to collect so much debris in such a relatively small area.

The next day, as the students entered the library with bags of plastic pollution they had collected at their homes and other spaces in the community, their outrage at the dangers plastic pollution poses to marine life was palpable, and they were committed to preventing plastic from reaching our waterways. They wanted to do something to help with the problem and were discussing ways the plastic pollution they had collected could be repurposed. To to provide inspiration, we again displayed images of Mandy Barker's artwork. Our students were immediately inspired by the powerful images Barker posts on her Instagram page. They worked for days to repurpose their plastic trash into unique pieces of art (see Figures 4 and 5) and attached contrasting captions to help communicate their messages.

Figures 4–5. Students working on their Mandy Barker–inspired artwork in an art-based, transdisciplinary makerspace.

The students photographed their images (see Figure 6) and shared them on the school's social media accounts. They were all thrilled and a bit starstruck when Mandy Barker "liked" the images on Instagram and encouraged them to "keep up the good work to raise awareness" (personal communication, November 17, 2018). The students felt empowered, as if they were on their way to becoming influential environmental art advocates against single-use plastic in the community. They realized their art could send a powerful message and make a difference.

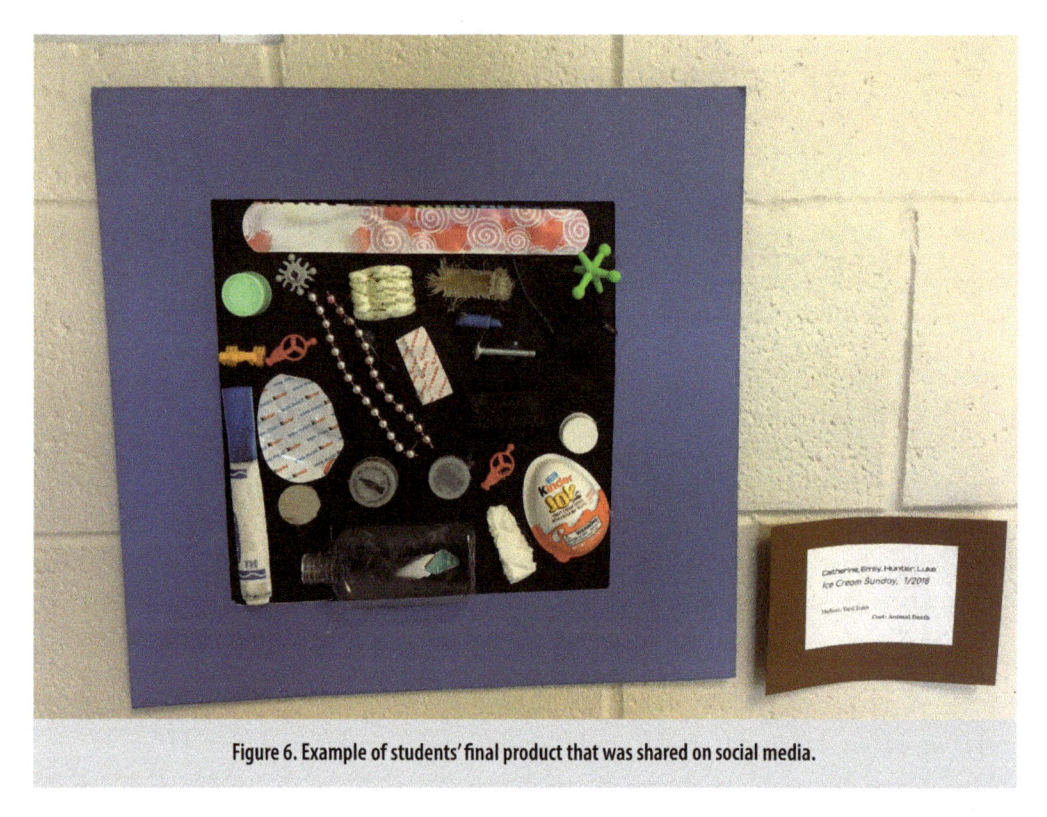

Figure 6. Example of students' final product that was shared on social media.

Findings

This project illuminates the possibilities when merging art, technology, and maker practices to create an interdisciplinary space for STEAM. Not only did the students engage with the traditional art practices related to photography, but they were able to gain inspiration, share their artwork, and connect with an expert via social media. The findings from this experience reveal the promise of combining art and maker practices to solve real-world problems in an art-based, interdisciplinary space that embraced STEAM.

Combining Art and Maker Practices

As demonstrated in the *making* of Mandy Barker–inspired art, the meeting of maker and traditional studio practices in the form of an art-based makerspace has the potential for merging the best of both worlds. *Making* in an interdisciplinary space that embraces STEAM involves the collaborative, active, hands-on production of physical and digital artifacts (Guyotte et al., 2015; Honey & Kanter, 2013). By purposeful intertwining of discipline-specific skills and knowledge, students are able to think through materials (Guyotte et al., 2014). In doing so, students can combine new technologies and practices with traditional materials and express themselves artistically (Peppler, 2016). Through this interdisciplinary overlap, they are able to innovate around complex social issues (Hunter-Doniger, 2020). An art-based makerspace reflects core makerspace characteristics, such as grappling with powerful interdisciplinary problems while engaging in material play. Uniquely, these spaces provide an environment where students can grapple with real-world problems.

Real-World Problems

As reflected in this example, powerful interdisciplinary projects provide the opportunity to reconfigure the artificial boundaries between STEAM disciplines in an art-based makerspace. Initially, the students were captivated by the threat plastic pollution poses to marine life, then immediately wanted to take action by creating works of art as their means of advocacy. The students simultaneously engaged in practices specific to all of the STEAM disciplines in ways reflective of arts and STEM professionals. The exploration of this complex, global issue provided a space that connected the students to the real world and helped them to discover that their artwork is important in ways that transcend the classroom.

Foregrounding Art Practices

STEAM and the maker movement provide important touchstones for contemplating how art education might progress in meaningfully integrating technology into the art curriculum (Patton & Knochel, 2017; Sweeny, 2017). Unique to the concept of interdisciplinary, art-based makerspaces is the practice of foregrounding historical and contemporary artmaking methods and theories. This practice has the potential to bring theoretical concepts into reality and contribute meaningfully to the STEM subjects while ensuring that art education is not diminished (Sweeny, 2017). For example, in this project, Mandy Barker's work was used as the foundation for advocacy. We discussed her technique of combining beautiful images, created from unconventional materials, with contrasting, hard-to-hear facts about pollution in the ocean to communicate her message. This practice inspired students to advocate for the world's oceans through their artwork.

Discussion: Connections to STEAM

Art is an important component to the STEAM curriculum and makerspaces (Knochel & Patton, 2015; Keifer-Boyd et al., 2019). Long-standing, academically sound traditions are an essential part of the history of art education and can contribute to artmaking within a makerspace (Sweeny, 2017). Combining traditional studio practices with maker practices, such as exploring solutions to real-world problems through material play while foregrounding art practices, situates students in an interdisciplinary space where each discipline is empowered. Additionally, individuals working in this space can learn a great deal from artists working in and between the fields of science, math, technology, and art. The interdisciplinary benefits of art education also include the multitude of ways that arts can be integrated across the curriculum.

Conclusion

Combining traditional art studio practices with maker practices provides art and general education teachers with a space to engage students in solving real-world problems while creating authentic art. Together, STEAM education and the maker movement can form a partnership that provides reciprocal benefits to all disciplines. Teachers can realize the potential of these spaces by engaging students in real-world problems and material play while foregrounding art practices. In turn, students can establish a rich palette of practices that are reflective of art education, the maker movement, and STEAM disciplines.

Melissa Negreiros, assistant professor in teacher education at the College of Charleston, served in South Carolina public schools as a classroom teacher, instructional coach, district coordinator, and principal. She currently teaches preservice teachers how to meaningfully integrate technology and problem-based learning to provide transformative experiences for students.

References

Barker, M. [@mandybarkerphotography]. (2018, November 17). They look amazing. [Instagram comment]. Instagram.

Blikstein, P. (2013). Digital fabrication and "making" in education—The democratization of invention. In J. Walter-Herrmann & C. Büching (Eds.), *FabLab: Of machines, makers and inventors* (pp. 203–222). transcript Verlag. https://doi.org/10.14361/transcript.9783839423820.203

Dougherty, D. (2012a). The maker movement. *Innovations, 7*(3), 11–14. https://doi.org/10.1162/inov_a_00135

Dougherty, D. (2012b, April 4). Makerspaces in education and DARPA. *Make:*. https://makezine.com/article/maker-news/makerspaces-in-education-and-darpa

Dougherty, D. (2013). The maker mindset. In M. Honey & D. E. Kanter (Eds.), *Design, make, play: Growing the next generation of STEM innovators* (pp. 7–11). Routledge. https://doi.org/10.4324/9780203108352-6

Groff, A. (2014). The maker movement in education: Designing, creating, and learning across contexts. *Harvard Educational Review, 84*(4), 492–494. https://doi.org/10.17763/haer.84.4.b1p1352374577600

Guyotte, K. W., Sochacka, N. W., Costantino, T. E., Kellam, N. N., & Walther, J. (2015). Collaborative creativity in STEAM: Narratives of art education students' experiences in transdisciplinary spaces. *International Journal of Education & the Arts, 16*(15). http://www.ijea.org/v16n15

Guyotte, K. W., Sochacka, N. W., Costantino, T. E., Walther, J., & Kellam, N. N. (2014). STEAM as social practice: Cultivating creativity in transdisciplinary spaces. *Art Education, 67*(6), 12–19. https://doi.org/10.1080/00043125.2014.11519293

Halverson, E. R., & Sheridan, K. (2014). The maker movement in education. *Harvard Educational Review, 84*(4), 495–504. https://doi.org/10.17763/haer.84.4.34j1g68140382063

Honey, M., & Kanter, D. E. (Eds.). (2013). *Design, make, play: Growing the next generation of STEM innovators*. Routledge. https://doi.org/10.4324/9780203108352

Hunter-Doniger, T. (2020). The A² curriculum ARTvocacy and autonomy: Giving a voice to the next generation. *Art Education*, *73*(4), 37–43. https://doi.org/10.1080/00043125.2020.1746160

IKEA Sverige. (2016, March 1). *IKEA art event 2016: Mandy Barker* [Video]. YouTube.https://www.youtube.com/watch?v=x-Zvhcv1KsU

Keifer-Boyd, K., Knochel, A. D., Patton, R. M., & Sweeny, R. (2019). Critical digital making: 21st century art education (in)formation. *Transdisciplinary Inquiry, Practice, and Possibilities in Art Education*. The Pennsylvania State University Libraries. https://doi.org/10.26209/arted50-12

Knochel, A. D., & Patton, R. M. (2015). If art education then critical digital making: Computational thinking and creative code. *Studies in Art Education*, *57*(1), 21–38. https://doi.org/10.1080/00393541.2015.11666280

Lu, L.-F. L. (2005). Pre-service art teacher negative attitudes and perceptions of computer-generated art imagery: Recommendations for pre-service art education programs. *Visual Arts Research*, *31*(1), 89–102.

Manifold, M. C. (2017). Making special, making art, or making things. *Studies in Art Education*, *58*(4), 360–364. https://doi.org/10.1080/00393541.2017.1368286

Martin, L. (2015). The promise of the maker movement for education. *Journal of Pre-College Engineering Education Research*, *5*(1), Article 4. https://doi.org/10.7771/2157-9288.1099

Martinez, S. L., & Stager, G. (2013). *Invent to learn: Making, tinkering, and engineering in the classroom*. Constructing Modern Knowledge Press.

Papert, S., & Harel, I. (1991). Situating constructionism. In *Constructionism* (pp. 1–11). Ablex.

Patton, R. M., & Knochel, A. D. (2017). Meaningful makers: Stuff, sharing, and connection in STEAM curriculum. *Art Education*, *70*(1), 36–43. https://doi.org/10.1080/00043125.2017.1247571

Peppler, K. A. (2010). Media arts: Arts education for a digital age. *Teachers College Record*, *112*(8), 2118–2153. https://doi.org/10.1177/016146811011200806

Peppler, K. (2016). ReMaking arts education through physical computing. In K. Peppler, E. R. Halverson, & Y. B. Kafai (Eds.), *Makeology: Makers as learners* (Vol. 2; pp. 206–226). Routledge. https://doi.org/10.4324/9781315726496-13

PSE STEAM Instructional Program. (n.d.). *Passion Projects*. Philip Simmons Elementary. Retrieved July 21, 2020, from https://sites.google.com/bcsdschools.net/psesteam/passion-project?authuser=0

Rideout, V. J., & Robb, M. B. (2019). *The Common Sense census: Media use by tweens and teens*. Common Sense Media. https://www.commonsensemedia.org/research/the-common-sense-census-media-use-by-tweens-and-teens-2019

Sweeny, R. W. (2017). Makerspaces and art educational places. *Studies in Art Education*, *58*(4), 351–359. https://doi.org/10.1080/00393541.2017.1368288

Thomas, S. (2016). *Future ready learning: Reimagining the role of technology in education*. Office of Educational Technology, U.S. Department of Education.

Digital Technology in the Art Room:
Breakfast Cereal Box Design

Rachel Wintemberg

This cereal-box-design science, technology, engineering, the arts, and math (STEAM) unit is the perfect blend of technology and art. The study of food-package design is an ideal gateway to interdisciplinary learning at the high school level. While this article focuses mostly on the design process and how to utilize Adobe software, I encourage STEAM educators to collaborate with biology teachers to analyze cereal nutrition information, as well as geometry teachers to delve into the mathematics and engineering of commercial package design. This project provided my class with the perfect platform to develop skills in both design technology and visual art, as well as the opportunity to explore careers in commercial art and communication design.

Like many children growing up in the pre-internet suburbia of the 1970s, I have fond childhood memories of shoveling down my sugary breakfast while reading the back of cereal boxes at the kitchen table. My high school students' formative impressions of commercial art and graphic design, forged as they were coming of age in a world bombarded by electronic media, were vastly different from the "five black-and-white TV channels (if you can adjust the rabbit ears just so), cartoons only on Saturday" experience that shaped my impressionable mind.

Happy memories of vitamin-fortified, sugar-and-carb-induced morning reverie, looking at engaging cartoon mascots, fun mazes, flashy lettering, and colorful logos while munching breakfast cereal, are some of the iconic childhood memories that young and old can still share.

When I was a child, every family had vinyl records, magazines, and newspapers laying around. High school graphic design assignments then, as now, reflected the world we grew up in. What 1980s high school student didn't have at least one magazine cover or album cover design in their portfolio? Today, as consumers switch to Kindle, Spotify, and electronic news subscription services, food packaging is one of the few remaining forms of print media still found in every home.

A high school graphic design classroom is both a laboratory and a think tank. It is a place where students can process, analyze, respond to, experiment with, and create visual design. What better way to introduce commercial art than with an assignment that combines typography, photography, cartooning, logo, and game design?

Instead of the pencil and paper of my own high school days, my students use Wacom tablets, Adobe Photoshop, and Adobe Illustrator. They have traded in drawing tables and T squares for iMacs and scanners, but my emerging designers still rely on the traditional elements and principles of design. Then, as now, the goal of the commercial artist is to communicate with the consumer through visual imagery.

I Offer You Breakfast Cereal Box Design: Digital Technology in the Art Room

My students were required to invent an original breakfast cereal and imaginary food company. They created a mascot and logo using Photoshop and Illustrator. We learned how to create 3D lettering and photograph food, and even created a game, puzzle, or maze for the back of the box. Figures 1 and 2 give examples of end products for this lesson prior to assembling.

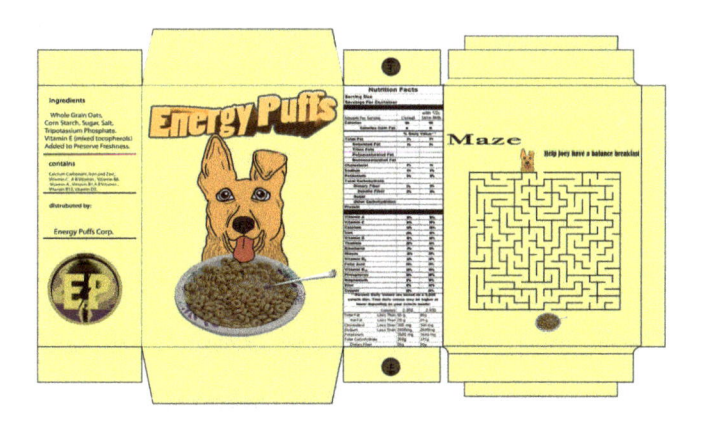

Figures 1–2. Examples of the finished cereal box project.

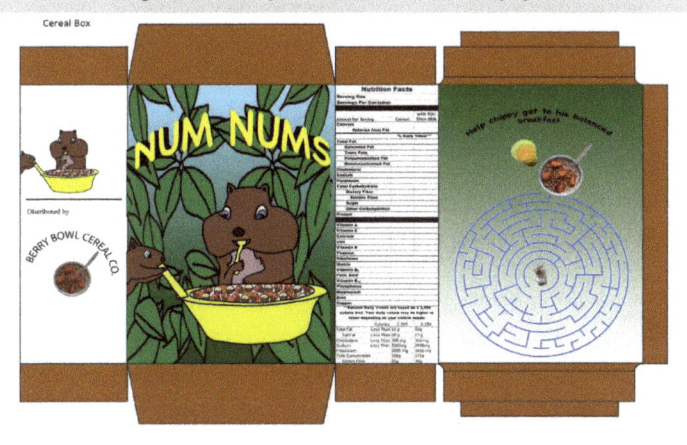

Our favorite day was the food photo shoot. Students cut fruit, poured milk and orange juice, and helped themselves to flakes, O's, and puffs before snapping pictures of each edible still life. After uploading our photos, we enjoyed eating our healthy breakfasts while gazing at the box designs, before cleaning up. Students incorporated their mascots and food photography into a maze for the back of the box. Their maze had to link the mascot to the food with an interactive story. Most students opted to start by using an online maze generator before adding text and other graphic elements. The designs of the mazes found in Figures 3 and 4 show a good example of how to incorporate the character and maze together.

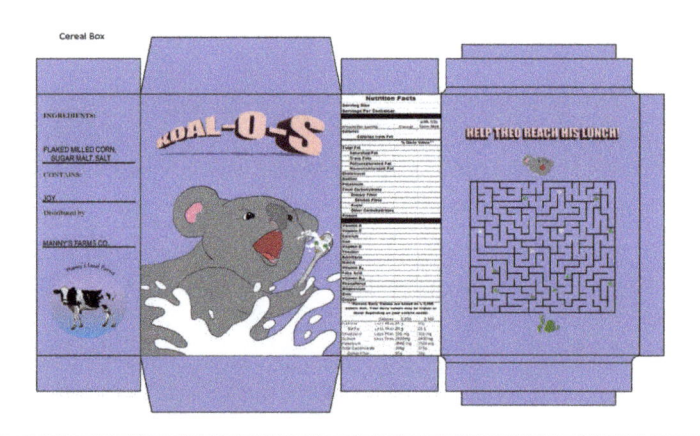

Figures 3–4. Examples of the maze design.

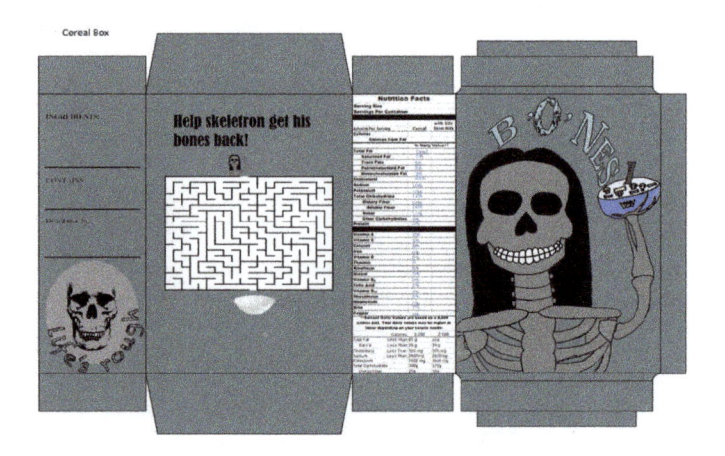

Classroom Environment

A key element to any good children's cereal is an appealing mascot. First, we looked at boxes of popular children's cereals and identified traits brand mascots have in common. My students broke into small, self-selected groups of three to five and sat together for this discussion.

While each student was required to design their own unique box, these groups also worked cooperatively during the food photo shoot. This enabled everyone to collaborate on their still life setups, direct each other to pour or hold items, and create more interesting pictures.

I photographed as many boxes as I could find in the supermarket cereal aisle and created a grayscale worksheet featuring all of them. Each group was instructed to brainstorm a list of common traits among the cereal mascot characters. Eliminating color from the worksheet helped us focus on just the cartoon features. I gave the class only about 5 to 10 minutes to generate their written lists before returning to a whole-class discussion. Figures 5 and 6 demonstrate examples of student mascot design.

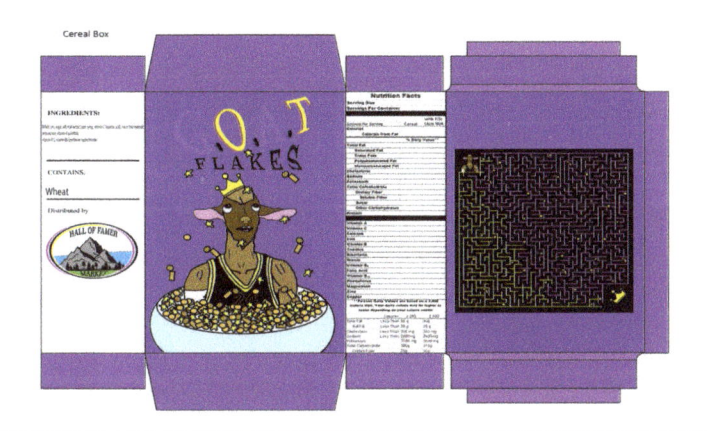

Figures 5–6. Examples of the character design.

The "turn and talk" technique works well for getting students to participate in class because people are often more comfortable sharing ideas with peers. One person from every group read off their list and, as they spoke, I wrote on the board. I taught this lesson to three different classes and every group noticed things that I hadn't previously considered.

Every group noticed that the mouths of the characters were disproportionately large and always opened and smiling, and that the characters were sometimes looking directly at the cereal and sometimes out at the viewer.

They observed that the characters all had a bouncy demeanor, as if they were vibrating with energy. Giant eyes and unusually large heads contributed to this look. These mascots weren't merely happy, they were ecstatic. They would do anything to eat their cereal.

Once we were done looking at the grayscale images, I presented color versions on the projector. Students noticed a universal use of bold, bright, flat primary and secondary colors.

Procedure

Materials:

- Computers
- Drawing tablets
- Paper
- Pencils
- Permanent markers
- Scanner
- DSLR cameras
- Green screen or green construction paper
- Adobe Photoshop
- Adobe Illustrator
- A variety of breakfast cereals, fresh fruit, milk, and orange juice

I see my digital art students daily for 42 minutes. The project took about 4 weeks.

Although this is a computer-based class, I often like my students to start out by sketching on paper. They drew their imaginary characters, outlining them with black permanent markers. We then scanned them and colored them using Photoshop. A drawing tablet may also be used instead of paper.

Some students wanted to use photo references. I had strict rules for the use of visual aids. If they wanted to use an image from the internet, it needed to be a copyright-free photograph, not a drawing or cartoon. I taught them to click "Tools" and "Usage Rights" when doing an image search. Regardless of copyright, my students were never allowed to copy an image, even a photograph, exactly. Instead, I taught them how to "make it their own" using the animation principle of exaggeration. They had to apply the lessons of our previous class discussion (the giant mouths, the googly eyes, oversize heads, etc.) to create an original cartoon loosely based on the photo reference. The principle of exaggeration was mastered by animators in the early 20th century. We viewed videos of these artists drawing from live models and zoo animals and discussed how the resulting cartoons differed from the originals.

I taught students how to use a scanner. I then uploaded the files to the school's cloud storage and shared them with students using their school email addresses. Students were required to use Adobe Photoshop to color their artwork. I taught students to download and open their files in Photoshop and click Select > Color Range > Shadows. Previewing the image and sliding the range selection ensured that only the black lines were selected. We clicked Edit > Copy and pasted them into a new document. Clicking Image > Image Size allowed us to reset the pixels per square inch to 300 and the image to letter size (8.5 x 11 inches). Resizing at the start of a project prevents the final work from appearing pixelated. We reselected the black lines in our new document and clicked Edit > Fill > Black. While the black lines were still selected, we clicked Select > Modify > Smooth. This guaranteed that the final mascot would have a crisp, black outline.

I showed the students how to use the Magic Wand tool to select each section they wished to color. The tool is sometimes difficult to find because it is hidden underneath the Quick Select tool. Photoshop is filled with hidden tools that are revealed when you click on the tiny triangle at the bottom right-hand corner of each icon in the tool menu. This can be confusing to beginners.

After using the Magic Wand tool, we clicked Select > Modify > Expand and expanded our selections by 3 pixels. We then clicked Select > Deselect and switched to the background layer before clicking Select > Reselect.

It is important that the "crawling ants," which are the dotted lines on the periphery indicating the area selected, are in the white background layer and not in the same layer as the lines. We then clicked Edit > Fill > Color. To switch colors, students double-clicked on the word "Color" in the drop-down menu of the pop-up box, and the Color Picker tool appeared. By expanding the selection and placing the color in the layer below the lines, students were able to create clean, professional-looking graphics. Failing to expand the selection results in an unsightly visible gap between color and outline. They then used the Burn tool to add shadows and the Dodge tool to add highlights. Like all tools in Photoshop, it is easy to adjust the width and hardness of the Burn and Dodge tools. A broad brushstroke with a soft edge will create convincing-looking shadows.

Once we were done coloring, we clicked Layer > Flatten Image. We then unlocked the layer by clicking on the lock in the Layer menu and used the Magic Wand tool to select and delete the white background. This can be accomplished by clicking Edit > Cut or by simply clicking the Delete or Backspace key on the keyboard. We then saved our finished mascots in PNG format. A PNG or Portable Network Graphic is a flat image that can be saved with a transparent background. For this project, all design assets needed to have transparent backgrounds so they could later be assembled to create the final composition.

Our next order of business was to invent the name of the imaginary cereal and use Adobe Photoshop to make 3D lettering. We created a letter-sized print document with a horizontal orientation and selected the Text tool. We then drew a large horizontal text box and adjusted the size to 60 point, centered the text, and chose a color other than black or white. Students selected a font from the drop-down menu. I encouraged them to pick an easy-to-read sans-serif style with thick, bold lines. We avoided cursive and heavily ornamental fonts that might ultimately be difficult to read.

At the top of the page in Photoshop is a small icon that looks like the letter T with a curved line under it. Clicking on that enables students to curve text. Sliders and drop-down menus in the pop-up window provide many options for giving text an exciting look. Be sure to warn the class that the words must still be easy to read. Next, I demonstrated how to click on the 3D icon at the top of the page so the text would appear to be three dimensional. They could then adjust the lighting and angle of the text in the 3D workspace. Next, they went to the layer menu (if they cannot see this menu, ask them to click Window at the top and then click Layers from the drop-down menu) and right-click on the 3D layer. Clicking Rasterize 3D Text from the drop-down choices will transform the text into a pixel-based image. Students should keep in mind that the spelling and words will no longer be editable. Next, they hid the background layer and saved the file as a PNG with a transparent background.

Students were required to select a photo from the food photo shoot for the final box design. This photo would be used for both the front of the box and the game on the back of the box. Students were required to resize the image, since our DSLR cameras create huge images. We clicked Image > Image Size and set the PSI to 300 and the width to 10 inches. Our goal now was to eliminate the table, leaving only a floating image of the food. We unlocked the background in the layer menu and clicked Select > Subject. This often resulted in an almost perfect selection that only required minor modification.

To add to or subtract from a selection, I directed them to go to the Quick Select tool (hidden under the Magic Wand tool). At the top of the page, students could choose how many pixels they wished to add or subtract at a time. Holding the Shift key down while modifying a selection allowed them to not lose the pixels they had already selected. This technique required some patience. I had my students use bright green construction paper and a green foamcore trifold as the backdrop for their photo shoot to make this process slightly easier. A green screen may also be used (see Figure 7). Once they had successfully selected the subject, I directed them to click Select > Inverse and then hit the Delete key on the keyboard. The background disappeared, and they were able to save the file as a PNG.

STEAM Education: An Interdisciplinary Look at Art in the Curriculum

Figure 7. Image of the green screen for the photo shoot day.

If your students use an online maze generator for the puzzle, be sure to remind them to also save that as a PNG. Next, have them open the maze in Photoshop and click Image > Canvas Size. Enlarge the canvas to create a few inches of blank space on all sides. Next, open the mascot and cereal photo files in Photoshop and temporarily resize them to about 2 inches across. Click Select > All and then Edit > Copy. Paste them into the maze file and then click Edit > Transform > Scale to resize them. Go back to the original mascot and food files and click Command-Z (or Ctrl-Z) to undo the last step before saving and closing. Remind them to be careful to not accidentally save them in thumbnail size. My students were able to resize files without risk since they had already turned their mascots and photos in via Google Classroom. If they accidentally messed up their original files, they could always redownload them from the cloud. My students were required to digitally submit each design asset on the day they finished it. This protected their work from any potential equipment failure that might require them to temporarily switch to a different computer and allowed me to stay up-to-date while grading their work.

Adding text to their mazes, asking children to help the mascot find their balanced breakfast, was next. The cereal photo was placed at the end of the maze and the mascot at the beginning. Many students created additional graphics to enhance the narrative and engage their target audience.

Next, I explained to the class that they needed to invent parent companies and create logos in Adobe Illustrator. Unlike Photoshop, images in Illustrator are vector based. I reminded them how in middle school they needed to plot points along x- and y-axes in math class and connect the dots to form a picture. They all remembered those math assignments fondly. I then explained that there are really an infinite number of points along the x- and y-axes, and that images in Illustrator are created using those points.

We learned how to use the Ellipse tool to create round logos. In Illustrator, the Ellipse tool is hidden underneath the Rectangular Shape tool. Holding down the Shift key will lock the aspect ratio, enabling you to create perfect circles. I also showed my students how to create lettering that goes around the circle. This tool is called Type on a Path. It is hidden underneath the Type tool. As in Photoshop, hidden tools are revealed when you click on the tiny triangle on the bottom right-hand corner of each icon in the toolbar. We also learned how to use the Image Trace feature in Illustrator. A mascot or photograph could be imported into Illustrator by clicking File > Place. Once the image is placed in Illustrator, it needs to be resized. I reminded them to use the Shift key when resizing in Illustrator to lock the aspect ratio. Next, the class should click Window > Image Trace. Once the pop-up window appears, they need to click the Preview box. Have them switch from default to six colors in the drop-down menu. They can modify the number of colors to get exactly the look they want. Next, show them how to click Object at the top of the page, then click Image Trace > Expand. Using the Direct Select tool, clicking on the white background, then hitting the Delete key will eliminate the white box around the design. The image is now a vector-based graphic with a clear background. If students do not remember to expand the selection, they will not be able to incorporate it into the logo because it will only be a preview.

For students who are accustomed to using Photoshop, Illustrator can be very confusing because all the menus are in different locations, yet the interface looks similar to Photoshop. Asking them to create a simple logo using the Type on a Path and Image Trace tools is a great way to introduce students to Illustrator. I created a step-by-step tutorial on YouTube, and each student worked through the process at their own pace, using the video's closed-captioning to minimize confusion.

It is easy to create a black-and-white cereal box template by unfolding a snack-sized container and placing it on a scanner, or students can just download one of the many free sample templates available online. Students can also add some math to this STEAM activity by designing their foldable containers from scratch. They can even create an unconventional box shape by combining simpler geometry nets. By choosing new background and foreground colors in Photoshop and using the Gradient tool, my students were able to create beautiful colors on their boxes before assembling their final designs. To add color, they unlocked the background on the template and used the Magic Wand tool to delete the white area outside the box pattern. Then they clicked Select > Color Range > Highlights and used the sliders to make sure only the white parts of the box were selected. The gradient works best if the foreground color is bright and cheerful, and the background color is white or a hue with an extremely light value. Experimenting with clicking and dragging will lead to the desired effect. Remind the class to keep in mind the colors of the mascot and lettering, and to choose a contrasting hue so the design assets appear to pop off the page.

Table 1. Factors to Keep in Mind When Assembling the Final Design

Term	Explanation
Overlapping	The cereal photo should be in the layer above the mascot, so the mascot appears to be looking out at both the food and the viewer. Overlapping also gives the design a sense of visual depth.
Bleed	The bleed area is the area near the folds or the edge of the document. Purposely having the mascot or cereal bowl photo visually extend beyond the bleed area is a good design practice, since it creates the illusion that the picture is part of a larger world that extends beyond its borders. I ask my students to imagine looking in a mirror and peering around the corner to see the world beyond the frame. To create this effect, you will need to erase the extra parts of the image precisely at the fold lines. To do this, make sure you are in the correct layer, click on a point on the fold with the eraser, choose another point on the fold, and hold the Shift key down before clicking. This will connect the two points with a straight line and erase a clean, straight path. It is poor design practice to stop an image right at the bleed line, since even a minor misprint or crooked fold will cause part of your picture to be cut off. Resize your assets to create a safe margin.
Centering an Image	If you wish to center something on one of the panels of your box, click View > Show > Grid. Be sure to hide the grid after you are done setting up your composition.
Asymmetrical Balance	Good visual design is based on the practice of balancing positive and negative space and light and dark values. If the composition is too central, the image looks static. To create more dynamic composition, try to offset areas of empty space on one side with an image of similar visual weight on the other side.

An effective cereal box design will draw the viewer's eye around the panel and use imagery to retell a timeless story. I created Table 1 as a helpful checklist for students to refer to before submitting their work. In this imaginary tale, the mascot is happy and excited about eating a wonderful treat. The mascot is both looking at their meal and looking out at you, the consumer. This simple tale, about a mischievous and cute character and a delicious food, has been told time and time again since ready-to-eat cold cereal was first invented in the 1800s. Because this tale will be so familiar to your students, usually evoking happy childhood memories, it is the perfect vehicle to introduce them to the new and unfamiliar medium of digital art and graphic design (see Figure 8). To find examples of this art form, they need only turn on their television, visit the supermarket, or look in their kitchen cabinets. The humble cereal box is the perfect vehicle for teaching students to examine the familiar with fresh eyes and explore new skills.

Figure 8. Example of a final product prior to assembling.

Where to Go From Here?

The acronym *STEAM* stands for science, technology, engineering, art, and math. This project provided my class with the perfect platform to develop skills in both design technology and visual art. If I were to teach this lesson again, I would ideally like to add engineering and mathematics to this unit by asking students to generate their own uniquely shaped box templates. There are numerous websites where students can download foldable geometry nets.

In future teachings of this unit, I plan to dedicate an entire class period to folding, cutting, and combining geometric forms. Ideally, I would love to coordinate the lesson with a geometry teacher and ask students to measure the volume of a cereal box and then calculate the necessary dimensions for an unconventionally shaped cereal box of their own design. I also plan to collaborate with a health teacher who has volunteered to be a guest speaker and show students how to analyze nutrition labels. The STEAM possibilities are endless.

After cutting out and assembling our boxes, my students staged a final photo shoot to document their work, and the finished projects were proudly placed in hallway display cases for the rest of the school community to enjoy.

Rachel Wintemberg teaches digital art and computer animation at Perth Amboy High School in Perth Amboy, New Jersey. You can reach her at rachwintemberg@paps.net.

Resources

Resources for teaching graphic design to high school students:
- https://www.aiga.org/resources/academic-design-education/graphic-design-curriculum

Resources for teaching typography:
- https://theartofeducation.edu/2018/12/20/5-exciting-ways-to-teach-typography-in-the-art-room
- https://bonfx.com/bad-typography

Resources for teaching logo design:
- https://www.khanacademy.org/partner-content/49ers-steam/49ers-art/49ers-elements-art-design/a/logo-design-challenge
- https://www.brandsoftheworld.com
- https://www.hongkiat.com/blog/logo-evolution

Resources for designing a brand mascot:
- https://99u.adobe.com/articles/58511/make-it-cuter-and-more-branding-lessons-from-the-weird-and-wonderful-world-of-japanese-mascot-design
- https://graphicmama.com/blog/21-famous-brand-mascot-designs-time

Resources for teaching food photography:
- https://expertphotography.com/complete-guide-food-photography-77-yummy-tips

Virtual Reality Art Education

Jeremy Blair

Virtual Reality Art Education (VRAE) is a professional development program for K–12 teachers in Putnam County, Tennessee. Founded by art professors David Gallop and Jeremy Blair at Tennessee Tech University, VRAE introduces teachers to the basics of virtual reality (VR) and science, technology, engineering, the arts, and math (STEAM) learning. In VRAE, participants receive a grant-funded Oculus Rift VR system for their classroom, develop engaging VR experiences for their students at the elementary and secondary levels, and critically reflect on VR's capabilities in the art classroom. Throughout this chapter, I present the foundations of VR and share the processes, discoveries, and barriers of three K–12 educators enrolled in the yearlong professional development program during the 2018–2019 school year.

A History of Virtual Reality

Virtual reality is an immersive sensory experience that digitally simulates an interactive environment (Pierre, 2008). VR systems commonly use head-mounted displays and are connected to high-powered computers to generate images, sounds, and sensations that simulate a physical presence in a virtual environment (Nite, 2014). VR has existed in various forms and conceptions throughout history (Blascovich & Bailenson, 2012). Panoramic murals from 19th-century Europe (Freina & Ott, 2015), as well as the Sensorama, an interfacing device introduced in the 1960s, were precursors to VR (Regrebsubla, 2015; Rheingold, 1991). The Sensorama simulated a ride through New York City by projecting street scenes, blowing wind, playing traffic noise, and releasing the city's smells (Regrebsubla, 2015; Rheingold, 1991). Many video game developers modeled arcade and console projects after the Sensorama, creating interfaces that transported users (Dan, 2000).

Jaron Lanier popularized the term "virtual reality" in the late 1980s when he developed the EyePhone, the first VR system for consumers (Sorene, 2014). Lanier's EyePhone used goggles and a "DataGlove" to see and move virtual objects in a simulated environment (Mokey, 2016; Sorene, 2014). The EyePhone had limited graphics, and the full system cost around $250,000 at the time (Sorene, 2014). Lanier eventually sold his company and patents. Still,

VR remained popular in the 1990s and influenced motion pictures and gaming systems (Mokey, 2016; Sorene, 2014). The technological and financial limitations of VR forced developers to wait for advancements in computing power and high-speed internet that would come decades later.

Virtual Reality Today

Today's VR systems look eerily similar to the EyePhone and rely on spatial immersion that surrounds the user with stimuli through a headset, sensors, and handheld controls (Bardi, 2019; Robertson et al., 1993). The Oculus Rift is named for the divide it creates between the real and virtual worlds. The Rift includes a tethered head-mounted display, touch controllers, software, and tabletop sensors that track user movements. It also uses a pair of screens in the headset that display two images side by side, one for each eye (Pritchard, 2022), and the goggles feature embedded sensors that monitor the user's head motions to adjust the image. Oculus offers many free and purchasable apps available for download, including artmaking and viewing experiences.

Following the completion of this study, the Oculus Rift was discontinued in April 2021 in favor of the wireless Quest, which subsequently underwent a rebranding to become the Meta Quest in 2022.

Virtual Reality in Education

VR has recently emerged as a valuable and accessible resource in education (Gregory et al., 2016; see Figure 1). VR's interactive, kinesthetic, and visual qualities embrace various learning styles, abilities, cultures, and interests and integrate well into any school subject (Leite et al., 2009; Roussou, 2004). Jeremy Bailenson (2018), the director of the Virtual Human Interaction Lab,

Figure 1. VR Painting, Billetto Editorial, Unsplash.

described VR as an on-demand human experience, emphasizing human connection over media consumption. Thus, VR is now prominent in higher education (Gregory et al., 2016). VR is used to study a variety of subjects, including learning sciences (Bailenson et al., 2008), cultures and museums (Blascovich & Bailenson, 2011; Stokrocki, 2014), teacher education (Anzalone, 2017; Shin & Ocansey, 2018), medicine (Blome et al., 2017; Kleven,

2014), interdisciplinary arts (*Yale University Art Students*, n.d.), and much more. Prominent VR centers include Stanford University's Virtual Human Interaction Lab, The University of Toledo's Virtual Immersive Reality Center, University of Colorado Boulder's ATLAS Institute, Yale University's Center for Collaborative Arts and Media, and Tennessee Tech's iCube.

An aspirational center for the VRAE program is the Center for Collaborative Arts and Media at Yale University. In 2017–2018, instructors at Yale introduced VR in their drawing courses. Anahita Vossoughi, the assistant director of the center, incorporated VR into instruction to broaden student horizons and to ensure traditional boundaries never limit students (*Yale University Art Students*, n.d.). Vossoughi commented that drawing in VR is particularly helpful with perceptual techniques because students are attempting to translate real-life objects in space onto a two-dimensional piece of paper. Having students draw these forms in VR first helps them better understand the world around them (*Yale University Art Students*, n.d.).

K–12 schools are also incorporating VR. Xennial Digital, an educational company, designs VR experiences for classrooms and studies the effectiveness of VR learning on-site through K–12 collaborations. Xennial Digital's most outstanding K–12 experiences include an interactive tour of the human heart and an echolocation experiment placing students in a virtual bat cave (Herndon & Gupta, 2019). Xennial Digital facilitates after-school programs where students brainstorm new concepts for VR learning, which has transformed their offerings.

Virtual Reality Art Education

Virtual Reality Art Education (VRAE) is a yearlong professional development program in Putnam County, Tennessee, that prepares K–12 educators to teach art with VR. The program includes quarterly meetings, hands-on workshops, demonstrations, and curriculum design. The program's sequence consists of identifying interested teachers, preparing and orienting teachers to VR, installing VR equipment in classrooms, and supporting participants in developing lessons and practices. The primary objectives of the program are:

- to advance visual arts education in Putnam County through VR
- to provide emerging experiential learning strategies for local art teachers
- to introduce a creative vehicle for empathy development and forming self

The 2018–2019 program included three teachers—an elementary STEAM coach, a middle school design and technology teacher, and a high school visual arts teacher. The program met professional development requirements in the Putnam County School System, and meetings and workshops were held at the art education studio at Tennessee Tech University in Cookeville, Tennessee.

Funding and Research

In 2018, VRAE administrators were awarded a $10,000 Faculty Research Grant from the Office of Research at Tennessee Tech University to develop the VRAE program. Equipment and supplies were purchased to compile VRAE technology kits for all three participants. The administrators, David and Jeremy, prepared all kits and technologies and provided tech support during the program. The individual kits consisted of the following items:

- Dell G5 15 Gaming Laptop, $1,250
- Oculus Rift with touch controllers and sensors, $450
- USB-C-to-HDMI adapter, $20
- leather inserts for headset, $10
- AA batteries, $5
- gaming backpack, $20

VRAE administrators collected qualitative data by asking research questions and documenting teacher progress. Administrators asked questions during group discussions and conducted interviews with individual teachers. They also wrote field notes during classroom observations and corresponded with participants over email. Participating teachers answered research questions at different stages of the program, which led to discussions on addressing the limitations of VR and designing practical VR lessons for students. Research questions included:

- In what ways does VR build upon or separate from traditional modes of artmaking?
- In what ways does teaching art with VR change or affect learning and engagement?
- Is VR a viable tool for standards-based art classrooms? If not, what are the limitations?

VRAE administrators presented the data gathered from teachers at the Tennessee Art Education Association Fall State Conference in Nashville, Tennessee, and at MANEUVER, a conference on manufacturing education using virtual environments in Cookeville, Tennessee. A detailed report was also submitted to the Office of Research at Tennessee Tech University, presenting the program's curricular strategies, teacher experiences, and findings.

Perceiving and Producing Art

The VRAE curriculum features two significant components, Perceiving Art and Producing Art. Administrators used *The Handbook for the National Core Art Standards for Media Arts* to develop both curricular elements (State Education Agency Directors of Arts Education, 2014). In Perceiving Art, teachers became aware of their physical senses by thinking, seeing, and understanding in VR. Participants visited art museums and galleries that offered VR field trips like the Kremer Collection VR Museum (Martin, 2020; Sandle, 2018), as well as

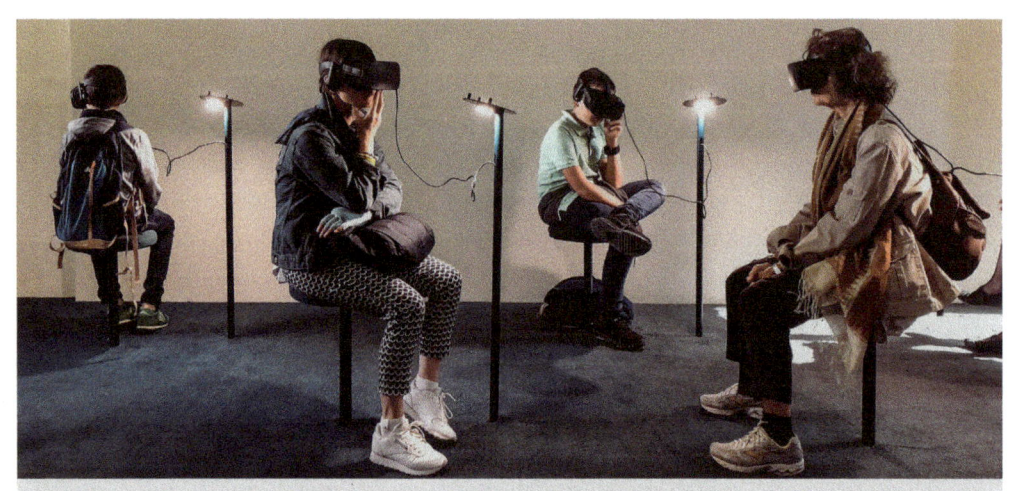

Figure 2. VR museumgoers, Lucrezia Carnelos, Unsplash.

museums that offer VR tours on-site (Coates, 2019; see Figure 2). In addition to VR tours, Perceiving Art promotes building awareness, being open to new interpretations, and looking closely while immersed in virtual environments. Achieving this mindset is beneficial when teachers model their skills to be present in VR spaces to their students. The Perceiving Art phase eased teachers into getting acquainted with the equipment and engaging with the basics of VR.

In the second phase, Producing Art, teachers reviewed VR artmaking processes and made their original art. Teachers met at Tennessee Tech University, and VRAE coadministrator David Gallop donned the Oculus Rift headset and demonstrated how to paint, draw, sculpt, and build using a variety of apps. After a quick demonstration, teachers experimented with artmaking apps, Medium and Quill. The group also reviewed how contemporary VR artists are painting, sculpting, animating, illustrating, and building new ways of seeing through interactive installations and blended realities with VR (Koenig, 2019; Nijholt, 2019; Raab, n.d.; Sharma, 2017; see Figures 3 and 4). VRAE teachers left the session with a foundation of skills and moved forward in developing VR experiences for their students.

Figure 3. VR silhouette, Stella Jacob, Unsplash.

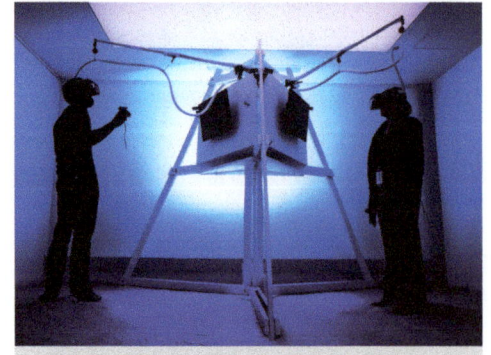

Figure 4. VR installation, Stella Jacob, Unsplash.

In both Perceiving Art and Producing Art, teachers gravitated toward apps that fit their interests and pedagogical practices in the program. Collectively, VR apps The Night Cafe, Dreams of Dalí, Quill, Medium, and Blocks emerged as favorites among the three participants. This short list is not exhaustive, but all five apps show high engagement and reliability and are free to download from the Oculus Store. Below is a brief media review describing the features and qualities of these select art applications.

Figure 5. The Night Café: A VR Tribute to Vincent van Gogh, Oculus Rift (screenshot).

Released in 2016, The Night Cafe: A VR Tribute to van Gogh, encourages users to explore van Gogh's enigmatic 1888 painting *The Night Cafe* (Tickle, 2015). Enter the post-Impressionist masterpiece and see the artist's vivid brush strokes, thick impasto, and vibrant colors never like before (see Figure 5). Van Gogh makes a personal appearance in the parlor, and users can open the window and view *The Starry Night* (1889) outside in the distance. This app impacted and sparked emotions in teachers, making it a potential staple in an art classroom.

Figure 6. Dreams of Dalí, Oculus Rift (screenshot).

Figure 7. Dreams of Dalí, Oculus Rift (screenshot).

Dreams of Dalí is a VR app where users navigate the memories, visions, and thoughts of famed surrealist Salvador Dalí. The main stage is an expansive desertscape (Rhodes, 2016) modeled after Dalí's masterpiece *Archeological Reminiscence of Millet's Angelus* (1935; see Figure 6). The eerie dreamscape backdrops imager' from Dalí's art and childhood, including enormous floating animals with elongated limbs flying overhead, reminiscent of *The Temptation of St. Anthony* (1946; see Figure 7). The dark, surreal themes and soundscapes make Dreams of Dalí well-suited for VR. This app was featured in a learning unit on surrealism by VRAE's high school visual arts teacher later in the program.

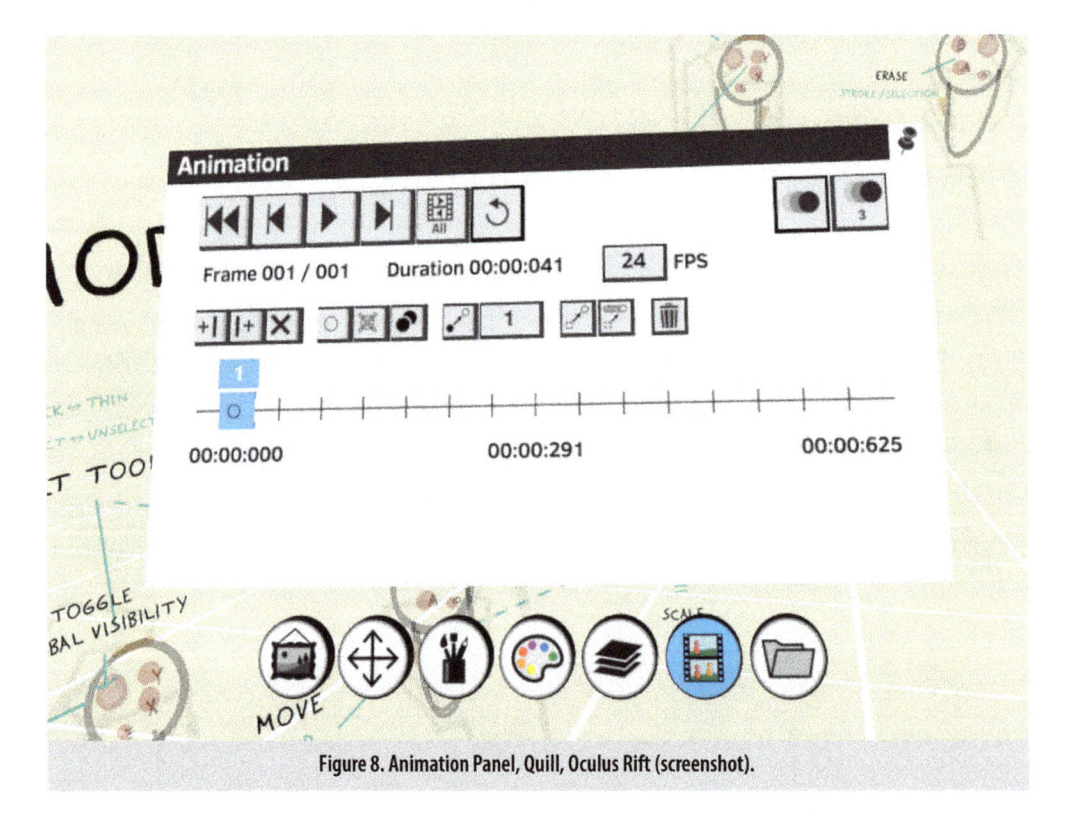

Figure 8. Animation Panel, Quill, Oculus Rift (screenshot).

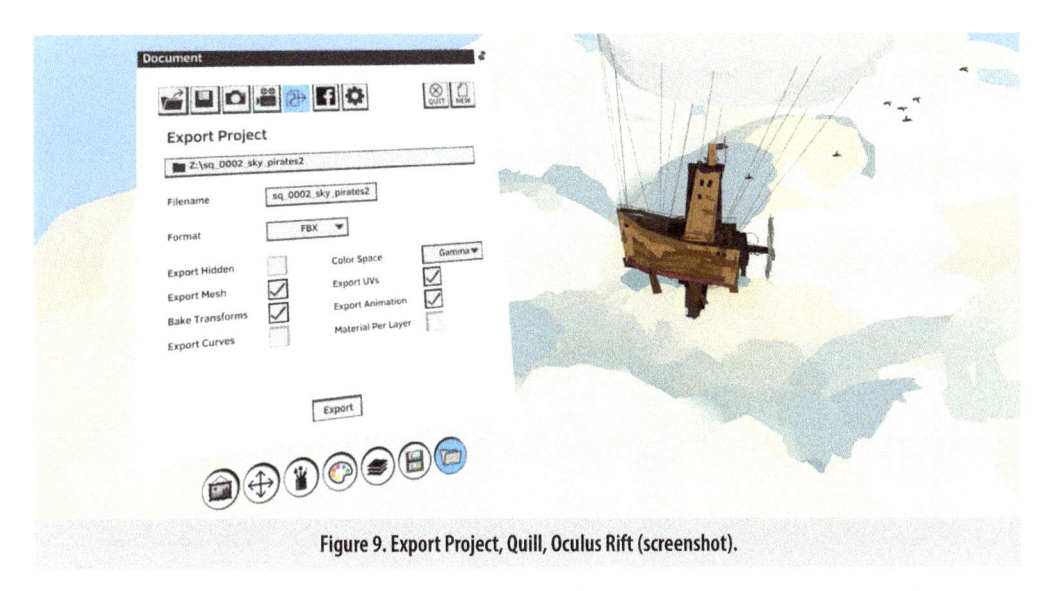

Figure 9. Export Project, Quill, Oculus Rift (screenshot).

Designed for amateur and professional artists, Quill transforms a handheld controller into a virtual paintbrush or pen (Constine, 2016). Quill invites users to virtually paint, sketch, collage, storyboard, and make movies in VR on an infinitely scalable canvas with unlimited colors and intuitive tools (Ku, 2018). Artists compose on a virtual canvas and fill it with original shapes and marks called "Quillustrations." These virtual illustrations can be animated with Quill by making interactive storyboards and animations (see Figure 8). Artists can upload images and alter them, and works can be exported as various file types and saved, printed, or shared on social media (see Figure 9). Artmaking with Quill was popular among all three participating teachers, but the sophisticated controls and intricate interface led to some frustrations.

Medium by Adobe is a VR sculpting app where users virtually airbrush volumetric clay medium, resembling foam, with an array of haptic controller functions (Carbotte, 2016). The virtual clay is sprayed, moved, rotated, shaped, expanded, and carved to sculpt raw shapes into complete forms (see Figure 10). Medium users can export their works as files for 3D printing. Medium is free to download from the Oculus Store and is a popular program among VRAE teachers and VR beginners but has a similar learning curve as Quill.

Figure 10. Sculpture tutorial, Medium by Adobe, Oculus Rift (screenshot).

Figure 11. Blocks tutorial, Google Blocks, Oculus Rift (screenshot).

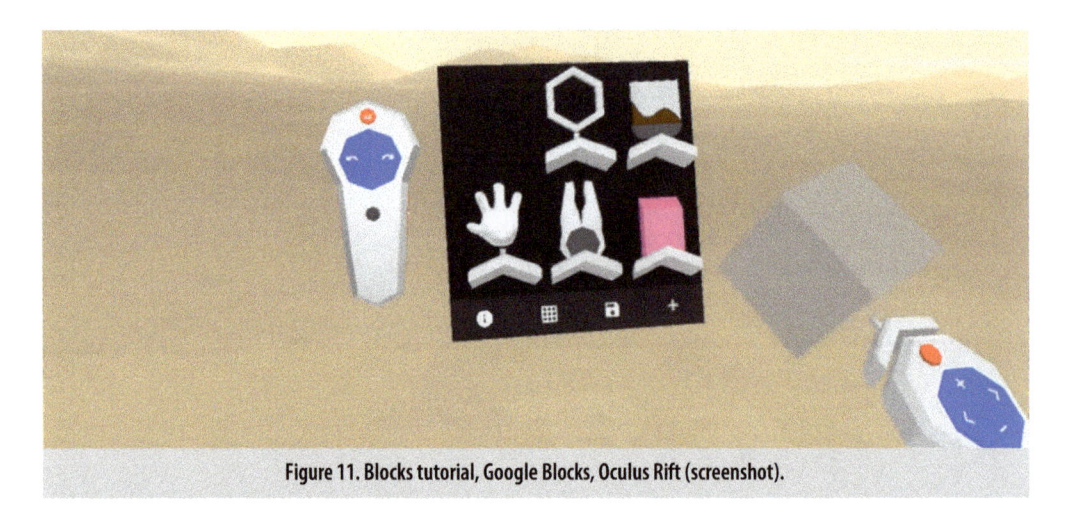

Lastly, Google Blocks, a *Minecraft*-esque modeling app, enables users to design objects, build structures, tell stories, and terraform environments using six simple tools: Shape, Stroke, Paint, Modify, Grab, and Erase (Li, 2017; see Figure 11). Google wants Blocks to feel like working with children's blocks rather than traditional 3D modeling software by starting with a simple set of shapes, a color palette, and intuitive tools (Hayden, 2017; Li, 2017). Users can infinitely manipulate blocks and experiment with virtual physics (Matthews, 2017). Artists can bring their designs to life by exporting them as animated GIFs or into specific file types for a 3D print, like Medium. Blocks is intuitive, like most Google products, making it optimal for the K–12 classroom. Blocks was a top choice of VRAE's elementary STEAM coach because of the app's child-friendly controls, futuristic interface, and seemingly boundless virtual sandbox.

Teaching With VR

VRAE teachers started developing activities in their classrooms after the initial orientation, two workshops, and technology kits were installed and connected. Teachers used the Rift primarily as an early-finisher activity but developed formal arts-based VR lessons at their schools as the year progressed. For example, VRAE's high school visual arts teacher designed a multimodal unit to learn the origins, concepts, and masterworks of surrealism. Using the Rift, students searched the psyche of surrealist Salvador Dalí in the Dreams of Dalí app, creating surreal artworks with traditional art materials. In this approach, VR was used as an interactive element to spark student

Figure 12. VR Club member, Monterey High School, Monterey, TN.

STEAM Education: An Interdisciplinary Look at Art in the Curriculum

Figure 13. (Above) VR cards for The Night Cafe, Alicia Upchurch @TeacherMermaid.

Figure 14. VR cards for Google Blocks, Alicia Upchurch @TeacherMermaid.

interest, and to provide context to Dalí's work. In addition to the surrealism unit, the teacher founded an after-school VR club for interested students to experiment and play with VR. Students in the club met periodically to experiment with apps and techniques, play games, and make works of art (see Figure 12). The club was choice-based, and students discovered best practices for how to use VR. Their efforts greatly benefited the teacher in integrating VR.

Several months into the VRAE program, teachers started to thrive in integrating and applying VR into their daily teaching practices. For example, VRAE's elementary STEAM coach designed a VR classroom station that students used in rotation with other activities in the classroom. The teacher custom-designed scavenger hunt clues, questions, and tasks printed on cards that guided students through virtual worlds. Guided by the cards, students used the Rift to meet Vincent van Gogh in The Night Café (see Figure 13) and imaginatively built structures in Google Blocks (see Figure 14). With this strategy, elementary students turned their virtual play into an investigation, problem-solving, and research exercise (see Figure 15).

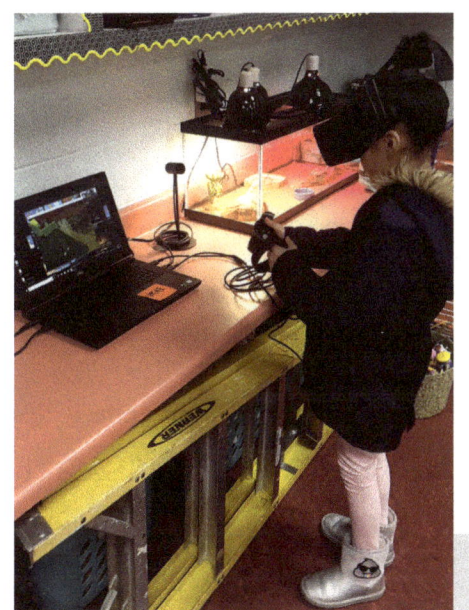

Figure 15. Child experiencing VR, Cane Creek Elementary School, Cookeville, TN.

Findings and Discoveries

VRAE teachers and administrators met for a final time at the end of the 2018–2019 school year. Teachers shared insights on their experiences in the program. Administrators analyzed discussions to establish findings and improve the program. The first finding was that teachers did not adopt new methods of teaching in reaction to using the technology. A quick example is that VRAE's elementary STEAM coach regularly gamified learning tasks, which is reflected in the VR scavenger hunt they developed. This finding illustrates that VR is a versatile tool that can weave, mesh, and evolve with the teacher.

A second finding was that the Rift became part of the room, and VR spaces inspired students to create with traditional art classroom materials. This inspiration was best evidenced in the high school students drawing and painting after experiencing the Dreams of Dalí. At the beginning of the year, VRAE administrators speculated if the Rift might cause a distraction in the three classrooms, but teachers confirmed that the Rift was a regular fixture in their rooms.

For the final discovery, teachers became tech-savvy and troubleshot their equipment and connection issues. Teachers received tech support from VRAE administrators, but they usually found solutions individually and collaborated on common problems. VRAE's middle school technology and design teacher was an invaluable liaison between the district's IT department and participants. This finding proves that VR technologies are not too advanced for the K–12 classroom and can be set up and maintained by teachers.

Limitations and Barriers

VR offered both opportunities and challenges for participating teachers and students. In the final meeting of the year, VRAE teachers also discussed the limitations and barriers of teaching with VR. Encountering perceptual apps like The Night Cafe and Dreams of Dalí was exciting, but surprisingly students at all three levels struggled to produce artworks in VR. Students used popular artmaking programs like Quill and Medium, but being immersed in a virtual environment was new and too abstract for most students. Anahita Vossoughi stated that drawing through space and not on paper was very difficult to teach, even with high-performing college students (as cited in *Yale University Art Students*, n.d.). Vossoughi also said they had to prepare and cultivate a different, quieter, and contemplative space for artmaking in VR with her college students (as cited in *Yale University Art Students*, n.d.). In hindsight, the VRAE program needed to better prepare students and teachers for the skills and mindsets required for making in VR. The entryway app, Oculus First Contact, was used as a tutorial to learn the basics of VR controls, but VR artmaking was still mostly unsuccessful.

Another barrier was that there was only one Oculus Rift per classroom, which drastically limited participation. Having only one headset and one set of controllers means students had to wait for days or weeks to participate, restricting collaboration and peer-based learning. VRAE administrators observed a student putting on the Rift headset and remarked on how the headset isolated them from the class, similar to a blindfold. This VR blindfold effect led teachers to connect their Oculus systems to overhead projectors and monitors in their rooms, to ensure the class could view the student's experience.

Another concern was that Oculus designs their VR headsets for adult users. Each headset comes equipped with adjustable straps, but the webbing cannot be adjusted tightly enough for a small child's head. To solve this, the elementary STEAM coach cut short sections of foam pool noodles and slid them over the straps of the headset, padding it and making a more secure fit that balanced the device's weight appropriately for smaller students.

The most significant limitations for applying VR in the Putnam County School System were the district's policies and restrictions on connected devices, equipment security, and unreliable internet connections. Teachers worked directly with the district's IT services for weeks to connect their VRAE laptops to the district's internet. VR apps require high-speed internet if they are played directly from the developer's site. To remedy this, teachers periodically took their laptops home and downloaded new apps and updated drivers and software using their home internet. Students could then play with the downloaded apps stored in the Oculus library, which did not require an internet connection at the school.

The most significant impediment to incorporating VR into education is the associated expense. Nonetheless, the latest VR systems offer untethered experiences with built-in computers in the headset, making them more accessible. While there are ways to raise funds, educators interested in adopting VR in their classrooms are encouraged to explore possibilities such as collaborating with local universities, K–12 schools, libraries, or VR-savvy organizations to test and determine the suitability of this technology.

Conclusion

VRAE administrators believe our technology-driven society requires new and innovative methodologies that access technology and culture to appeal to the next generations of teachers (Delacruz, 2009). Through the yearlong program, administrators discovered that VR is a creative vehicle that belongs in K–12 schools, but barriers exist that need to be overcome. Educational companies like Xennial Digital, and centers like the Virtual Human Interaction Lab and the Center for Collaborative Arts and Media, are pioneering how teachers can creatively engage students with VR. The VRAE program challenged teachers to reconsider their conceptions of technology, teaching, and exploring the intersections of VR and art. New media artist Chris Milk stated that with VR, you're not interpreting the medium: You're in the medium, and the medium disappears as you use it, becoming a state of consciousness (as cited in Butet-Roch, 2017). The properties of VR force students to investigate and examine more than other mediums, because they are inside of it, leading to moments of significant inquiry and creative problem solving.

Teachers in the VRAE professional development program confirmed that VR is an asset for art and STEAM educators. VR and STEAM education have similar frameworks that equally value and merge the interdisciplinary fields of science, technology, engineering, art, and math (National Art Education Association, 2014/2022). Like STEAM education, VR is a technology that can un-silo academic disciplines, illuminate universal connections, allow students to practice critical thinking, and prepare students for careers and life. To conclude, arts education is always adopting new technologies to expand the toolbox for students, improving with highly engineered systems like VR (*Yale University Art Students*, n.d.). VRAE teachers proved that VR provokes students to choose new adventures, take risks, move their bodies, and empathically enter the minds and masterworks of artists in the art classroom. Hopefully these virtual adventures will lead to more and continued adventuring later in student lives.

***Jeremy Blair** is an assistant professor of art education at Tennessee Tech University. Blair holds degrees from Miami University and the University of North Texas.*

References

Anzalone, C. (2017, June 29). *Virtual reality simulates classroom environment for aspiring teachers* [News release]. University at Buffalo News Center. http://www.buffalo.edu/news/releases/2017/06/038.html

Bailenson, J. (2018). *Experience on demand: What virtual reality is, how it works, and what it can do.* Norton.

Bailenson, J. N., Yee, N., Blascovich, J., Beall, A. C., Lundblad, N., & Jin, M. (2008). The use of immersive virtual reality in the learning sciences: Digital transformations of teachers, students, and social context. *Journal of the Learning Sciences, 17*(1), 102–141. https://doi.org/10.1080/10508400701793141

Bardi, J. (2019, March 26). What is virtual reality? VR definition and examples. *Defy Reality.* https://www.marxentlabs.com/what-is-virtual-reality

Blascovich, J., & Bailenson, J. (2011). A museum of virtual media: The brain doesn't much care whether an experience is real. *Natural History, 119*(8), 20–28.

Blascovich, J., & Bailenson, J. (2012). *Infinite reality: The hidden blueprint of our virtual lives.* Morrow.

Blome, T., Diefenbach, A., Rudolph, S., Bucher, K., & von Mammen, S. (2017, September 6–8). *VReanimate—Non-verbal guidance and learning in virtual reality.* 9th International Conference on Virtual Worlds and Games for Serious Applications (VS-Games), Athens, Greece. https://doi.org/10.1109/vs-games.2017.8055807

Butet-Roch, L. (2017, March 14). The 5 virtual reality films you should experience right now. *Time.* https://time.com/4685993/five-virtual-reality-experiences

Carbotte, K. (2016, November 21). *"Oculus Medium": Sculpt with digital clay.* Tom's Hardware. https://www.tomshardware.com/news/oculus-medium-touch-art-program,33061.html

Coates, C. (2019, July 1). *Museum VR & AR: New ways to entertain and inform.* Blooloop. https://blooloop.com/museum/in-depth/museum-vr-museum-ar

Constine, J. (2016, January 26). *Oculus "Quill" turns VR painting into performance art.* TechCrunch. https://techcrunch.com/2016/01/26/oculus-quill

Dan, C. (2000). Growing old in new media. In A. W. Balkema & H. Slager (Ed.), *Screen-based art* (pp. 73–78). Brill. https://doi.org/10.1163/9789004495005_011

Delacruz, E. M. (2009). Art education aims in the age of new media: Moving toward global civil society. *Art Education, 62*(5), 13–18. https://doi.org/10.1080/00043125.2009.11519032

Freina, L., & Ott, M. (2015). A literature review on immersive virtual reality in education: State of the art and perspectives. *Proceedings of eLearning and Software for Education, 11*(1), 133–141. https://doi.org/10.12753/2066-026x-15-020

Gregory, S., Lee, M. J. W., Dalgarno, B., & Tynan, B. (2016). *Learning in virtual worlds: Research and applications.* AU Press. https://doi.org/10.15215/aupress/9781771991339.01

Hayden, S. (2017, July 6). *Google announces "Blocks", a VR app like "Tilt Brush" for modeling 3D objects.* Road to VR. https://www.roadtovr.com/google-announces-blocks-vr-app-like-tilt-brush-modeling-3d-objects

Herndon, C., & Gupta, N. (Hosts.). (2019, June 6). XR for Education—Lorenzo Vallone—Xennial Digital (No. 25) [Audio podcast episode]. In *Virtuality Podcast.* https://www.iheart.com/podcast/263-virtuality-podcast-29573598/episode/25-xr-for-education-lorenzo-45775774

Kleven, N. F. (2014). *Virtual university hospital as an arena for medical training and health education* (Unpublished doctoral dissertation). https://ntnuopen.ntnu.no/ntnu-xmlui/handle/11250/253752

Koenig, R. (2019, October 31). *Virtual reality experiences can be "violent" and intrusive. They need an artist's touch.* EdSurge. https://www.edsurge.com/news/2019-10-31-virtual-reality-experiences-can-be-violent-and-intrusive-they-need-an-artist-s-touch

Ku, A. (2018, August 15). Oculus Quill—Tools and hotkeys. *Inborn Experience (UX in AR/VR).* Medium. https://medium.com/inborn-experience/oculus-quill-tools-and-hotkeys-330ae2ccfe8c

Leite, W. L., Svinicki, M., & Shi, Y. (2009). Attempted validation of the scores of the VARK: Learning Styles Inventory with multitrait–multimethod confirmatory factor analysis models. *Educational and Psychological Measurement, 70*(2), 323–339. https://doi.org/10.1177/0013164409344507

Li, A. (2017, July 6). *Google VR releases Minecraft-esque "Blocks" tool to create objects, scenes for VR/AR.* 9to5Google. https://9to5google.com/2017/07/06/google-vr-releases-minecraft-esque-blocks-tool-to-create-objects-scenes-for-vrar

References continued

Martin, A. (2020, May 15). The 10 best virtual museum and art gallery tours. *Elite Traveler*. https://www.elitetraveler.com/design-culture/10-best-virtual-museum-tours

Matthews, K. (2017, July 31). *What Google's Blocks could mean for the future of virtual reality*. UploadVR. https://uploadvr.com/googles-blocks-mean-future-virtual-reality

Mokey, N. (2016, December 19). *We have virtual reality. What's next is straight out of "The Matrix."* Digital Trends. https://www.digitaltrends.com/computing/dt10-we-have-virtual-reality-whats-next-is-straight-out-of-the-matrix

National Art Education Association. (2022, March). *NAEA position statement on STEAM education*. (Original work published 2014). https://www.arteducators.org/advocacy-policy/articles/552-naea-position-statement-on-steam-education

Nijholt, A. (Ed.). (2019). *Brain art: Brain–computer interfaces for artistic expression*. Springer International. https://doi.org/10.1007/978-3-030-14323-7

Nite, S. (2014). *Virtual reality insider: Guidebook for the VR industry*. New Dimension Entertainment.

Pierre, S. (2008). Characterizing e-learning networked environments. In G. D. Putnik & M. M. Cruz-Cunha (Eds.), *Encyclopedia of networked and virtual organizations* (Vol. 1; pp. 181–186). IGI Global. https://doi.org/10.4018/978-1-59904-885-7.ch024

Pritchard, T. (with Andronico, M., & Smith, S. L.). (2022, October 26). *What is the Oculus Rift? Everything you need to know*. Tom's Guide. https://www.tomsguide.com/us/what-is-oculus-rift,news-18026.html

Raab, J. (n.d.). Virtual reality is for artists. *Time*. https://time.com/vr-is-for-artists

Regrebsubla, N. (2015). *Determinants of diffusion of virtual reality* [Diploma thesis, Berlin Institute of Technology]. GRIN Verlag. https://www.grin.com/document/318329

Rheingold, H. (1991). *Virtual reality: Exploring the brave new technologies of artificial experience and interactive worlds—From cyberspace to teledildontics*. Secker & Warburg.

Rhodes, M. (2016, January 26). Oculus Rift takes you inside the wild mind of Salvador Dalí. *Wired*. https://www.wired.com/2016/01/oculus-rift-takes-you-inside-the-wild-mind-of-salvador-dali

Robertson, G. G., Card, S. K., & Mackinlay, J. D. (1993). Three views of virtual reality: Nonimmersive virtual reality. *Computer*, 26(2), 81–90. https://doi.org/10.1109/2.192002

Roussou, M. (2004). Learning by doing and learning through play: An exploration of interactivity in virtual environments for children. *Computers in Entertainment*, 2(1), Article 1. https://doi.org/10.1145/973801.973818

Sandle, T. (2018, September 26). *Virtual reality exhibit brings art to life (includes first-hand account)*. Digital Journal. http://www.digitaljournal.com/entertainment/entertainment/virtual-reality-exhibit-brings-art-to-life/article/533085

Sharma, S. (2017, June 26). The 10 VR artists you need to see to believe. *Dextra*. Medium. https://medium.com/dextra/the-10-virtual-reality-artists-you-need-to-see-to-believe-c66cfde4dcb8

Shin, H., & Ocansey, T. S. (2018, June 8). Stepping into a virtual reality classroom for teacher training. *State of the Planet*. Columbia Climate School. https://news.climate.columbia.edu/2018/06/08/virtual-reality-teacher-training

Sorene, P. (2014, November 24). Jaron Lanier's EyePhone: Head and glove virtual reality in the 1980s. *Flashbak*. https://flashbak.com/jaron-laniers-eyephone-head-and-glove-virtual-reality-in-the-1980s-26180

State Education Agency Directors of Arts Education. (2014). *Customize handbook: National Core Arts Standards*. https://www.nationalartsstandards.org/customize-handbook?bundle_name[4]=4&sm_vid_Process[1]=1&include[eu/eq]=eu/eq

Stokrocki, M. (Ed.). (2014). *Exploration in virtual worlds: New digital multi-media literacy investigations for art education*. National Art Education Association.

Tickle, G. (2015, May 11). A virtual reality tribute to Vincent van Gogh and his famous painting "The Night Café." *Laughing Squid*. https://laughingsquid.com/a-virtual-reality-tribute-to-vincent-van-gogh-and-his-famous-painting-the-night-cafe

Yale University art students explore painting in 3D with VR and Tilt Brush. (n.d.). Google for Education. https://edu.google.com/why-google/case-studies/yale-vrar/?modal_active=nonecl

SECTION IV
Engineering/Design

Section IV engages the readers with a variety of authentic interdisciplinary lessons. A prime example of an interdisciplinary lesson is found in "Engineering Joy: Toying With Process in Expanded Media Arts," teaching students to explore the intersection of art, engineering, and technology. Engineering includes building and constructing structures, as in the chapter "Building Forts at Recess: When Student-Initiated Creativity Becomes STEAM Learning," as well as creating kinetic sculptures in the chapter "How Might We Make This Work? Using Design Thinking to Engineer Kinetic Sculptures in the Art Room." Connecting classroom lessons and activities, the chapter "Engineering Intersections of STEAM: Maker-Centered Learning to Support Teachers' Engineering Confidence and Connections Between Design Processes" is an investigation of the design process.

… *Engineering Joy:* Toying With Process in Expanded Media Arts

Engineering Joy:
Toying With Process in Expanded Media Arts

Sean Justice

> " *I know, I'm a monster. I destroyed a child's dream… their precious toy. But let me just say this: I learned more about toys and how they work by breaking them open than all of the years that I've played with them as the manufacturers intended.*
>
> —preservice art educator, 2019[1]

Science, technology, engineering, the arts, and math (STEAM) learning works because intersections between domains reveal play spaces that support a special kind of fun—hard fun (Papert, 2002). The student quoted above encountered hard fun when she reverse engineered an animatronic Snoopy to bring forth a whirling dancer (Figure 1). Her classmates encountered hard fun when they made toys that waved, blinked, sang, screamed, and danced.

Figure 1. Before and after. A Snoopy remix brings forth a whirling ballerina. Photo courtesy of Bethany Kornacki.

–118–

Seymour Papert wrote passionately about the need for schools to cultivate time and space for children to explore real materials, serious tools, and powerful ideas to build things that truly matter to them. Papert believed that when learning matters, it's hard, but *because* it matters, it's fun. Children know this, and so should we.

This is a story about learning to teach something hard. Typically, teaching ends in a product. Students make something, or they prove they've learned something by scoring well on a test. But my story flips the objective upside down. Instead of the product, the focus is on process. Getting started on this journey was hard, and figuring out how to teach differently was hard—because breaking through bias is *always* hard. But learning together with my students has brought joy: "Finally! Our mechanisms were free!!! The feeling of finally having it completely separated from the plastic shell after so much hard work was exhilarating" (preservice art educator, 2019).

This chapter describes Toy Hack Remix, a hybrid art and engineering activity in my digital methods course in the art education program at Texas State University. I'll begin by exploring intersections between art and engineering, as well as explaining how toy remixing fits into my curriculum. To describe what students learn, however, depends on shifting the objective from product to process. I'll reflect on why this shift to process-oriented learning is sometimes difficult for students and teachers and share what I think I've learned by trying to do it.

STEAM Intersections

> *I have never felt more like a mad scientist in my whole life and I loved it.*
> —preservice art educator, 2020

Imagine each letter of the STEAM alphabet as a separate planet with its own gravitational field. As we know from the Moon's effect on the Earth's oceans, gravitational fields do not exist independently. Rather, each influences the others. Accordingly, neither art nor engineering (nor science, technology, or math) exist entirely in their own spheres, even though we paint them as structurally isolated inside schools. Teachers know, however, that there are moments where individual gravitational fields intersect.

As an educator, I'm interested in transitional zones where tools and thinking routines from one domain intersect routines from other domains. These intersectional spaces generate interest-driven learning. For instance, when a student uses classroom French on a street corner in France, the purpose of learning French becomes newly meaningful, almost visceral in its immediacy, sparking an exhilarating self-efficacy. Teachers who leverage these intersections to enhance student engagement know that newly useful skills open learners to unexpected connections and increase their motivation to just keep learning.

In art and engineering, drawing matters because it engenders thinking routines that matter in each domain: depicting relationships between components in one case, and exploring experience and emotion in the other. Achieving the skills to render these relationships with depth and dimension creates immediacy that suffuses the work with emotion, whether depicting machine part, portrait, or streetscape. For learners of vastly different abilities, creating a skill-based threshold unleashes explosive engagement and self-efficacy. If the curriculum can accommodate the enthusiasm, teachers can harness that engagement to launch students onto learning trajectories of ever-increasing complexity. This suggests that *what* learners do is perhaps less important than just engaging them with *anything* that builds self-efficacy.

For example, most art teachers I know would welcome my student's joyful mad scientist because her engagement would galvanize her classmates. Notwithstanding that no domain answers to a "joy" standard, educators agree that positive engagement is critical to good learning, even in engineering. In *A Whole New Engineer*, Goldberg and Somerville (2014) name joy as the first of five pillars of strong engineering education (along with trust, courage, openness, and community). While admitting that joy "seems like the last word one would use to describe engineering education" (Goldberg & Somerville, 2014, p. 128), the authors argue that research into productive innovation suggests "that positive emotions bathed in freedom are more effective in the development of bold, initiative-taking engineers than fear cloaked in coercion and rigid requirements" (p. 125).

Art educators value positivity and reject coercion as well; as a digital media arts teacher, Meeken (2020) emphasizes forgiveness. Students already know a lot about making art with digital tools, including what to do if they make a mistake—just hit Undo and keep going. Meeken suggests teachers should do so, too. And from a traditional tools perspective, Beal (2001, p. 3) sees materials as "being as much the teacher as [she is]," suggesting that teachers might forgive students *and* themselves for not knowing everything about everything.

The National Art Education Association (NAEA, 2015/2019) defined *media arts* as "an expanding field [of] objects, spaces, and experiences, film, video, computer programming, interactive animation, digital fabrication, games, virtual and augmented reality" (para. 6). This expansion presents opportunities to connect isolated learning domains across the curriculum. More bodies in motion equals more intersections, more transitional zones— they're everywhere. Leveraging the power of that abundance depends on how we perceive the goal of our teaching.

As an art educator, I hope my students learn to engage with tools and materials as a meaningful response to the world, a mix of self-expression, experimentation, and wild flights of fancy. The million moving pieces they'll juggle as teachers will sometimes present stumbling blocks that trip up classroom learning, but I hope I'm teaching them to rely on just getting to work, and on trusting their students' own sense of self-efficacy. Rather than pin those hopes on any singular pedagogy, I want students to recognize that "process" itself will bring joy and curiosity to their classrooms.

Process as a tool or material of the curriculum provides an intersection between learning domains. Goldberg and Somerville (2014) describe a new awareness among progressive engineering educators: Engineering is about designing "not a body of knowledge but a process, a way of thinking" (R. Miller, as cited in Goldberg & Somerville, 2014, pp. 5–6). This shift in the learning objective changes universities and STEM programs in schools when designing and making things switch places with a prolonged study of theory or technique. Goldberg and Somerville (2014, pp. 42–44) explain that when students make something—like an electronic heat sink—before understanding the math and engineering at a deep level, their successes and failures amplify intrinsic motivation, catapulting them forward on interest-driven learning trajectories. It didn't work! Why not!? When students *need* to know, they'll stop at nothing to find out.

The Play Space

Toy Hack Remix appears in my digital methods course at about the halfway point of the semester. The stated purpose of the course is to familiarize art education students with the computational tools they will encounter as teachers. Since these tools change faster than any of us can keep up with, my actual objectives don't dwell on the tools themselves. For instance, there aren't specific Photoshop or 3D printing objectives, though students are encouraged to play with those tools, among many others.

Rather, the focus is on learning how to learn and work meaningfully with media arts tools. I want students to confront, embrace, and overcome the frustrations that sometimes accompany unfamiliar tools. Students begin by saying "I hate technology," but I focus on accepting their misgivings and moving beyond them. In this class we approach media arts materials as we would paint, clay, cardboard, or wood—by learning what the material wants, how it moves, what kind of meanings it invites. This strategy, which I've called *material learning* (Justice & Cabral, 2019), works reliably, and students find themselves engaged in creative meaning-making with tools they had previously held at a distance (if they had held them at all).

The course is based on inquiry activities. Each inquiry centers on different materials, not all of which are digital. We begin with structure and flow: bare copper wire, coin cell batteries, and LED lights. I invite students to design freestanding wire sculptures incorporating working LEDs, without using tape or other adhesives. Very little direct instruction is given at the start of class, although examples, lists of materials, and pdfs are posted on the university learning management system. As students enter the room, I ask them to explore the materials table, where everything is laid out and labeled, like a buffet counter. Then they watch me work with the wire, following where it will go, twisting, bending, and balancing batteries and LEDs.

Some students become discombobulated, perhaps because I'm not telling them what to do, or maybe they fear doing it wrong, even though "it" hasn't been explicitly defined.

Inevitably, however, some students start playing with the wire and LEDs. After 30 minutes or so, many students have a structure that stands up and lights up, at least intermittently, so we take a break to look at their explorations; discuss what the materials want; and ask questions about circuits, current, and flow. When the session ends it's not unusual for some students to ask about taking materials home to continue building their ephemeral circuits. Of course, the answer is always yes.

Reflecting on structure and flow, one student wrote:

> After getting started I felt frustration and then soon anger.... For this first inquiry, we were asked to explore the materials, make a simple circuit, and then make it stand on its own while lit up. At first, I thought it was kind of stupid. I didn't understand why [Professor Justice] couldn't just tell us what to do.... After going back and forth between being confused, frustrated, and angry I felt something new. After finally getting the light to work while standing, I felt such elation. (preservice art educator, 2020)

Elation means learning. Other inquiries invite students to notice and play with cardboard, computer programming, motors, robot parts, augmented reality, handmade animations, and, of course, toys. The materials differ, but elation, exhilaration, and joy remain consistent. In fact, students' journeys are similar from one inquiry to the next: confusion, perhaps followed by frustration, followed by excitement, laughter, and fist bumps.

The trick is to start. But that can be challenging, perhaps because instructions aren't step-by-step, or maybe we're tired, distracted, or stressed by challenges elsewhere in our lives. Sometimes, difficulty fuels the frustration that brightens the glory of success. But at other times, multiple missteps and failures bring anger.

During an inquiry activity, my goal is to remain calm, open to expressions of emotion, and available to help. Sometimes I need to defuse expectations that I will tell someone explicitly what to do. I also need to make a safe space for exploration and failure. This contradiction—remaining supportive but neutral—is the most difficult aspect of my pedagogy, and I have to psyche myself up for it before each inquiry starts.

At the end of an inquiry, students submit process portfolios with photographs, videos, sketches, and screenshots, including a brief reflection about what they learned and how the learning felt. Students are not graded on what they have made but on their process documentation. Completing a circuit sculpture or remixing a toy is not the point, but documenting and reflecting on the process is key. Some students take a while to catch on to the structure of the cycle (there are six to eight inquiries each semester), and they ask for more time to "finish" or worry that their grade will suffer if they don't make a "good" whatever-it-is. Eventually most everyone gets it, and by midsemester, when Toy Hack Remix comes up, "process" has become a buzzword.

Toy Hack Remix: What and How

The context of Toy Hack Remix and the way it appears in my course, as described above, is critical to understanding how it unfolds in practice. To be clear, taking a toy apart and putting it back together was not my invention. In fact, as a learning activity, it's been around for a while.

Background

I first encountered toy remixing with Christa Flores, a science teacher and makerspace coordinator in Asheville, North Carolina, during a workshop at South by Southwest EDU 2017 in Austin, Texas. My setup today is based on the materials she continues to share and revise for whoever would like them (Flores, 2019). In turn, Flores credits her enthusiasm for toy remixing to San Francisco's Exploratorium (n.d.; see also Wilkinson & Petrich, 2014), and to thinking routines developed by the Artful Thinking project at Harvard's Project Zero, particularly *Parts, Purposes, Complexities* (Project Zero, 2010). But toy remix variations are plentiful, showing up at professional learning events for teachers all over the country. Among these, a favorite is Angie O'Malley's (2019) 5th-grade "Toy Hacking for Accessibility," where students design hacks that make toys accessible for children with disabilities.

Figure 2. Plush toys with animatronic features work best, but almost any motorized toy will do, as long as it works. Photo courtesy of Tyler Vinklarek.

My version of toy remixing relies on a simple setup and few instructions (the fewer the better). Skills and procedures gleaned from prior inquiries work like stepping stones and might or might not play a role in a student's approach to toy remixing. That is, inquiries aren't scaffolded, but skills and materials from prior activities remain available to future activities. To prepare for toy remixing, the one thing students have been asked to do is purchase a toy of their own. I've found that secondhand thrift stores often have a good selection. Plush animatronic toys are best (Figure 2), but almost any motorized toy will do, as long as it works (note to self: bring fresh batteries).

The What and How

On Day 1 of Toy Hack Remix, students find a smorgasbord of tools and materials spread out across the room—screwdrivers, chisels, hacksaws, seam rippers, power drills, glue guns, many kinds of tape, safety goggles, gloves, and boxes of spare parts left over from prior take-apart activities. Stacks of handouts and copies of the Exploratorium book (Wilkinson & Petrich, 2014) are also available. At the start of class, I repeat the safety protocol for sharp instruments (i.e., how not to hurt yourself), and remind students to read the handouts.

Step 1: Before deconstructing the toy, explore it from the outside and sketch what you think is inside. What do you think makes it work? (See Figures 3–4.)

Step 2: As you take the toy apart, document components and the connections between them. How accurate were your predictions? Revise your sketch as you go. (See Figure 5.)

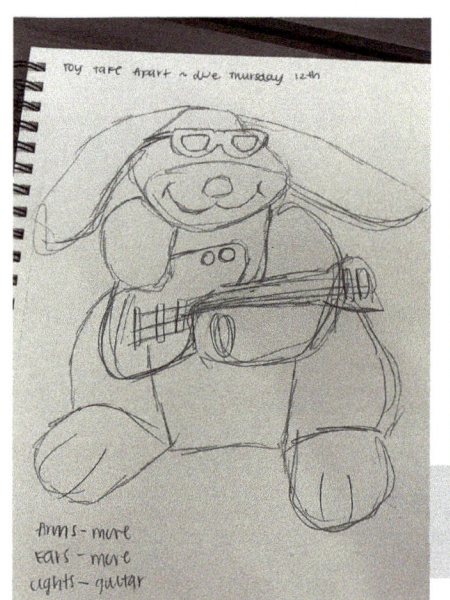

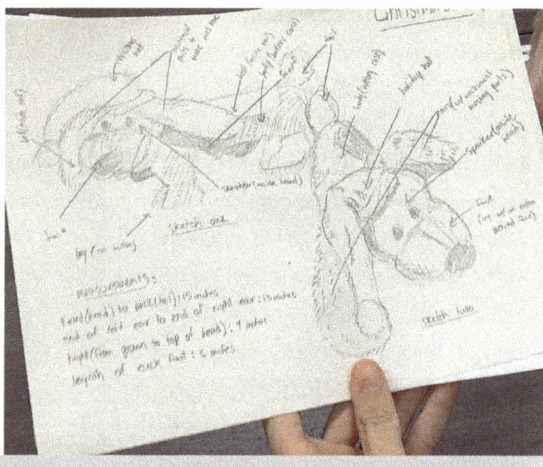

Figures 3–4. Step 1: Before taking your toy apart, explore it from the outside and sketch what you think is inside. Be sure to label your drawing. Drawings by Emmanuel Zygmont and Claire Drew.

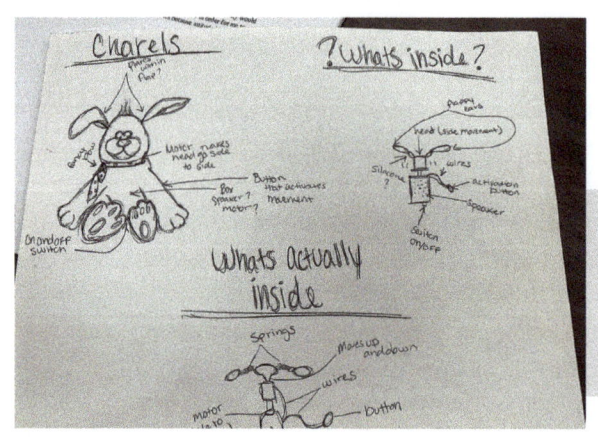

Figure 5. Step 2: As you take the toy apart, document components and the connections between them, revising your sketch as you go. What surprises you? How do the parts work together? Drawing by Belinda Lara.

Step 3: Put the toy together again. Remember that your reconstruction should *translate* some aspect of the toy's original motion. For example, if the toy waves left and right, the reconstructed toy might undulate up and down. Or, if it bounces, it might whirl, crawl, jiggle, or dance.

The key to translation is paying attention to the toy itself and remaining open to the serendipity of discovering how its parts work together. The act of attending to possibility makes moments of transmediation available (Manovich, 2002)—the notion that things and thinking change as they transit from one materiality to another. Awareness of structure invites a critique of the conventions that shape the toy, prompting students to imagine themselves as designers who can break free of manufacturers' constraints (See Figure 6). As the inquiry begins, I wander around the studio, pointing to tools and materials that might have gone unnoticed, reminding students to hold expectations loosely, and urging them to pay attention to what's unfolding in front of them.

Figure 6. Step 3: Put the toy together again. The reconstruction should *translate* some aspect of the toy's original motion into a different kind of motion, e.g., perhaps back-and-forth becomes up-and-down. Remixed toy by Belinda Lara.

Outcomes

Toy Hack Remix is often the most affective inquiry of the course, as evidenced by the emotional resonance in students' reflections. Students write about the serendipity and flow of material learning, which they've just begun to notice: "Part of the fun here is that I didn't go in with a plan. Every decision was an in-the-moment light bulb idea," (preservice art educator, 2020). And

> as I took the toy apart, I was immediately obsessed. I forgot to eat, or take a break, and I completely lost track of time. This brought me great joy and recreated a state of mind [from] adolescence… creativity that I thought I was not capable of anymore. (preservice art educator, 2020)

Students also discuss shared learning: "I was so proud of all my classmates because I know some people really had trouble at first, but in the end, there was not a single failure" (preservice art educator, 2020). And "I started to feel more comfortable operating on Snoopy and when I saw what my classmates were doing with their toys, I felt very motivated" (preservice art educator, 2019).

Recognizing *process* as a component of their learning is evident in the way students imagine what comes next:

> My fear of the unknown is much smaller [and] I'm beginning to look at things around me and think about what is making them tick. If I can inspire "I wonder" to pop into a child's mind, I think I will be a successful teacher. (preservice art educator, 2019)

And

> What the hell was all that? None of what I expected is even remotely close to what I experienced. Once I finally understood that, it sparked a memory... the moment I decided to be an educator. My first experience teaching was dance to children, [but] I thought I would hate it. I didn't expect to come out loving to teach, just like I didn't expect this process of toys to take apart. Maybe, just maybe, if I can rebuild a toy then I can rebuild a child's learning process. (preservice art educator, 2019)

What Comes Next

In schools, what is learned and how it is learned depends on what students do and how they do it. But what comes next—*why* the learning matters—requires remixing learning itself. Toy remixing *begins* with a product and *becomes* a process. The upside-down object—process *as* product—prompts thinking about learning itself. I see it in students' reflections. Not only do they write passionately about their experiences, ideas, memories, aha moments and new skills (as quoted throughout this chapter), but they connect their individual learning to classmates' learning, which opens them to imagining their role as designers of interdependent learning.

As described above, process portfolios require brief reflections about the experience of learning. Two questions are consistent across all inquiry activities: *How would you bring somebody along the learning path you have traveled?* And *Why would you want to do so?* In blog posts students often address the first question with step-by-step procedurals. The second question often spools out unexpectedly, pragmatic but entangled with poetry, ambition, and longing. Why would you want to bring somebody along this path? Students write, "To...

"...feel better equipped for everyday life."

"...remove the fear or hesitation that can keep you too close to 'safe.'"

"...learn about my own creative process, patience, and surrender."

"…rebuild a child's learning process."

"…inspire 'I wonder' to pop into a child's mind."

Distinguishing process from product frames learning as a shared community asset to be remixed for the benefit of others. This requires the skill to notice and leverage expertise as a shared structural relationship. Acquiring this skill requires experiencing the exhilaration and purpose of learning together. Doing that requires authentic encounters with materials, tools, and ideas to build things that truly matter. Getting there isn't easy:

> I started off hating [process] learning, but by the second inquiry, I wished I had learned this way more growing up. A lot of the time, teachers just tell students how to do something and the students just repeat, [but] I love thinking of learning as a journey. I feel much more confident in myself and my ability to explore and learn. (preservice art educator, 2020)

Some Final Thoughts

> *I have recently noticed that in some things, I resist change with every fiber of myself, and often I am unaware of it.*
> —preservice art educator, 2019

In his book about craftsmanship as a way of thinking and as a civilizing process, Sennett (2008) explains that archaic Greek hymns celebrate the *public* good that comes from building *individual* skills. In those days, hundreds of years before Plato and Aristotle, the unity "between skill and community" had not yet dissolved (p. 24). Flash forward to today, and Bogost (2016) warns we've lost the ability to pay attention to the wonder of everyday things like pop songs, sitcoms, sonnets, games, and of course, toys: "Our world is jam-packed full of splendor and mystery, most of which we never notice as we play the demands and dissatisfaction of our selfish lives" (p. 25).

Toy Hack Remix sometimes shatters students' resistance to process-centered learning, empowering them to attempt wonderful, impossible things. Sometimes it nearly shatters me, too. Getting students to the point of breakthroughs is difficult, though I believe we get there together. For students, a spark of new awareness reveals glimmers of the wonders and dissatisfactions they will encounter when they become teachers. For teachers, exhausted as we often are, breakthroughs can spark a desire to just keep going and the hope it will matter in the lives of our students, and of their students. These are the intersectional spaces I'm seeking: joy, curiosity, trust, community.

Toy Hack Remix can be remixed by anyone, for any age or skill level. The *reason* for remixing is equally open, but with O'Malley (2019) and Flores (2019), I value openings toward meaningfulness. For me, the goal is to challenge the isolation of individual expertise and product-centeredness. That might not be the learning objective in every classroom, but toying with process-centered learning together with my students has unexpectedly taught me how to engineer joy.

Endnote

[1] Quotes from preservice art educators appearing throughout the chapter are excerpts from reflective blog posts written by students and shared with classmates.

> ***Sean Justice*** *is an associate professor of art education at Texas State University in San Marcos. His teaching and research address teacher education in the age of computing and digital networks. As an artist, he has exhibited photographs, videos, and computer animations both nationally and internationally. His book* Learning to Teach in the Digital Age: New Materialities and Maker Paradigms in Schools *was published by Peter Lang in 2016. He publishes regularly in art, education, and human development journals.*

References

Beal, N. (with Miller, G. B.). (2001). *The art of teaching art to children: In school and at home*. Farrar, Straus and Giroux.

Bogost, I. (2016). *Play anything: The pleasure of limits, the uses of boredom, and the secret of games*. Basic Books.

Exploratorium. (n.d.). *Toy take apart*. https://www.exploratorium.edu/tinkering/projects/toy-take-apart

Flores, C. (2019). Maker education and the STEM monster. In P. Blikstein, S. L. Martinez, H. A. Pang, & K. Jarrett (Eds.), *Meaningful making 2: Projects and inspirations for Fab Labs and makerspaces* (pp. 104–107). Constructing Modern Knowledge Press. https://fablearn.org/fellows/meaningful-making-book

Goldberg, D. E., & Somerville, M. (with Whitney, C.). (2014). *A whole new engineer: The coming revolution in engineering education*. ThreeJoy. https://doi.org/10.4271/0986080004

Justice, S., & Cabral, M. (with Gugliotta, K.). (2019). The crayon doesn't do that. In R. L. Garner (Ed.), *Exploring digital technologies for art-based special education: Models and methods for the inclusive K-12 classroom* (pp. 122–132). Routledge. https://doi.org/10.4324/9781351067928-12

Manovich, L. (2002). *The language of new media*. MIT Press.

Meeken, L. (2020). System error: Versatility and facility as empowering values for the digital arts classroom. *Art Education*, *73*(3), 22–28. https://doi.org/10.1080/00043125.2020.1717816

National Art Education Association. (2019, March). *NAEA position statement on media arts*. (Original work published 2015). https://www.arteducators.org/advocacy/articles/523-naea-position-statement-on-media-arts

O'Malley, A. (2019). Toy hacking for accessibility. In P. Blikstein, S. L. Martinez, H. A. Pang, & K. Jarrett (Eds.), *Meaningful making 2: Projects and inspirations for Fab Labs + makerspaces* (p. 145). Constructing Modern Knowledge Press. https://fablearn.org/fellows/meaningful-making-book

Papert, S. (2002, June 24). How to make writing "hard fun." *Bangor Daily News*. https://archive.bangordailynews.com/2002/06/24/how-to-make-writing-hard-fun

Project Zero. (2010). *Parts, purposes, complexities*. Harvard Graduate School of Education. https://pz.harvard.edu/resources/parts-purposes-complexities

Sennett, R. (2008). *The craftsman*. Yale University Press.

Wilkinson, K., & Petrich, M. (2014). *The art of tinkering: Meet 150+ makers working at the intersection of art, science and technology*. Weldon Owen.

Building Forts at Recess:
When Student-Initiated Creativity Becomes STEAM Learning

David Rufo

Clouds hung low in the early December sky as a persistent north wind threatened to usher in the first storm of the winter season. However, this did not seem to concern my students as they excitedly worked in cooperative groups to analyze problems, find solutions, engage in critical discourse, and resolve conflicts among themselves. As an elementary classroom teacher, I found moments like these extremely satisfying. This instance was particularly interesting because the children were not working on an activity that I had assigned as their teacher, but on one they had initiated a few months prior. They also chose to do this work during their recess time and to do it outside despite the weather. The children were working on a series of fort structures they erected in a copse of sumac trees near the playground at our school in upstate New York.

Student Agency, Self-Initiated Creativity, and STEAM

In our classroom, my teaching partner and I designed hands-on and project-based learning activities that privileged student choice in an attempt to foster meaningful and relevant learning experiences (Lattimer & Riordan, 2011). We also embraced the notion of student agency to encourage them to become independent learners who were willing to take risks and explore new ideas. Project-based learning is an approach designed to engage students in the "investigation of authentic problems" (Blumenfeld et al., 1991, p. 369) and allow students' agency to engender intrinsic motivation (Deci & Ryan, 1985). Further, studies show that empowered children become enthusiastic and productive learners (Anning, 2002; Grube, 2009). I found that combining these practices in my classroom led to an increase in self-initiated creativity, which correlates with research literature that suggests student autonomy boosts creativity (Fairweather & Cramond, 2010; Jaquith, 2011). Granted, self-initiated or student-initiated creative actions produce artifacts that are not part of teacher-directed lessons or school-sanctioned activities. Nevertheless, this type of creativity requires curiosity, divergent thinking, and imagination, which in turn leads to authentic, relevant, and challenging learning experiences (Grube, 2009; Hawkins, 2002). The fort-building activity in which my students took part provides a good example of this pedagogical approach as it was initiated by the students, enacted in areas which they selected, and engaged in of their own volition.

Fort building remained the dominant recess activity from 2009 until 2014, when I left the school to complete my dissertation. This is not surprising, as my 4th and 5th graders were in the midst of what David Sobel (2002) designates as middle childhood—that "critical period in the development of the self and in the individual's relationship to the natural world" (p. 52). Sobel goes on to illustrate how fort building provides a way for children to have a role in shaping their worlds and satisfy their "place-making impulses" (2002, p. 52). During those 5 years, I was able to witness how the fort-building activities "afforded opportunities for creative play that other parts of the school grounds did not" (Blizzard & Schuster, 2004, p. 57), as well as the myriad ways children spontaneously incorporate science, technology, engineering, the arts, and math (STEAM) explorations into their play-based learning experiences. Schools traditionally organize curriculum as separated subject areas (Fan & Yu, 2017, p. 107), whereas STEAM learning provides opportunities for students to engage in "disciplines that were previously perceived as disparate" (Guyotte et al., 2014, p. 12). In some respects, the fort-building activity was the consummate STEAM learning experience as it provided students with a domain in which to grapple with problems that required scientific, technological, engineering, arts-based, and mathematical solutions.

The Beginning

The activity began in October when a handful of students who were not interested in playing soccer, four square, or games that involved the usual array of playground equipment wanted to explore a hillside on the other side of a 3-foot-high chain-link fence that enclosed the playground. Under his supervision, my teaching partner allowed the group to climb the fence so they could survey the area and wander among the tall grasses and underbrush. Over the next few days, these students spent their recess time collecting downed branches gathered from nearby woods to construct rudimentary lean-to frames they called forts. Upon seeing the forts, other students joined in; within a few weeks, the hillside became dotted with small hovels made of sticks and branches.

As the hillside became more crowded, so did the main trail that ran between the forts. A group of students complained about the congestion and asked permission to build at a new location on an adjacent hillside. As they began to make a clearing, it was discovered that the long tangles of wild grasses pulled from the earth could be formed into dense cushions of soft thatch and placed on the hard-packed dirt floors of the forts. They also found that the thatch provided an effective insulating material when stuffed between the increasingly complex network of branches, sticks, and twigs that made up the walls and roof of each fort structure. This serendipitous discovery led them to abandon their plans to relocate and instead, they began using the grasses they harvested as barter for desirable fort-building materials such as long, straight branches or rocks with squared edges and flat sides that could be easily stacked or used as foundational supports.

Roles and Responsibilities Established

By November, the students had self-organized into working groups based on their talents and interests, reminiscent of medieval guilds. Some worked as framers, finding the right type of branches and then fitting them together at the worksite to erect the framework for each fort. Others specialized as reapers, fashioning crude tools from sticks that had hooked ends or raked edges to facilitate the pulling and cutting of the thick masses of entangled grasses. At the same time, another group bundled the grasses into enormous clumps and loaded them on sleds for efficient transport to the fort sites. Still other students spent their time as weavers, carefully and meditatively interlacing and inserting the thatch throughout the framework of each fort. Students who had an understanding of scale and proportion formulated new designs that included fortified roofs to support second floors while others constructed rock foundations to level floors fashioned from old pallets taken from the school dumpster.

Finally, there were those students who were not interested in harvesting, gathering, building, or designing but possessed skills of persuasion, inspiration, and interpersonal discernment. These were the students who oversaw various aspects of the construction, such as locating potential building sites, settling disputes, and rallying those who became disheartened when faced with new and unforeseen challenges.

STEAM Learning Through Fort Building

Although the fort-building activities had become routine, it was not until that day in early December that I began to realize the extent to which STEAM learning was embedded in the fort-building activity and what student-initiated creativity could teach me about the way children go about the learning process.

At first, I was hesitant to accept my students' invitation to enter their fort, as it would be necessary for me to crouch low and crawl through the small hole framed by a U-shaped branch that served as the entryway. Once inside, I would have to squat and it might have been difficult to move about the inside the child-sized structure. The earliest forts, this one included, were built on the top edge of a steep hillside overlooking the sports field. I envisioned losing my balance, tilting backward, crashing through the back wall, and somersaulting down the rocky hill. But that day the temperature had dropped precipitously, bringing with it gusting winds and a frigid windchill, so I accepted the invitation to enter the fort.

Once inside, the transformation was surreal. The bedding of thatch on the floor, as well as the portions pressed into the walls and ceiling, provided ample protection from the howling wind. Inside, sounds became muted as a soft light permeated the dense weave of branches, sticks, and grasses. Not only did the fort provide warmth and protection from the elements, but it offered psychological benefits as well. This meditative space brought back memories of my own childhood and especially those instances when learning happened through exploration, experimentation, and play.

The Reggio Emilia approach to education regards the classroom space as "a third teacher" (Strong-Wilson & Ellis, 2007, p. 41). During the fort-building activity, outdoor spaces beyond the confines of the playground became a third teacher, providing the materials and motivation, along with a host of playful problems to be solved. Through the convergence of student agency, self-initiated creativity, and integrated learning, the children had created structural spaces that demonstrated the power of STEAM education. The students employed *scientific* concepts as they explored their natural surroundings, foraging for resources like branches, sticks, grasses, and rocks to use as construction materials. They developed new *technologies* as they found increasingly efficient methods and tools to regulate and systematize the building process. They employed *engineering* techniques as they laid foundations, erected frameworks, constructed roofing structures, developed insulation and waterproofing systems, and established a network of pathways between the forts. *Arts-based* thinking led to the creation of fort structures with aesthetically pleasing exteriors, as well as interiors that provided the children with serene, safe spaces "created from the raw materials of the natural world and their flexible imaginations" (Sobel, 2002, p. 160). *Mathematics* was required to estimate the size and shape of each fort structure, the square footage necessary to comfortably accommodate each fort member, and the amount of materials needed for each phase of the project prior to sending out search parties to gather and transport the items back to the jobsite.

STEAM Spontaneity

Over time, I noticed that the more choice and agency my students had in their learning, the more they engaged in self-initiated creativity. Freed from the constraints of scripted and standardized curricula, my students demonstrated how children spontaneously go about the learning process and how that process frequently involves STEAM competencies. The fort-building activity illustrated how choice-based learning promotes STEAM inquiry, leading to relevant and meaningful in-depth understandings (Starko, 2009). When my teaching partner and I assumed the roles of guides and facilitators, following the children's lead and attending to their interests, they became problem solvers, engineers, designers, innovators, and inventors.

David Rufo is a visual artist and an assistant professor of childhood education at Utica University in upstate New York. Previously, Rufo worked for 2 decades as an elementary classroom teacher.

References

Anning, A. (2002). Conversations around young children's drawings: The impact of the beliefs of significant others at home and school. *International Journal of Art & Design Education, 21*(3), 197–208. https://doi.org/10.1111/1468-5949.00317

Blizzard, C., & Schuster, R., Jr. (2004). "They all cared about the forest": Elementary school children's experiences of the loss of a wooded play space at a private school in upstate New York. In K. Bricker & S. J. Millington (Eds.), *Proceedings of the 2004 Northeastern Recreation Research Symposium* (pp. 57–63). U.S. Department of Agriculture.

Blumenfeld, P. C., Soloway, E., Marx, R. W., Krajcik, J. S., Guzdial, M., & Palincsar, A. (1991). Motivating project-based learning: Sustaining the doing, supporting the learning. *Educational Psychologist, 26*(3 & 4), 369–398. https://doi.org/10.1207/s15326985ep2603&4_8

Deci, E. L., & Ryan, R. M. (1985). *Intrinsic motivation and self-determination in human behavior.* Plenum Press. https://doi.org/10.1007/978-1-4899-2271-7

Fairweather, E., & Cramond, B. (2010). Infusing creative and critical thinking into the curriculum together. In R. A. Beghetto & J. C. Kaufman (Eds.), *Nurturing creativity in the classroom* (pp. 113–141). Cambridge University Press. https://doi.org/10.1017/cbo9780511781629.007

Fan, S.-C., & Yu, K.-C. (2017). How an integrative STEM curriculum can benefit students in engineering design practices. *International Journal of Technology and Design Education, 27*(1), 107–129. https://doi.org/10.1007/s10798-015-9328-x

Grube, V. (2009). Admitting their worlds: Reflections of a teacher/researcher on the self-initiated art making of children. *International Journal of Education & the Arts, 10*(7). http://www.ijea.org/v10n7

Guyotte, K. W., Sochacka, N. W., Costantino, T. E., Walther, J., & Kellam, N. N. (2014). STEAM as social practice: Cultivating creativity in transdisciplinary spaces. *Art Education, 67*(6), 12–19. https://doi.org/10.1080/00043125.2014.11519293

Hawkins, B. (2002). Children's drawing, self-expression, identity and the imagination. *International Journal of Art & Design Education, 21*(3), 209–219. https://doi.org/10.1111/1468-5949.00318

Jaquith, D. B. (2011). When is creativity? Intrinsic motivation and autonomy in children's artmaking. *Art Education, 64*(1), 13–19. https://doi.org/10.1080/00043125.2011.11519106

Lattimer, H., & Riordan, R. (2011). Project-based learning engages students in meaningful work. *Middle School Journal, 43*(2), 18–23. https://doi.org/10.1080/00940771.2011.11461797

Sobel, D. (2002). *Children's special places: Exploring the role of forts, dens, and bush houses in middle childhood.* Wayne State University Press.

Starko, A. J. (2009). *Creativity in the classroom: Schools of curious delight* (4th ed.). Routledge. https://doi.org/10.4324/9780203871492

Strong-Wilson, T., & Ellis, J. (2007). Children and place: Reggio Emilia's environment as third teacher. *Theory Into Practice, 46*(1), 40–47. https://doi.org/10.1080/00405840709336547

Engineering Intersections of STEAM:
Maker-Centered Learning to Support Teachers' Engineering Confidence and Connections Between Design Processes

Shaunna Smith

The hot glue works into overdrive as plastic bottle caps roll across the table. Cardboard tubes are cut and transformed into buildings and portals. A produce clamshell is transformed into a wheeled vehicle to help the Tortoise speed past the Hare. Abandoned plastic grocery bags become a parachute to help Rapunzel escape her tower. Giggles and high fives mix with questions of how something functions. "What if" and "transform that" echo throughout the room as teachers test their prototypes during an introductory novel engineering activity, which challenges them to use recyclables to design solutions for storybook characters' problems. This is not how these teachers thought they would be spending their Monday evenings in a graduate-level science, technology, engineering, the arts, and math (STEAM) course.

This chapter focuses on the impact a graduate-level STEAM course had on teacher participants' ability to recontextualize design processes and influence their confidence in the engineering design process. The 15-week course focused on interdisciplinary STEAM learning, which explored intersections of STEAM content and design processes in the context of educational makerspaces and K–12 classrooms. This chapter reports on logistics of facilitating reflective learning in the STEAM course and examines recurring reflections that document participants' engagement in the engineering design process.

Literature Review

Maker-centered learning is a theoretical framework that focuses on using design as an active learning approach to encourage dispositions such as creativity and agency (Blikstein et al., 2016; Clapp et al., 2017), as well as discipline-specific knowledge and skills (Bevan, 2017; Rodriguez et al., 2018; Smith, 2018). It is inspired by the global DIY maker movement and crafting culture that draws upon diverse mindsets, techniques, and tools, including nondigital craftsmanship traditions of the past and advanced digital technologies (Martin, 2015; Martinez & Stager, 2013; Peppler et al., 2016; Vossoughi et al., 2016). Embedded assessments are critical to maker-centered learning, particularly reflection (Petrich et al., 2013; Schwartz, 2016; Smith, 2018).

Making and Reflection

Reflection in maker-centered learning instills a sense of intentionality because it allows teachers to "frame it and reflect upon it to make sure learning happens" (Schwartz, 2016, para. 2). When learners are encouraged to document reflections of what they are doing, they provide critical records of their creative ideas, experimentations, systematic procedures, and design processes (Smith, 2018). This can be used by others to assess their work (e.g., formative and summative, engineering notebooks, artist journals) and become a longitudinal record of self-assessment, enabling them to see their personal growth over time (Blikstein et al., 2016). Embedding reflection within maker-centered learning facilitates deeper meaning-making by connecting active in-class participation to previous experiences and conceptual understanding (Petrich et al., 2013; Schwartz, 2016). Reflection can be especially helpful for learners to engage with STEAM content.

Making and STEAM

Maker-centered learning serves as an effective STEAM approach because content and design processes from various disciplines intersect. When learners engage in design and make artifacts, they apply interdisciplinary skills, including creativity, critical thinking, problem solving, and communication (Clapp et al., 2017; Petrich et al., 2013). Likewise, maker-centered learning often requires learners to apply knowledge from various disciplines and leverage design processes and tools that are typically connected to certain fields of study (Bevan, 2017; Martinez & Stager, 2013; Rodriguez et al., 2018; Smith, 2018). With the ability to address various dispositions, knowledge, and skills, making is especially useful for teaching engineering concepts.

Making and Engineering Education

Researchers and teacher educators assert that maker-centered learning can be used as an engaging strategy to integrate engineering into K–12 learning (Bevan, 2017; Martin, 2015; Rodriguez et al., 2018; Thomas & Besser, 2017). Engineering is about solving problems through designing solutions, and making provides an authentic mechanism (Bevan, 2017; Rodriguez et al., 2018). The Next Generation Science Standards integrate engineering to strengthen K–12 students' scientific understanding, including Science and Engineering Practices and Crosscutting Concepts (Bybee, 2014; Willard, 2014). While there are a variety of engineering design process models, the most common K–12 model is the Engineering is Elementary (EiE), which involves five phases: (1) ask, (2) imagine, (3) plan, (4) create, and (5) improve (Cunningham, 2018; see also https://eie.org). This model assists students with exploring engineering design through intentionally engaging in problem-focused design and systematically documenting their processes. Research shows that teachers without prior engineering experience range significantly in their understanding of and confidence in integrating engineering design concepts into the classroom (Hynes et al., 2017). Because most teachers did not experience engineering in their teacher preparation, it is important to engage them in active learning of engineering practice to increase their confidence to teach engineering concepts to K–12 students (Bybee, 2014; Cunningham, 2018; Cunningham & Carlsen, 2014). This study examines the impact of a graduate-level STEAM course on teacher participants' confidence in the engineering design process.

Methods

The methods for this chapter were constrained by the STEAM course itself as well as the participants. The logistics, participants, and data collection are below.

STEAM Course Logistics

The overarching goals for this course included engaging in and reflecting on the intersections of STEAM content and design processes through diverse materials, tools, and contexts. Unit topics were arranged in a sequence with multiple weeks per topic, including intersections of STEAM (2 weeks), 2D design (3 weeks), 3D design (3 weeks), electronics and interactive design (5 weeks), and final autoethnographic reflection (2 weeks). Each weekly topic included (1) 5E lesson structure; (2) inspirational examples from artists, makers, and industry; (3) scaffolded techniques using familiar nondigital materials and advanced digital materials; (4) in-class discussion; and (5) recurring reflection. Techniques focused on a variety of design themes and materials, including common crafts, recyclables, free design software, inexpensive digital fabrication hardware, and user-friendly electronics. Each unit culminated with a choice-based design project where students choose one or more unit techniques to create their own artifact.

Procedure and Logistics for Facilitating Multimodal Reflection

A key theme in this course was reflection on the design process (i.e., *What learning occurs while I design an artifact?*). Diverse strategies were embedded throughout the course to ensure a variety of formative and summative assessments, including multimodal opportunities to reflect using multimedia to document weekly creative process and artifacts.

In-class discussion was facilitated through questions about STEAM content connections, design process, and craftsmanship. *Weekly reflections* were facilitated using Edmodo to respond to the weekly thematic prompt; reflect on design processes used during in-class activities; identify three things they learned, two things they want to learn more about, and one thing they were proud of; and share multimedia documentation of their experience (e.g., photo, URL, video).

Self-Assessment

The Engineering Design Process (EDP) reflection included self-assessment of engineering design process confidence at the end of each design unit using an online Google Form. *Culminating autoethnographic reflective video* was completed at the end of the semester using free software (e.g., Adobe Spark, iMovie, WeVideo) to document their semester-long evolution, including design processes they engaged in, artifacts they created, and implications for their personal creativity and professional practice.

Research

A convergent mixed-methods design was used, which included qualitative and quantitative data that were collected, analyzed, and reported separately, then converged for triangulation, comparison, and interpretation (Creswell & Plano Clark, 2018). Research questions included:

1. How do teacher participants use recurring weekly reflections to communicate the differences and similarities between the design processes of different fields?

2. How does teacher participants' engineering design self-efficacy change during a semester-long STEAM course?

Participants

Participants included five in-service teachers from diverse content areas, who taught grade levels spanning from kindergarten (age 5) through Grade 12 (age 18; see Table 1). All participants were given pseudonyms to protect anonymity.

Table 1. Participant Demographics

Participant	Gender	Grade level	Discipline	Years of teaching
Diana	Female	5	English language arts & social studies	3
Clara	Female	K–5	art	4
Donya	Female	6–8	art	10
Kathryn	Female	6–8	mathematics	6
Melissa	Female	9–12	mathematics	1

Qualitative Data Collection and Analysis

Qualitative data included reflections collected weekly for 15 weeks (August–December) using Edmodo. Qualitative data was analyzed using deductive coding techniques described by Miles et al. (2014), including terms related to maker-centered learning, interdisciplinary learning, STEAM content concepts, and design processes.

Quantitative Data Collection and Analysis

The EDP reflection was created by the author and included 28 closed-ended questions with a five-level Likert scale (i.e., 1: not confident at all, 2: slightly confident, 3: somewhat confident, 4: fairly confident, 5: completely confident). Twenty-one questions were based on Carberry et al.'s (2010) Engineering Design Self-Efficacy instrument that evaluates confidence, motivation, expectation of success, and anxiety. These questions were reformatted to align with the EiE engineering design process (i.e., ask, imagine, plan, create, improve). Seven questions were added to evaluate confidence in identifying design process connections, interdisciplinary connections, and classroom integration strategies. The EDP reflection was completed at the end of each unit (2D design in September, 3D design in October, electronics and interactive design in November) using a Google Form. Descriptive statistics were used to calculate means and changes.

Findings

The findings from this study were rich with detail and demonstrated several factors, including communicating differences and similarities of the design process, makerspaces as intersections of art, 2D design, 3D design, electronics, reflections, and self-efficacy.

Communicating Differences and Similarities of Design Processes

Qualitative findings are organized sequentially in the context of the 15-week course to demonstrate how participants reflected on the differences and similarities of design processes from different fields.

Makerspaces as Intersections of Art and Everything

The course began with an introduction to STEAM concepts and design processes, including a novel engineering challenge (use recyclables and common craft materials to prototype a solution for a storybook character), and an exploration of pedagogical roots of the global maker movement and K–12 maker education.

During the novel engineering activity, Kathryn acknowledged similarities and differences between art and engineering design process by stating, "While solving the problem was not necessarily 'personally meaningful' like art, it was exciting to be able to think deeply about how to solve a problem that another is experiencing" (Week 1; see Figure 1).

Figure 1. Produce clamshell transformed into a wheeled vehicle to help the Tortoise speed past the Hare, designed by Diana and Kathryn.

Similarly, Donya reflected that intersecting design experiences could help improve students' interdisciplinary mindsets by

> guiding them in thinking more like artists, designers, engineers and makers and helping them to understand that it is a messy process that involves mistakes, problem-solving, rethinking, testing, retesting, and documenting how they make multiple changes and adaptations along the way. (Week 2)

2D Design

This unit included free vector-based design software (i.e., Inkscape, Silhouette Studio), 2D CNC machines (i.e., Silhouette Cameo paper- and vinyl-cutting machine, digital sewing and embroidery machine), and 2D materials (i.e., paper, vinyl, textiles).

While expanding her knowledge of design beyond her experience as an elementary art teacher, Clara reflected,

> I'm beginning to see the similarities in design process methods but the differences in intention. Art is expressive and about sharing a message. Engineering is about systematically solving a problem. Science is about discovery. All three use design in similar ways, yet are also unique and different. (Week 4)

Kathryn's 2D project celebrated engaging in the engineering design process and applying STEAM concepts inspired by mathematician George Hart:

> I found his geometric sculptures and puzzles exciting and I loved the art and mathematical connection, which is a passion of mine. After researching his work I chose to use Silhouette Studio to create one of his designs, The Tunnel Cube. (Week 5, see Figures 2 and 3)

Figure 2. Kathryn's Tunnel Cube, designed using Silhouette Studio, crayon, cardstock paper, and Silhouette Cameo.

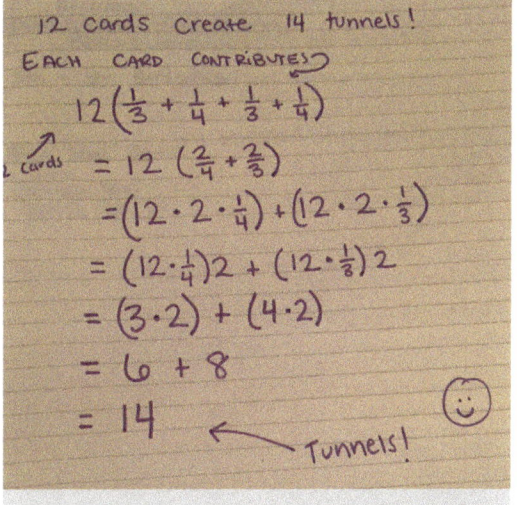

Figure 3. The mathematical explanation of the Tunnel Cube.

3D Design

This unit explored sculpture and additive manufacturing, including free 3D CAD modeling software (i.e., Tinkercad, Blender), 3D materials (i.e., hot glue guns, 3D pens, modeling clay, recyclables), and 3D printers (MakerBot Replicator Mini).

Accustomed to traditional 3D sculptural techniques, Donya was surprised by how 3D CAD software benefited her iterative design process:

> I think the advantages to using 3D modeling software over non-digital techniques are how precise you get to be. You can easily add details, exact measurements, and view all angles of the design before printing; therefore it is much easier to make changes. (Week 6)

Melissa's 3D design project reflection exemplified this:

> I had to create multiple design iterations to have functioning cookie cutters. I also had to think about how I was going to place these on the cookie dough and consider size, depth, and strength for reuse. These were ideas that I hadn't realized were an important part of the engineering design process. (Week 8, see Figure 4)

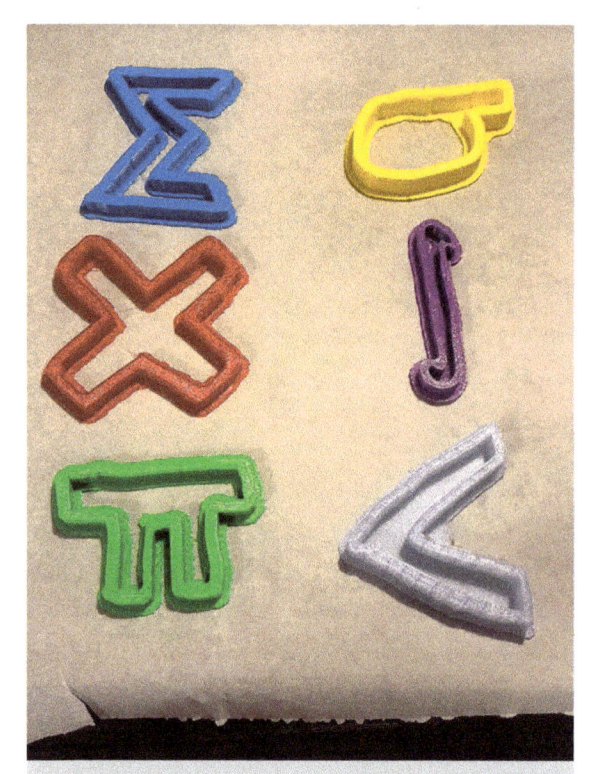

Figure 4. Melissa's mathematical cookie cutters, designed using Tinkercad and Makerbot Replicator Mini 3D printer.

Electronics and Interactive Design

This unit focused on simple electronics and computer programming that were easily accessible for beginners, including kits (i.e., littleBits, Snap Circuits), conductive materials (i.e., alligator clips, pencil, paint, tape, thread), electrical components (i.e., LED lights, motors, sensors), microcontrollers (i.e., Arduino, Makey Makey), and free computer programming software (i.e., Scratch, Python).

Surprised by the accessibility of using paper circuits, Kathryn reflected, "I love that these scaffolded resources exist allowing you to make sense of how circuits work by having a clear hands-on visual aid to help you explore and learn by DOING" (Week 9, see Figures 5 and 6).

Figure 5 (below). Paper circuit created with paper, copper tape, LED, CR2032 battery, and binder clip.

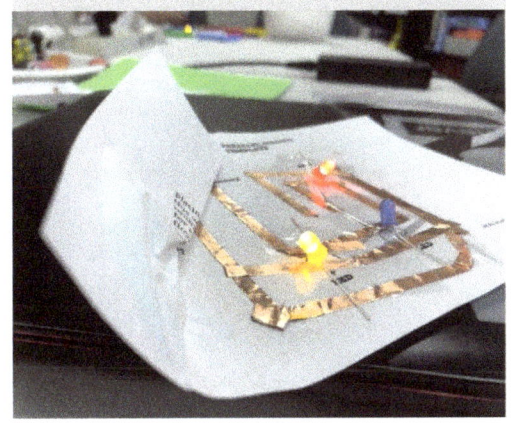

Figure 6 (left). Kathryn's greeting card designed with paper, marker, and paper circuit.

Melissa reflected on connections between design and her mathematical process while troubleshooting her sewable circuits:

> I was able to get the LEDs to light up before sewing the two fabric parts together, but for some reason I couldn't make the LEDs work after I sewed the two parts together. I thought I may have somehow interfered with the electrical path during sewing so I redrew my electrical path on paper, compared with the sewn circuit on my stuffed monster, and was able to identify and fix the error. It's a lot like the process I use to fix a mathematical error. (Week 11, see Figures 7 and 8)

Figure 7 (left). Soft circuit designed using felt, conductive thread, LED light, and CR2032 battery.

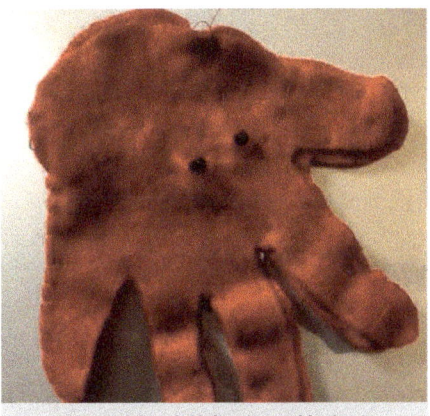

Figure 8 (above). Melissa's sewable circuit prototype and Soft Monster.

–143–

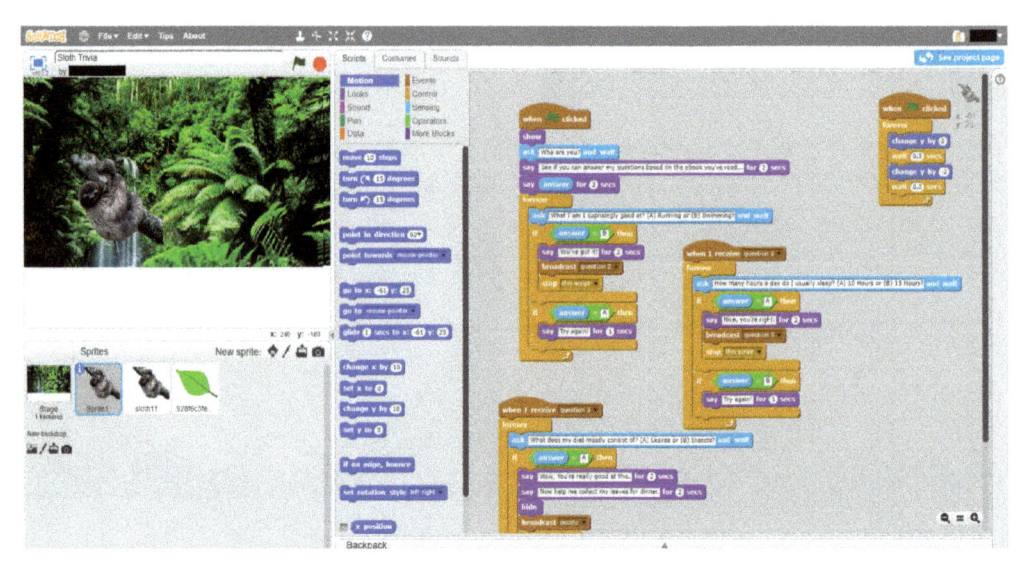

Figure 9. Diana's interactive game, designed in Scratch.

In addition to trying new materials and gaining confidence to complete an advanced project, Diana shared her new comfort with these techniques and ability to connect to her 5th-grade language arts classroom:

> Prior to this, I had zero experience using Scratch. After spending some time learning the basics, I saw that programming and expository writing were similar. I created a text-based game that asks multiple choice questions about a topic. I decided to make a prototype that I could bring into a nonfiction writing project my students will be working on in the future. (Week 13, see Figure 9)

Culminating Reflective Experience

Last, participants created a culminating autoethnographic reflective video project, allowing each participant to share their own creative evolution throughout the course. Participants presented their video at the final class meeting.

By the end of the semester, each participant highlighted different points of growth in their reflections. Kathryn pointed to an awareness of transdisciplinary learning, "I have had a parallel experience of coming to class to learn new skills and techniques, then bringing those skills to my students to connect art and engineering design in my math classroom" (Week 15, see Figure 10).

Donya acknowledged how the recurring reflection allowed her to examine her own thinking and application, "This has really soaked in and I noticed that with each project I thought more of how I was applying engineering and design processes" (Week 15). Diana expressed an awakened sense of connection to the design process despite the initial unfamiliarity of the course topics: "These were things I had never done before. However, I quickly realized that the engineering design process is something that I engage in all the time, when planning lessons or problem-solving" (Week 15). Highlighting the benefits of reflecting on her weekly design process, Melissa acknowledged, "If I hadn't reflected each week I might not have seen the connections or my own growth" (Week 15).

Changes in Engineering Design Self-Efficacy

Figure 10. Kathryn brought the paper circuit activity to her school makerspace for students to try.

Quantitative results are presented as group means, which is an average of the five participants' EDP reflection scores from three separate administrations. Increases were seen in participants' confidence in engaging in the engineering design process throughout the semester. The mean change from the first administration in September (4.07: fairly confident) and the third administration in November (4.41: completely confident) was 8.51%. There was a decrease between the second administration and third administration, particularly for Phases 3–5 (3: Plan, 4: Create, and 5: Improve). This could possibly be due to participants having more familiarity with 2D and 3D design techniques and less familiarity with electronics. Table 2 and Figure 11 display mean group scores and percentage changes to compare group confidence for each of the five phases of the engineering design process.

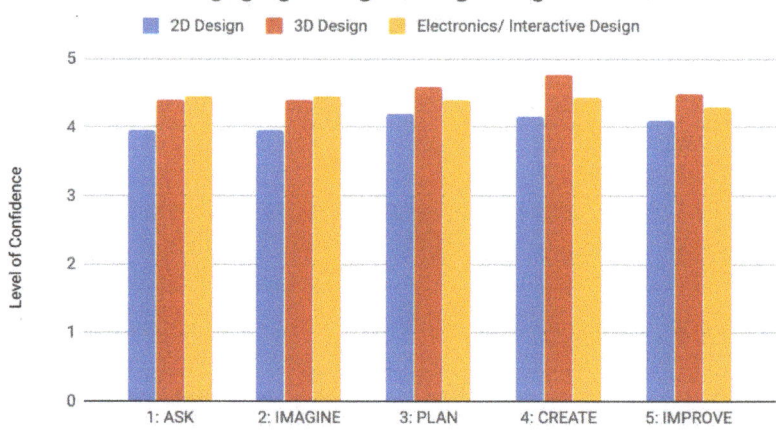

Table 2. Comparing Group Confidence in the Five Phases of Engineering Design Process

	2D design (September)	3D design (October)	Electronics/ interactive design (November)	% change between 2D and electronics
1: Ask	3.95	4.40	4.45	12.66%
2: Imagine	3.95	4.40	4.45	12.66%
3: Plan	4.20	4.60	4.40	5.06%
4: Create	4.16	4.76	4.44	7.09%
5: Improve	4.10	4.50	4.30	5.06%
Mean	4.07	4.53	4.41	8.51%

Figure 11. Comparing Group Confidence in the Five Phases of Engineering Design Process

(Note: Scale is 1–5, where 1 is not confident at all and 5 is completely confident.)

Participants experienced increases in their confidence to integrate engineering design process into the classroom. The mean change from the first administration in September (3.6 - somewhat confident) and the third administration in November (4.47 - completely confident) was 21.94%. Table 3 and Figure 12 compare mean group scores and percentage change for group confidence in integrating engineering design into the classroom.

Table 3. Comparing Group Confidence in Integrating Engineering Design in the Classroom

	2D design (September)	3D design (October)	Electronics/ interactive design (November)	% change between 2D and electronics
Design process connections	3.60	4.20	4.40	20.25%
Transdisciplinary process connections	3.60	4.20	4.40	20.25%
Classroom facilitation	3.60	4.40	4.60	25.32%
Mean	3.60	4.27	4.47	21.94%

Figure 12. Comparing Group Confidence in Integrating Engineering Design in the Classroom

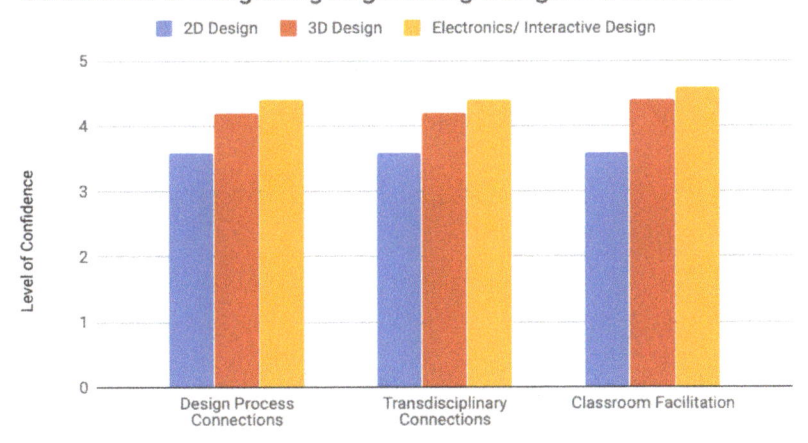

(Note: Scale is 1–5, where 1 is not confident at all and 5 is completely confident.)

Discussion

Quantitative data shows that semester-long engagement in the engineering design process increased participants' personal confidence and professional confidence in their ability to facilitate design in their own classrooms. Qualitative data illustrated this increased confidence through participants' gradual acknowledgment of how they enacted the engineering design process in a variety of ways. Likewise, the qualitative data illustrated how participants began to see connections between engineering, interdisciplinary skills, and the content areas they taught. This ability to recontextualize STEAM content and design processes afforded participants personal and professional confidence to integrate within their own classrooms.

Implications for Teacher Education

The scaffolded instructional approach used in this STEAM course positively impacted participants' confidence in the engineering design process by merging familiar explorations of materials and techniques with the unfamiliar. This has implications for preparing teachers in different disciplines, including art, generalists, and secondary STEM. Embedding time for recurring reflection encouraged teacher participants to engage in reflective practice that examines their personal and professional creativity in a variety of modes, including quantitative self-assessment for each unit project, weekly reflections with text and multimedia, and a culminating autoethnographic video.

Integration Ideas for K–12 Teachers

- Assist learners to see connections between STEAM content and processes by leading units with diverse representation of how artists, crafters, engineers, makers, scientists, and others apply interdisciplinary concepts while engaging in design. Point out specific applications of common concepts and techniques. Ask students to compare and contrast to examine deeper connections.

- Increase technical confidence by scaffolding nondigital and digital techniques to bridge familiarity and inspire possibilities. Encourage examination of the affordances of digital fabrication tools, including instrumentation, precision, scaling, iteration, and efficiency.

- Embed multimodal reflective assessments to encourage documentation of the learning process, engagement in intentional design, and self-examination of personal growth over time. Consider apps like Seesaw to document process or Flip to create video reflections and responses.

- Try activities that merge traditional craft and common materials with advanced STEAM concepts and digital design techniques:

    - **2D design:** Use Silhouette Studio software and Silhouette Cameo cutting machine to create paper craft inspired by historical *kirigami* techniques (i.e., *jianzhi, monkiri, wycinaki, schrenschnitte, papel picado*). Explore symbolism and positive and negative space while testing the structural integrity of paper, fabric, and other 2D media.

- **3D design:** Challenge students with novel engineering (https://www.novelengineering.org) where students use the engineering design process to design solutions that solve problems presented in books. Explore the integration of design thinking to empathize with characters' problems. Host gallery walks or "shark tank-esque" sessions to get feedback.
- **Electronics and interactive:** Integrate conductive paint and simple electronic components (LEDs, batteries, microcontrollers, sensors) to create interactive paintings that sense light, motion, and sound in the style of Jie Qi (artist and engineer; https://technolojie.com).

Limitations and Future Research

This study is limited by a small sample size but is strengthened by the longitudinal mixed-methods approach used to examine participant experiences over 15 weeks. Future research can examine how this type of longitudinal interdisciplinary design experience can be enacted by teachers in their own classrooms, as well as what impact it has on K–12 students' confidence in the engineering design process, awareness of the intersections of STEAM, and ability to learn STEAM content.

Conclusion

Maker-centered learning highlights the intersections of STEAM content and processes, which can empower teachers to negotiate the boundaries between exploratory "fun" activities and the practice of interdisciplinary skills. Embedded reflection can promote deep learning within maker-centered learning environments through intentional documentation of design process and connect active in-class participation with previous experiences.

Throughout the 15-week STEAM course, participants in this study were able to authentically reflect on how design processes cross boundaries of discipline and context. Whether as artists or makers who express themselves through creating artifacts, engineers who design solutions, mathematicians who design proofs, scientists who design experiments, or teachers who design instruction; everyone engages in design processes that apply creativity, critical thinking, and problem solving. Often thought to be unrelated, "the difference between science and the arts is not that they are different sides of the same coin or even different parts of the same continuum, but rather, they're manifestations of the same thing" (Jemison, 2002, 09:00).

Shaunna Smith has experience as a secondary art and digital media teacher, associate professor of educational technology (Texas State University) and STEM specialist at the STEM Pre-Academy (University of Hawaii System). She specializes in professional development for teachers on topics of art, engineering, and STEAM integration.

References

Bevan, B. (2017). The promise and the promises of making in science education. *Studies in Science Education, 53*(1), 75–103. https://doi.org/10.1080/03057267.2016.1275380

Blikstein, P., Martinez, S. L., & Pang, H. A. (Eds.). (2016). *Meaningful making, projects and inspirations for Fab Labs and makerspaces*. Constructing Modern Knowledge Press.

Bybee, R. W. (2014). NGSS and the next generation of science teachers. Journal of *Science Teacher Education, 25*(2), 211–221. https://doi.org/10.1007/s10972-014-9381-4

Carberry, A. R., Lee, H.-S., & Ohland, M. W. (2010). Measuring engineering design self-efficacy. *Journal of Engineering Education, 99*(1), 71–79. https://doi.org/10.1002/j.2168-9830.2010.tb01043.x

Clapp, E. P., Ross, J., Ryan, J. O., & Tishman, S. (2017). *Maker-centered learning: Empowering young people to shape their worlds*. Jossey-Bass.

Creswell, J. W., & Plano Clark, V. L. (2018). *Designing and conducting mixed methods research* (3rd ed.). SAGE.

Cunningham, C. M. (2018). *Engineering in elementary STEM education: Curriculum design, instruction, learning, and assessment*. Teachers College Press.

Cunningham, C. M., & Carlsen, W. S. (2014). Teaching engineering practices. *Journal of Science Teacher Education, 25*(2), 197–210. https://doi.org/10.1007/s10972-014-9380-5

Hynes, M. M., Mathis, C., Purzer, S., Rynearson, A., & Siverling, E. (2017, January). Systematic review of research in p-12 engineering education from 2000-2015. *International Journal of Engineering Education, 33*(1B).

Jemison, M. (2002, February). *Teach arts and sciences together*. TED2002. https://www.ted.com/talks/mae_jemison_teach_arts_and_sciences_together

Martin, L. (2015). The promise of the maker movement for education. *Journal of Pre-College Engineering Education Research, 5*(1), Article 4. https://doi.org/10.7771/2157-9288.1099

Martinez, S. L., & Stager, G. S. (2013). *Invent to learn: Making, tinkering, and engineering in the classroom*. Constructing Modern Knowledge Press.

Miles, M. B., Huberman, A. M., & Saldaña, J. (2014). *Qualitative data analysis: A methods sourcebook* (3rd ed.). SAGE.

Peppler, K., Halverson, E. B., Kafai, Y. B. (2016). *Makeology: Makerspaces as learning environments* (Vol. 1). Routledge. https://doi.org/10.4324/9781315726519

Petrich, M., Wilkinson, K., & Bevan, B. (2013). It looks like fun, but are they learning? In M. Honey & D. E. Kanter (Eds.), *Design, make, play: Growing the next generation of innovators* (pp. 50–70). Taylor & Francis. https://doi.org/10.4324/9780203108352-10

Rodriguez, S., Harron, J., Fletcher, S., & Spock, H. (2018). Elements of making: A framework to support making in the science classroom. *Science Teacher, 85*(2), 24–30. https://doi.org/10.2505/4/tst18_085_02_24

Schwartz, K. (2016, September 14). Don't leave learning up to chance: Framing and reflection. *Mind/Shift*. https://www.kqed.org/mindshift/46316/dont-leave-learning-up-to-chance-framing-and-reflection

Smith, S. (2018). Children's negotiations of visualization skills during a design-based learning experience with non-digital techniques and digital fabrication technologies. *Interdisciplinary Journal of Problem-Based Learning, 12*(2), Article 4. https://doi.org/10.7771/1541-5015.1747

Thomas, A., & Besser, D. (2017). The maker movement and engineering. *Bridge, 47*(3), 32–36.

Vossoughi, S., Hooper, P. K., & Escudé, M. (2016). Making through the lens of culture and power: Toward transformative visions for educational equity. *Harvard Educational Review, 86*(2), 206–232. https://doi.org/10.17763/0017-8055.86.2.206

Willard, T. (Ed.). (2014). *The NSTA quick-reference guide to the NGSS, elementary school*. NSTA Press.

How Might We Make This Work?
Using Design Thinking to Engineer Kinetic Sculptures in the Art Room

Kristin Vanderlip Taylor

> "This is impossible!" one student said in frustration. Tinkering with the project a bit, another suggested, "But wait, what if we glue it?" After the assemblage was complete, a third exclaimed, "Ok, I think it's working now—look at it move!

In 2016, the Innovation Collaborative (IC), which "provides information about how effective integration of the arts, sciences, humanities, engineering, math, and technology (STEAM) can reinforce innovative thinking" (n.d.-a, "Purpose" section), began a national research project examining K–12 effective practices in transdisciplinary learning. My colleague and I coauthored and submitted a STEAM project titled Art in Motion: Kinetic Sculptures, combining visual art, science, and engineering (IC, n.d.-b). Upon acceptance, we were invited to contribute to the study as Innovation Fellows; we tested various transdisciplinary lessons, documented data, and evaluated findings using rubrics designed to measure how the intersections of these disciplines promoted creative and innovative thinking. After teaching this kinetic sculpture lesson in our individual art classes, we presented our research and findings virtually to the IC Research Thought Leaders (nationally known multidisciplinary education researchers) and other Innovation Fellows at the first convening (IC, n.d.-b).

During this time, I taught art at a suburban public school in Los Angeles County to students in Grades K–8. My two middle school elective classes each contained nearly 40 students in Grades 6–8, with some in general art (Year 1 of middle school) and advanced art (Year 2). All students previously had art with me during their elementary school years unless they were new to the school. My curriculum was fairly open-ended while centered around big ideas, and I supported students' individual interests in researching and exploring a range of topics through art. Each year, I incorporated several collaborative projects to engage students with their classmates or younger students across campus, hoping to build community while strengthening communication and problem-solving skills. The STEAM lesson presented here provided opportunities for all these elements, as students worked collaboratively using the design thinking process to brainstorm, develop, test, document, and refine sculptures that could move in some way.

Social Constructivism and Design Thinking for Transdisciplinary Learning

Designed to facilitate social-constructivist learning, this kinetic sculpture lesson required students to communicate ideas and cooperatively solve problems. Vygotsky's (1978) theory of social constructivism asserts that learning is a social process, and knowledge is co-constructed as people interact with each other. Providing opportunities to actively learn together through investigations and experimentations (Goldman & Kabayadondo, 2017; Gross & Gross, 2016) encouraged students who might not otherwise work together to do so, building community in our classroom.

These activities included brainstorming discussions, sketching, manipulating various materials for prototyping, documenting, interviewing, reflecting, revising, and presenting together. Because my classes contained mixed grade and ability levels, students were assigned to specific tables for approximately 2 months, then rotated during the school year for variety. This allowed for peer mentoring between younger and older students, as well as support for those who needed additional guidance. This choice in grouping was based on Vygotsky's (1978) Zone of Proximal Development, in which students maximize their learning with support from adults or peers. It also served to eliminate the clustering of students by grade levels that often occurs when leaving seating arrangements open, compelling students to engage with a variety of classmates of different ages and abilities.

In developing the lesson, the design thinking process became a foundational component for how students would collaboratively create a three-dimensional movable work of art, one of the objectives of this learning experience. While there are many varied definitions of design thinking, Goldman and Kabayadondo (2016) summarize it succinctly by explaining that it "is a method of problem-solving that relies on a complex set of skills, processes, and mindsets that help people generate novel solutions to problems" (p. 3). Design thinking in the art room allows students to experiment with materials, ideas, and the possibility of failure, encouraging revisions to demonstrate new understandings from their practice (Gross & Gross, 2016), opportunities they may not have in other classes. Utilizing the design thinking process to create kinetic sculptures engages a hybridity of exploration without discipline boundaries—transdisciplinary learning (Graham, 2020; Knochel, 2018; Quigley & Herro, 2016)—with equal focus in visual arts, engineering, and science concepts to ensure the sculptures not only meet visual arts standards in craft and design but also effectively move based on engineering and the forces or energy enacted upon them.

Kinetic Sculpture Inspiration

To excite students about the assignment, I introduced kinetic sculptures designed by Theo Jansen, Alexander Calder, and Rube Goldberg. Engineered from plastic tubes and soda bottles, Jansen's *Strandbeests*, or "beach animals," are powered by the wind as it acts upon the different components (neural systems, legs, wings, and water feelers) to move the sculptures along the beach, at the same time keeping them from getting stuck in the ocean or trapped in the sand (Jansen, n.d.). While aesthetically beautiful in their own right, the math and engineering knowledge required to set these works in motion are clearly evident in the spacing and placement of each component. Calder's kinetic sculptures have been a long-standing example of movable art in my art curriculum, as he, too, worked primarily with air as the force for making his works kinetic (Calder Foundation, n.d.). Knowing access to mechanical devices may be limited in schools, the use of everyday inexpensive materials was important, and I wanted to show work from artists who did not rely on supplies that might be unattainable for my students.

Rube Goldberg's illustrated machines provided yet another source of inspiration, as they were humorously designed using the mechanics of simple machines and accessible materials to complete simple tasks through overly complex motions (Wolfe, 2000). Because Goldberg never actually built his machines, other examples constructed by artists inspired by his work were also shared, including the OK Go (2010) video for the song "This Too Shall Pass" and student-created machines for various Rube Goldberg contests. While viewing these kinetic works, I asked the following questions:

- How do you think the artist made the artwork?
- Where do you think they got the idea?
- What do you think the artist used?
- What is causing it to move?
- What question would you ask the maker?

Students responded first with ideas about the media used; explanations of how the works were made were based on close observations identifying objects seen in the still photographs or videos displayed. Students then shared guesses about how the works moved—via air, human interaction, or possibly hidden motors—describing, too, how the artists might have planned to create movement when designing the sculptures. When asked what might have inspired the artists, some students immediately said "animals!" and "dragons!" about the Strandbeests. One student said that Calder's sculptures reminded them of the toy hanging above their baby brother's bed, which I identified as a mobile, and I explained that Calder was known for making both *stabiles* (nonmoving sculptures) and *mobiles* (moving sculptures). The words "kinetic" and "force" were then introduced and explained to provide students with new foundational language for discussing these ideas.

Design Thinking in Action: Kinetic Sculpture Teamwork

While some brainstorming occurred immediately following the viewing of artworks, introducing the design thinking process was critical at this point to help students understand the iterative work they would be engaging in. Different than other projects in our art room, this collaborative learning experience would require specific steps, including

1. Asking questions: identifying possible solutions
2. Planning: brainstorming, documenting, and sketching
3. Building: constructing a prototype collaboratively
4. Testing: recording data regarding movement
5. Sharing results: discussing what works or doesn't with another team
6. Revising and refining: making adjustments, retesting, recording data, sharing results

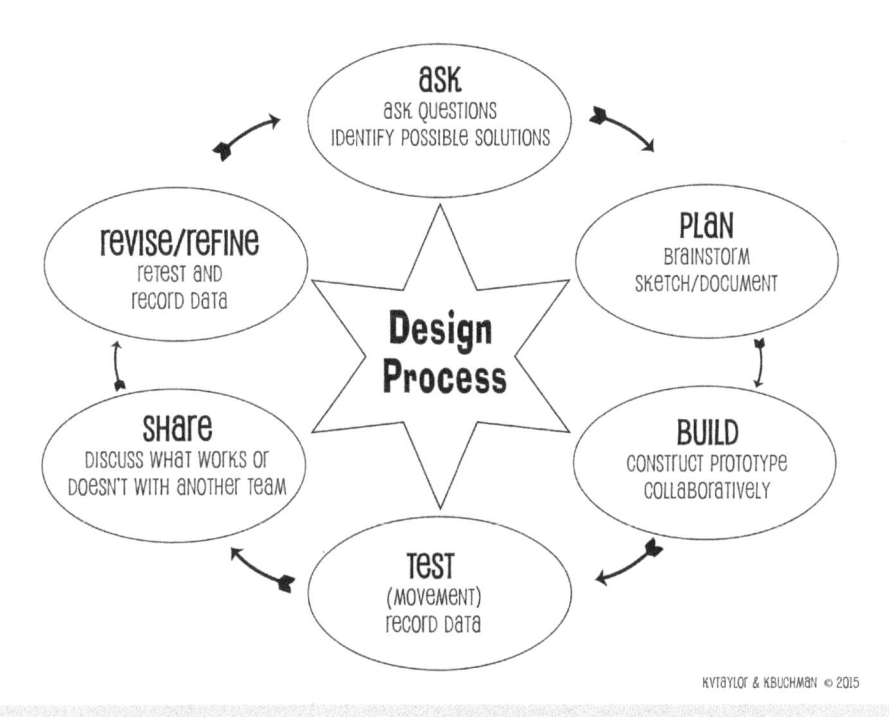

Figure 1. Design Thinking Process handout, 2015. Courtesy of the author and K. Buchman.

These steps were adapted from a range of design thinking sources to specifically fit the needs of this project. They were provided as a handout (see Figure 1) to be kept as a reminder of the various stages involved as students engineered their designs. Students were informed that they would create *process books* with their groups, documenting all evidence (sketches, notes, peer interviews, and data) to be turned in at the conclusion of the project. Filming was also an option, and students were shown how to upload videos to our class Dropbox.

Building from the Big Idea *Artists use the design process to create kinetic works of art*, the objectives were for students to:

- collaboratively utilize the design process: identify the problem, brainstorm possibilities, choose a direction, construct prototype, test and record data, revise and refine model.

- experiment with materials to collaboratively create a three-dimensional work of art that can move in some way (i.e., kinetic sculpture).
- present their findings to one other small group of peers, accepting input for revisions before refining the model.

Because this project integrated visual art, it was important for students to consider how their sculpture was designed, activating prior knowledge of art terms and 3D construction concepts. However, while we discussed ideas for what made something "aesthetically pleasing," specific criteria were not established as part of the final rubric, something identified as a potential deficit when evaluating student work, particularly for an art grade. My students, however, came to love describing how their work was aesthetically pleasing, using this term whenever possible. After sharing initial thoughts with peers, students made individual sketches and planning notes for possible sculptures (see Figures 2 and 3). I introduced lessons over several days on simple machines with activities for practice. I also consulted our middle school science teachers for additional materials and resources on engineering design, as well as forces and interactions, to ensure alignment with the Next Generation Science Standards (NGSS Lead States, 2013).

Students then regrouped with peers to name their teams and determine whether they would select one group member's sketch to construct or combine ideas to create a newly envisioned kinetic sculpture. This discussion required students to decide what kind of force they might use for movement, how that could be done, and what materials they might use,

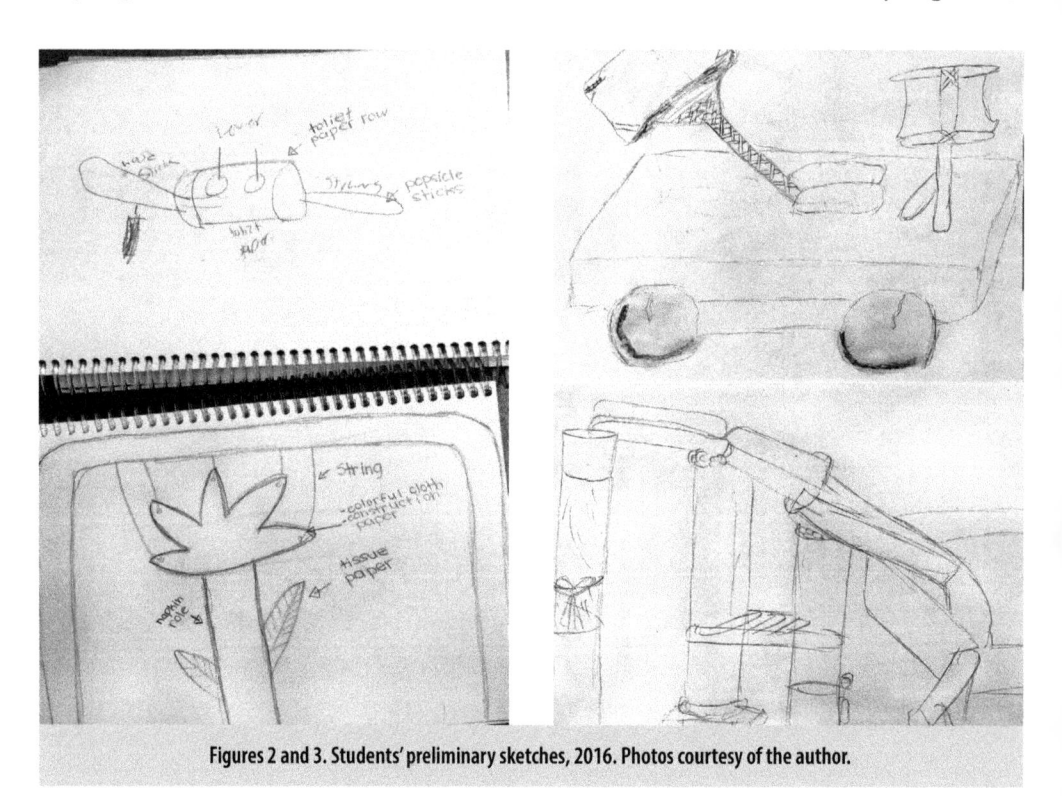

Figures 2 and 3. Students' preliminary sketches, 2016. Photos courtesy of the author.

STEAM Education: An Interdisciplinary Look at Art in the Curriculum

Figure 4. Prototype with wheels, 2016. Photo courtesy of the author.

from anything available in the art room to recycled materials or other objects from home. Each team also decided on roles for their members, some of which included illustrator, text documenter, photo or video documenter, materials manager, time keeper, and cleanup leader. Once prototyping began (see Figure 4), students were immersed in collaborative construction for nearly 3 weeks, as the need for modifications in plans arose even prior to testing for movement.

Data were documented using an "in progress data" handout (see Figures 5 and 6).

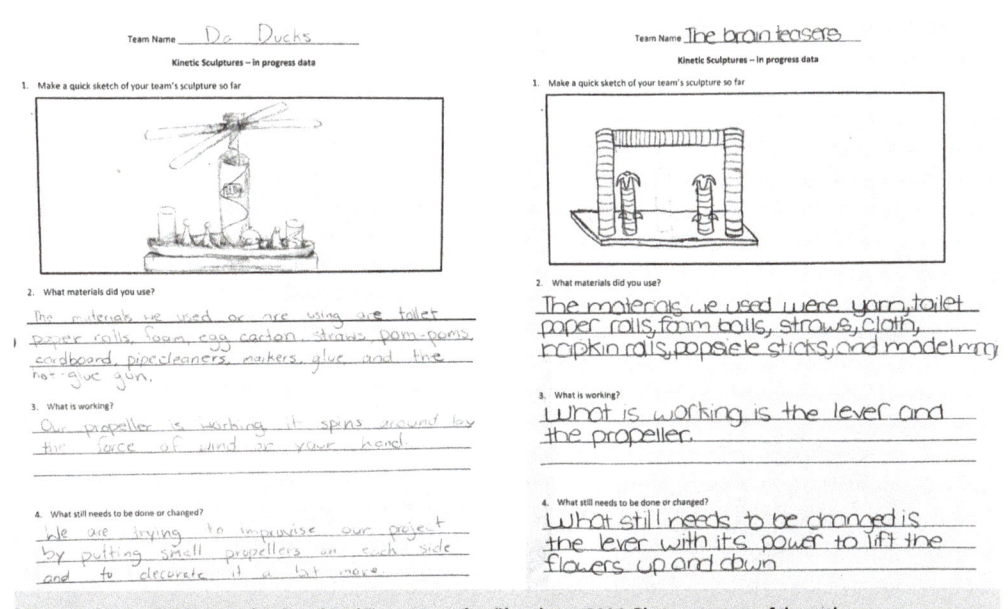

Figures 5 and 6. Completed "in progress data" handouts, 2016. Photos courtesy of the author.

Figure 7. Prototype with lights added, 2016. Photo courtesy of the author.

Some groups struggled through multiple failed attempts; designs were revised, new materials used, and two groups decided to add electrical components to their sculptures (a motor and lights; see Figure 7).

When the initial builds were complete, students tested the sculptures for motion, documenting evidence through notes, photos, videos, and group discussions. Then, each student was required to interview someone from another group, asking about their prototyping and testing processes to discuss what worked and what didn't (see Figures 8 and 9).

This step was intended to provide multiple perspectives about possible revisions from someone outside the immediate group, while helping students learn how to talk about their work analytically with peers. After completing this task, students once again regrouped to determine necessary changes for their team's sculpture, followed by refining, retesting, and reflecting on the revisions to complete their process books (see Figure 10). At the conclusion, groups presented their work and shared personal takeaways from the experience through written reflections.

Figures 8 and 9. Completed peer interviews, 2016. Photos courtesy of the author.

Figure 10. One group's finished kinetic sculpture and process book, 2016. Photo courtesy of the author.

Synthesis of STEAM Learning

Overall, this lesson provided students with multiple positive outcomes. The transdisciplinary nature of the assignment enabled students to synthesize disparate ideas about science, engineering, and art while creating their sculptures, prompting them to think like artists, engineers, and scientists all at the same time. Even though I regularly encourage students to reflect on and revise their work, the latter is often unrealized, as many are simply ready to move on. This learning experience shifted that outcome, as the design thinking process required students to make revisions as needed to ensure effectiveness.

Listening and responding to different peers' perspectives also encouraged empathy, as many students interviewed or worked with unfamiliar peers. I noticed unlikely partnerships between 6th- and 8th-grade students during peer interviews, and I saw students attentively listening to each other while documenting feedback. This component seemed to deepen students' understandings of the applied concepts through the sharing of experiences, as it provided new insights from nongroup members. Additionally, the ability to document the learning through traditional and digital methods allowed students to work in formats they were comfortable with and had access to. All groups had at least one member digitally recording the process and outcomes using the technology of their phones, either through photos or videos, which allowed other group members to participate in different ways (constructing, testing, or notating data). This provided relief for students who did not have their own digital devices or did not know how to upload files to Dropbox. Feedback from students about the assignment was positive; there were only a couple situations during the process when I was asked to intervene to ensure group members were all equally contributing. All students responded in written reflections that they enjoyed working collaboratively on this project.

Effective Strategies and Unexpected Discoveries

From personal experience, I've observed that collaborative learning is not always welcomed by all students in the art room, as art can be a very individualized process. It can be difficult for some to be open to others' perspectives and to relinquish ownership of ideas. However, using design thinking as a framework to guide students through this collaborative learning experience seemed to alleviate these obstacles, as all group members focused on specific tasks while they worked through the stages of the assignment. By grouping students as I had, the range of skills and knowledge varied among teams, encouraging students with relevant science and engineering knowledge to mentor those who had not yet learned the information. Similarly, those with advanced art experience were able to provide support for teammates who were not as familiar with applying knowledge of design principles in creating sculptural work. These strategies can be effective across all subjects, particularly for teachers who wish to shift to a more transdisciplinary approach to teaching.

This lesson employed language from the National Core Art Standards (NCCAS, 2015) that aligned with science and engineering vocabulary, such as *new ideas, materials,* or *methods; experimenting; innovating;* and *taking risks.* Terms including *design, craft,* and *aesthetics*

Assessment Rubric

	5	4	3	2	1
Brain-storming and Planning	Group generates and documents more than 3 ideas/sketches/concepts for their model.	Group generates and documents 3 ideas/sketches/concepts for their model.	Group generates and documents 2 ideas/sketches/concepts for their model.	Group generates and documents 1 idea/sketch/concept for their model.	Group does not generate or document any ideas/sketches/concepts.
Prototype/Model And Testing/Plan for Redesign	Group builds a working model that can be tested for movement using appropriate tools, materials and resources. Group clearly documents what works or doesn't (*data) and proposes many options for improvement.	Group builds a working model that can be tested for movement using appropriate tools, materials and resources. Group documents what works or doesn't (*data) and proposes more than one option for improvement.	Group builds a working model that can be tested for movement using appropriate tools, materials and resources. Group provides little documentation of what works or doesn't (*data) and proposes an option for improvement.	Group builds a model but it can't be tested for movement. Group provides no documentation of what works or doesn't (*data).	Working model is not built.
Redesign	Group uses data to redesign the working model into a more effective kinetic sculpture. Group clearly and completely documents the results of the redesign.	Group uses data to redesign the working model. Group documents the results of the redesign.	Group uses some of the data and/or minimally redesigns the working model. Group documents some of the results of the redesign.	Group does not use their data to redesign the working model. Group minimally documents the results of the redesign.	No redesign is attempted.
Group Process Book	Process book includes: brainstorming and planning documentation, prototype model testing documentation, plan for redesign, documentation of redesign, and reflective peer interviews for all group members.	Process book includes most of the components required.	Process book includes some of the components required.	Process book includes few of the components required.	Process book is not turned in.

* Examples of data to be evaluated or revised: sturdiness, successful movement based on initial plan, material selection, sizes, shapes, type of force used (can it work with a different force)

Figure 11. Assessment rubric, 2016. Courtesy of the author and K. Buchman.

had not been specified as criteria for grading, as previously noted. The rubric (see Figure 11) focused more on the stages of design thinking, ensuring that students met each step with documentation to demonstrate their learning. As a class, we discovered this missing component through dialogue about each artwork, as students first discussed how each sculpture looked, rather than the effectiveness of engineering and movement. Because students themselves placed equal value on the artistic portion of the assignment, many expressed desire to be graded on it, proportionate to the emphasis on the design process and scientific learning. Their acknowledgment that all subjects explored in this STEAM lesson deserved parallel emphasis (Graham, 2020; Knochel, 2018) demonstrates their understanding of transdisciplinary learning in a way I did not expect.

Reflective Takeaways

Sharing these findings with the IC Research Thought Leaders and other Innovation Fellows deepened my own reflection about my students' collaborative processes and my understanding of what effective transdisciplinary learning looks like. I discovered new ways that I, too, benefit from collaboration, especially in planning learning experiences such as this. Working with my colleague to develop, test, reflect on, and revise our lesson paralleled the work my students did as they employed design thinking, yet I hadn't viewed it in this way until presenting the results. Removing the divisions between isolated subjects allows for students—and teachers—to envision learning that mirrors the reality of our world (Gross & Gross, 2016), and as art educators, we have the flexibility to bridge these boundaries, making cross-disciplinary connections in our curriculum.

Acknowledgments

I would like to thank my colleague, Kerry Buchman, for her collaboration in writing, testing, documenting, and revising this lesson for our students and for use within the Innovation Collaborative's research study, to contribute to their work in "fostering creativity [and] innovation… in teaching and learning" (IC, n.d.-a, "Our Mission" section). I would also like to thank the IC Research Thought Leaders and Innovation Fellows for their feedback and support as we continue navigate this important work together.

Kristin Vanderlip Taylor is an associate professor of art education at California State University, Northridge and is National Board certified in Early/Middle Childhood Art.

References

Calder Foundation. (n.d.). *Introduction*. Retrieved June 13, 2020, from http://www.calder.org/introduction

Goldman, S., & Kabayadondo, Z. (2017). Taking design thinking to school: How the technology of design can transform teachers, learners, and classrooms. In S. Goldman & Z. Kabayadondo (Eds.), *Taking design thinking to school: How the technology of design can transform teachers, learners, and classrooms* (pp. 3–19). Routledge. https://doi.org/10.4324/9781317327585

Graham, M. A. (2020). Deconstructing the bright future of STEAM and design thinking. *Art Education*, *73*(3), 6–12. https://doi.org/10.1080/00043125.2020.1717820

Gross, K., & Gross, S. (2016). Transformation: Constructivism, design thinking, and elementary STEAM. *Art Education*, *69*(6), 36–43. https://doi.org/10.1080/00043125.2016.1224869

Innovation Collaborative. (n.d.-a). *Mission and goals*. https://www.innovationcollaborative.org/mission-and-goals.html

Innovation Collaborative. (n.d.-b). *Research thought leaders convening*. https://www.innovationcollaborative.org/convene.html

Jansen, T. (n.d.). *Explains*. Retrieved June 13, 2020, from https://www.strandbeest.com/explains

Knochel, A. D. (2018). An object-oriented curriculum theory for STEAM: Boundary shifters, materiality and per(form)ing 3D thinking. *International Journal of Education Through Art*, *14*(1), 35–48. https://doi.org/10.1386/eta.14.1.35_1

National Coalition for Core Arts Standards. (2015). *National core art standards: A conceptual framework for arts learning*. Rights administered by State Education Agency Directors of Arts Education. http://www.nationalartsstandards.org/content/national-core-arts-standards

NGSS Lead States. (2013). *Next Generation Science Standards: For states, by states* (Vol 1–2). National Academies Press.

OK Go. (2010, March 2). *OK Go—This too shall pass—Rube Goldberg machine—Official video* [Video]. YouTube. https://www.youtube.com/watch?v=qybUFnY7Y8w&feature=emb_title

Quigley, C. F., & Herro, D. (2016). "Finding the joy in the unknown": Implementation of STEAM teaching practices in middle school science and math classrooms. *Journal of Science Education and Technology*, *25*(3), 410–426. https://doi.org/10.1007/s10956-016-9602-z

Vygotsky, L. S. (1978). *Mind in society: The development of higher psychological processes* (M. Cole, V. John-Steiner, S. Scribner, & E. Souberman, Eds.). Harvard University Press. https://doi.org/10.2307/j.ctvjf9vz4

Wolfe, M. F. (2000). *Rube Goldberg: Inventions!* Simon & Schuster.

SECTION V
Art (Performing Arts)

Since the majority of the chapters in this book focus on STEAM and visual arts education, this section features the performing arts. The pandemic hit the arts hard, but the chapter titled "COVID-19 Leads to Powerful STEAM Lessons in Music" discusses how children in a virtual classroom created instruments resembling guitars or cellos. "When the 'A' Stands for Dance: Transdisciplinary STEAM Education That Dances to Connect Disciplines" makes connections through a case study on preservice educators and specifically discusses how STEAM is consistently interdisciplinary. The last chapter in this section, "'But What About the Eyeballs?': Devised Theatre as Interdisciplinary Knowledge-Generation Tool" is about theatre and how the production of a play can be a springboard for students to become engaged in science and technology.

COVID-19 Leads to Powerful STEAM Lessons in Music

Rodney Harshbarger

Skylines and STEAM

One game I like to play with my wife is "What city is it, quick, quick, quick?" Often, in a movie, sitcom, or even a sporting event, the broadcast starts with an aerial view of the city before it zooms in or switches cameras to a specific building or individual. There is something aesthetically pleasing about skylines and aerial views of a city. It is the art! What makes San Francisco enjoyable to look at or unique? It is the Transamerica Pyramid, the Golden Gate Bridge, and Lombard Street with its eight hairpin turns. Every time I see a photo or watch a movie set in San Francisco, my heart makes a connection with the first time I sailed under the Golden Gate Bridge on the *USS Halsey*. I was a young man who had just enlisted in the U.S. Navy, fresh out of high school, and I had never seen such a big city—much less been to a location where a lot of movies were filmed. There was a connection. San Francisco is not alone; other cities have visual imagery iconic to each of them that can spark a connection. For Seattle, it is the Space Needle. For Toronto, it is the CN Tower. Could you imagine any pleasure in this game if every major city was built from a cookie-cutter spec-sheet? It is the artistic design that makes it so satisfying and the connections so explicit.

Now, envision this game in a musical format. Could you picture children learning the ABC's without using the ABC song? It is the redundancy of the chord changes and rhythms that make using music so easy to learn the alphabet in this fashion. How about a graduation without "Pomp and Circumstance"? People experience a sentimental connection when they hear this song that brings them back to a milestone life experience. Educators need to embrace teaching science, technology, engineering, the arts, and math (STEAM) in a curriculum successfully (Hwang & Taylor, 2016). Integrating the "A" into STEM is as essential as incorporating STEM in the performing arts. The following discussion tells a story, but also gives attention to how to implement and teach a STEAM music lesson.

Literature Review: Picking Up STEAM

Since the turn of the century, there have been numerous studies and articles written on STEM education. STEM involves thinking across curricula collectively, instead of studying subjects in an isolated fashion (Jolly, 2014; Morrison & Bartlett, 2009). Even when the term was new, some scholars recognized that STEM was larger than just the disciplines recognized by each letter. One definition describes STEM as teaching or learning that involves one or more of the STEM subject areas, or incorporating an outside discipline with a STEM subject area (Sanders, 2009). Certainly, literature pertaining to moving from STEM to STEAM has gained momentum in the past few years. This need for including the arts into STEM education is not exclusive to the United States; Middle Eastern countries have started to include arts education in STEM in an effort to reduce the gap in knowledge between recent graduates and the skills needed for 21st-century jobs (El-Deghaidy, 2017). Recent studies have started addressing the importance—and flat-out need—to include the arts along with the other disciplines, creating the acronym STEAM. Combining the elements of art into the STEM disciplines strengthens STEM education (Mahmud et al., 2018). Integrating the arts into a child's education creates a scholar closer to meeting the demands of the 21st-century workforce (Lachman, 2018). With the acceptance of the arts, adding the "A" to the acronym STE(A)M opens more opportunities for more students to take part in closing the workforce gap (Land, 2013). The ties between STEAM and 21st-century skills needed to thrive in today's workforce—the four Cs (communication, collaboration, critical thinking, and creativity)—are not missing, but they are not abundant (Harshbarger & Harshbarger, 2016). In the near future, scholars will research and report the parallel benefits of both STEAM and the four Cs (Liao et al., 2016). For example, from a music standpoint, music, STEM, and 21st-century skills have an interdisciplinary relationship. Performing music involves using creativity, innovation, critical thinking, problem solving, math, science, technology, communication, and collaboration, as well as flexibility and adaptability (Platz, 2007). Whether a student is practicing their individual part in a practice room, practicing with their instruments or instrument family, or playing with the entire band, the end product will involve numerous disciplines. For the purpose of this elementary lesson, "Building a String Instrument," students used science, technology, engineering, art, and math to fulfill the requirements.

COVID-19 Leads to Powerful STEAM Lesson

In March 2020 a global pandemic, COVID-19, swept through the United States. As Central Florida teachers were preparing to leave for spring break, my elementary principal called an emergency faculty meeting, giving explicit directions on how we were going to move forward academically in a virtual setting because of the virus. Our special-area rotation schedule was to remain as planned. This meant each special-area teacher saw one class from every grade level for a 2-week time frame. Before going our separate ways, the 3rd-grade lead teacher told me they had just started studying sound in their science classes. Instead of the students having a separate link for music instruction as planned, I asked the 3rd-grade teachers if they would be open to combining music and science to expand their "Science and Sound" unit. They welcomed the idea. I had done similar units with other teachers, but I had never attempted this with students as young as 3rd grade or worked with this group of colleagues in a STEAM lesson or other project-based learning lesson.

Our spring break was extended by a week to address the logistical nightmare of a rapid shift from face-to-face to virtual instruction. Our technology department collected information on students' access to digital devices, such as a computer or tablet, and internet access. They then dispersed the necessary technology and made sure everything was functional. Prior to school starting after the break, the 3rd-grade teachers informed their students that they would be meeting for a 1-hour videoconference every Monday, Wednesday, and Friday morning, and they emailed the students a link to access the sessions.

Beginning the Lesson

The following Monday, we were up and running. I attended Ms. B's first virtual conference, and we explained that we would be combining science and music in a project-based lesson. We told the students they would be given a choice between building a musical instrument that resembled an acoustic guitar or one that resembled a cello. They would use their instrument to perform pizzicato, a playing technique in which performers pluck the strings instead of playing them with a bow. Under normal conditions, students could choose to work in small groups, but the restrictions of a statewide quarantine prevented this. We did not issue many parameters to the construction of their instruments, other than requiring at least three "strings" and for students to be able to play either "Hot Cross Buns" or the first two lines of "Twinkle, Twinkle Little Star" as the culminating activity.

I reviewed the characteristics of the four families of musical instruments, which are strings, woodwinds, brass, and percussion. Then I briefly performed, plucking each string of both an acoustic guitar and a cello one at a time and talked about how the pitches were different but mathematically related. The longer the string, the lower the frequency. The shorter the string, the higher the frequency. And a string divided in half plays the same note exactly one octave higher. I discussed the terms "sound," "sound waves," "pitch," "vibration," and "tone." Then Ms. B discussed other science terms we would be studying in the unit: "energy," "medium," "frequency," and "wavelength." We closed the science segment of the first virtual meeting by inviting questions. Students asked what materials were allowed and if siblings or parents could help. Similar to a science project, we encourage family participation and tell the students as long as they (the student) could play the instrument and explain their musical creation it was fine. We asked each student to think about which musical instrument they would like to build and email both teachers with their preference. Students could also state that they did not have a preference, allowing us a little flexibility to ensure at least a few of each instrument would be built.

During the second virtual meeting, students were offered the opportunity to ask questions about how musical instruments produce sound. I had taken a number of instruments from each instrument family home in preparation for my virtual music instruction. We discussed how frequency and pitch are the same concept, but they are referred to by different names in different disciplines. Without the quarantine, students would have been able to interact with actual instruments to find answers to their questions. In the spirit of honesty and full disclosure, it would have been a more authentic and hands-on learning experience in person; think of the difference between dissecting a frog and watching a video of someone else dissecting a frog. I concluded by asking them to think about and begin collecting anything they might use in the construction of their instrument.

The Progress

For our third videoconference, I asked volunteers to share their progress. Most students displayed parts and pieces of household items they were planning on using to construct their instrument. Ms. B encouraged the students to start assembling their musical instruments if they had not started already and reminded them that weekends were a good time to recruit help from adults that worked during the week. Finishing the construction of the instrument over the weekend, or at least coming close, would give students the needed time to practice for their upcoming performance. I reminded them of the definite learning curve for playing an instrument, and that it would require a bit of time and determination to master the assigned tasks—an important lesson for students who are looking for instant gratification. About half of the class laughed and raised their hands as we discussed this.

At the fourth meeting, I gave the instructions for the week, including exactly what artifacts would be due that Friday. Artifacts included students recording themselves explaining the materials they used in their musical creation, and whether the instrument was intended to be more closely related to a guitar or a cello. Students also needed to state any modifications made to the instrument, if any, and why they were necessary. Further, students were to explain how their instrument played different pitches, using both scientific and musical vocabulary. Finally, each student was to attempt to play either "Hot Cross Buns" or the beginning of "Twinkle, Twinkle Little Star" and email the video to both the homeroom teacher and myself. After giving the instructions for the week, I asked volunteers to share any progress they made or points of frustration.

Sharing both proved to be effective in promoting collaboration and critical thinking, skills essential in a project-based STEAM assignment and 21st-century workforce skills (Harshbarger & Harshbarger, 2016; Larmer & Mergendoller, 2010). After each student shared, we invited other students to interact, offering a compliment, a question about construction, or a suggestion to help a student overcome frustration. What was initially planned as a short activity turned into a marathon of rich, meaningful conversation. Ms. B and I let it continue for about 45 minutes because there was such a high level of engagement. I closed my portion of the day's lesson by letting the students know I was going to break them into four groups and would meet with each group virtually on Wednesday. I also told them to stay near their phones Tuesday morning, because I wanted to touch base with everyone to see if they needed to discuss any particular items without the rest of the class in the session.

On Monday afternoon, the homeroom teacher and I talked on the phone to create the groups. I shared with her what I thought made sense musically, and she shared with me who did and did not play nice together. The next day I contacted every student to inform them about the virtual meeting the following day. Ms. B and I spent Wednesday's virtual conferences fielding a few questions, but most of each miniconference was spent listening to excited students showing off their instruments and discussing what they used, and how they constructed their musical instruments.

The second Friday, the last day of our music rotation, students were invited to share with the entire class if they were comfortable with it. The students were so excited to show off their musical instruments that the science portion of the videoconference lasted almost the entire hour! Students laughed, smiled, (mostly) played well, and almost everyone complimented each other by visually clapping, giving a thumbs-up, or commenting in the chat portion of the video platform supporting each other in one way or another (See Figures 1–3).

Figure 1. Maddox with his cello.

Figure 2. Jenny's guitar.

Figure 3. Mia's tools.

Full STEAM Ahead

The students had a great time with this lesson! One thing I found interesting is that when I have teamed up with a teacher in the past to organize a similar lesson, we always gave some sort of formative and summative assessment. No matter how much we tried to put the students' minds at ease, there were a lot of questions surrounding the grading process. Conversely, this time around, with the hand we were dealt with COVID-19, students were getting credit for just being present in the video chats and constructing a musical instrument. This really seemed to act as a stress reducer. However, without the students' knowledge, or even addressing anything near the word "assessment" or "test," Ms. B and I checked for content mastery during our phone calls and breakout video sessions. With some poking and prodding, every student used both science and music vocabulary terms discussed throughout the lesson when talking about their instruments, and they used the terms in such a way that showed mastery of the content. The students reported that they really enjoyed the project, and they appreciated the autonomy of getting to create their own instrument. It was a welcome shift from a teacher-controlled to a student-controlled lesson (Marzano et al., 2001). Scientific terms and concepts were used numerous times throughout this lesson.

Technology for this STEAM lesson came in the form of students needing to repurpose common household items to create their musical instruments. The engineering component seemed to be the students' favorite part, and the part they will remember the most, based on our videoconferences. Many measurements and calculations took place to create their musical instruments. One student, Kyle, reported that his wood glue did not hold during the first strum of checking the instrument's playing ability. Kyle reported that his dad, sensing his disappointment, decided it was the right time to teach him how to use a drill. Kyle spoke in detail about how he got to put his hand on the drill with his dad's hand on top of his, and how his dad made him wear safety glasses in case of any flying debris. You could tell that Kyle was totally engaged in this project and it made a meaningful connection to his father's work in the real world.

Overall, there was a high level of engagement. There were a few gaps in participation across the grade level, but this was not exclusive to the music and science portions of online learning. Some students submitted few or none of their virtual assignments. Additionally, one student had a family member who was affected by the COVID-19 virus and immediately stopped attending school.

I'd Like to Buy an "A," Please

STEAM opportunities present themselves in various lessons, and teachers should take advantage of the connections between subject areas, and to the real world. STEAM should be thought of and taught as one cohesive entity, and not constantly taught in five different silos (Piro, 2010). Many times, students' eyes have lit up when I started teaching different time signatures in music; students immediately raise their hands to compare time signatures to fractions that they have studied. It is too good of an opening to not spend a moment interjecting a quick STEAM correlation to what we are studying.

There is not one musical, on or off Broadway, or one CD produced, that does not use science, technology, engineering, and math to put a successful product together. It does not matter how functional a kitchen cabinet is (using the greatest that science and technology has to offer, coupled with the best engineering and mathematical formulas), it is not going to make it through my front door if my wife does not find it aesthetically pleasing! Just like the CN Tower and the skylines, aesthetics are important to not only our senses, but also our success in the future.

Rodney Harshbarger was born and raised in Dayton, Ohio. After spending 4 years in the Navy, he attended the University of Louisiana at Lafayette, where he majored in music education. He holds a master's degree from the University of Florida and an EdD from the University of Central Florida. Harshbarger is National Board Certified and a former Indian Trails Teacher of the Year, as well as a former Flagler County Teacher of the Year. He was named a quarterfinalist for the Grammy Educator Award multiple times, and he has presented workshops involving STEAM all over the United States at both music and science conferences.

References

El-Deghaidy, H. (2017). STEAM methods: A case from Egypt. In A. J. Sickel & S. B. Witzig (Eds.), *Designing and teaching the secondary science methods course: An international perspective* (pp. 71–87). Sense. https://doi.org/10.1007/978-94-6300-881-5_5

Harshbarger, D., & Harshbarger, R. (2016). *Learning in the 21st century: A study addressing educational trends and implications* [Doctoral thesis, University of Central Florida]. University of Central Florida STARS. https://stars.library.ucf.edu/cgi/viewcontent.cgi?article=6042&context=etd

Hwang, J., & Taylor, J. C. (2016). Stemming on STEM: A STEM education framework for students with disabilities. *Journal of Science Education for Students With Disabilities, 19*(1), Article 4. https://doi.org/10.14448/jsesd.06.00017

Jolly, A. (2014, November 18). STEM vs. STEAM: Do the arts belong? *Education Week.* https://www.edweek.org/teaching-learning/opinion-stem-vs-steam-do-the-arts-belong/2014/11

Lachman, R. (2018, January 17). *STEAM not STEM: Why scientists need arts training.* The Conversation. https://theconversation.com/steam-not-stem-why-scientists-need-arts-training-89788

Land, M. H. (2013). Full STEAM ahead: The benefits of integrating the arts into STEM. *Procedia Computer Science, 20,* 547–552. https://doi.org/10.1016/j.procs.2013.09.317

Larmer, J., & Mergendoller, J. R. (2010). Seven essentials for project-based learning. *Educational Leadership, 68*(1), 34–37. https://www.ascd.org/el/articles/seven-essentials-for-project-based-learning

Liao, C., Motter, J. L., & Patton, R. M. (2016). Tech-savvy girls: Learning 21st-century skills through STEAM digital artmaking. *Art Education, 69*(4), 29–35. https://doi.org/10.1080/00043125.2016.1176492

Mahmud, S. N. D., Nasri, N. M., Samsudin, M. A., & Halim, L. (2018). Science teacher education in Malaysia: Challenges and way forward. *Asia-Pacific Science Education, 4*(1), Article 8. https://doi.org/10.1186/s41029-018-0026-3

Marzano, R. J., Pickering, D., & Pollock, J. E. (2001). *Classroom instruction that works: Research-based strategies for increasing student achievement.* ASCD.

Morrison, J., & Bartlett, R. V. (2009). STEM as curriculum. *Education Week.* https://www.edweek.org/teaching-learning/opinion-stem-as-a-curriculum/2009/03

Piro, J. M. (2010, March 9). Going from STEM to STEAM. *Education Week.* https://www.edweek.org/teaching-learning/opinion-going-from-stem-to-steam/2010/03

Platz, J. (2007, October). *How do you turn STEM into STEAM? Add the arts!* Ohio Alliance for Arts Education. https://oaae.net/2007/10/01/how-do-you-turn-stem-into-steam-add-the-arts

Sanders, M. (2009, December/January). STEM, STEM education, STEMmania. *Technology Teacher.* https://vtechworks.lib.vt.edu/bitstream/handle/10919/51616/STEMmania.pdf?sequence=1&isAllowed=y

When the "A" Stands for Dance:
Transdisciplinary STEAM Education That Dances to Connect Disciplines

Alison E. Leonard

As I walked around the room, I could see the students working in pairs, actively engaged in both programming a dance for their virtual characters and creating accompanying choreography for themselves. Many were hunched over their laptops, with one student controlling the mouse and their partner pointing and gesturing to the action on the screen. Others were split with one student at the laptop and the other standing, rehearsing their dancing. Several pairs could be seen rehearsing their dances together, occasionally pausing to restart their virtual character's dance on their laptops so they could sync their virtual–physical performances. No matter where the students were in the process of this project, nor how they were negotiating their partnership and charge of creating a virtual–physical dance, it was clear that these students were engaging in the work of programmers, of engineers, of artists, of choreographers: drafting, iterating, rehearsing. Their engagement was transdisciplinary, connecting all disciplinary content, literacies, and habits of mind involved. In other words, their project required and relied on both the dancing and the programming; without one, the project would fall apart. Unlike most science, technology, engineering, the arts, and math (STEAM) projects I had seen or been involved with before, where the visual arts or design played the central role, here, the "A" stood for dance—and not just dance as a means to represent knowledge as the final showcase of a project. Here, the dancing was the process; it was both the inquiry and the performance.

Dance in STEAM Education

Dance as the "A" in STEAM education remains rather underutilized, and similar to what you might find when searching for dance in schools, examples of STEAM education using dance is not the norm. In practice, often STEM becomes STEAM by "adding on the arts" as a means of representing knowledge in presentation and performance, versus as a form of inquiry as well. However, evidence of shifting perspectives about dance in education and related to STEAM can be seen with recent collaborative projects connecting scientists and dancers, including the Dance Your PhD contest (American Association for the Advancement of Science & *Science Magazine*, n.d.; Stolberg, 2006). Sousa & Pilecki's 2013 book, *From STEM to STEAM*, provides two dance examples: one at the elementary level, exploring the solar system, and the other at the secondary level, studying DNA.

Available resources and research also include the work of Schaffer and Stern (http://www.mathdance.org) and Schaffer et al. (2001), who have long written, presented, and performed about the connections between dance and mathematics in performance and education. Another teaching artist, Rosenfeld (2016), writes and teaches about math inquiry through percussive dance, which is a rhythmic, musical dance form that utilizes precise foot patterns. Education research provides several examples in STEAM education in which dance is utilized to explore numerous concepts, including chemistry (Tay & Edwards, 2015), geometry (Leonard & Bannister, 2018; Moore & Linder, 2012), the transformation of energy (Simpson Steele et al., 2016), the life cycle of a butterfly (Stapp et al., 2018), the human life cycle (Silveira et al., 2014), and robotics (Sullivan & Bers, 2018). As more resources for integrating dance into other subject areas in preK–12 classrooms increase (Kaufman & Dehline, 2014; Sousa & Pilecki, 2013), there continues to be immense potential and opportunities for dance to play a role in STEAM education.

Dance and Technology Through Virtual Environment Interactions

I recently had the opportunity to work on a collaborative project involving dance, virtual reality, computer science, and digital production arts. Our team of researchers and graduate students pioneered the design and development of a virtual environment aimed at teaching computational thinking through dance. Through our program Virtual Environment Interactions (VEnvI), we worked with upper elementary and middle school students (5th through 8th grades) during in-school, after-school, and summer-camp contexts, examining how an interactive dance-centered curriculum and a virtual platform supported computer programming education. Through the project, students had the opportunity to program a virtual dancing character and choreograph a corresponding dance for themselves to perform along with a projection of their virtual character (Figures 1 and 2).

Figure 1. The virtual–physical dance performance. Two students perform their dance choreography using chairs as props in front of a screen projecting their virtual choreography.

Figure 2. A virtual–physical dance battle. Two students dance battling their virtual dancing character on the screen behind them. They choreographed and programmed their performance so that the character would dance first, then they would try to "one-up" the character, and so on.

Dance and arts education have long emphasized embodied ways of thinking as central and inextricable to the learning process (Dils, 2007; Hanna, 2014; Minton & Faber, 2016; Warburton, 2011). Aligning with theories of embodied cognition that explore how thinking depends on and occurs through the body and experience (Barsalou, 2008; Lakoff & Johnson, 1999; Minton & Faber, 2016; Warburton, 2011; A. D. Wilson & Golonka, 2013; M. Wilson, 2002), we called upon dance's embodied strategies as novel in this context. We aimed to broaden opportunities and foster inclusion in computer science for students not necessarily previously engaged in computing. Here, dance as embodied inquiry is viewed as playing a central role in our global digital lives with great potential in coding contexts (Lombana-Bermudez, 2016; Owen et al., 2016).

We found that utilizing dance in both physical and virtual worlds as a purposefully embodied means to explore computational-thinking concepts (e.g., sequences, loops, functions, variables), practices (e.g., debugging, iterating), and perspectives (e.g., seeing computing as a profession and as a means of expression; Brennan & Resnick, 2012a, 2012b; Wing, 2006) appealed to students, helped increase their understanding of the computational concepts, and allowed for embodied engagement (Daily et al., 2014; Daily et al., 2015; Daily et al., 2016; Isaac & Babu, 2016; Jörg et al., 2014; Leonard & Daily, n.d.; Leonard et al., 2021; Leonard et al., 2015; Lin et al., 2017; Parmar, 2017; Parmar, Babu, et al., 2016; Parmar, Isaac, et al., 2016).

Dance and programming might seem like complete opposites if you envision a person dancing on their feet and another seated at a computer typing code; however, both parallel each other as forms of composition. For example, dance relies on the sequencing of a series of moves, just as programming uses a series of code sequences to execute a task. In dance choreography, the use of repetition allows for a movement motif to be showcased, similar to how programming requires certain sequences to be looped. Unison in dance creates a cohesive look, similar to the use of parallelism or "doing together" in programming that allows for processes to be carried out simultaneously. In partner dancing, one leads, and another follows. That idea, along with choreographic theme and variation, uses similar concepts to conditional branching in computing that use if-then Boolean logic constructs. Likewise, theme and variation use repeated motif movements, and the rearranging and reordering of them in new ways in a dance composition is similar to reusing and recycling code in programming. These compositional strategies mirror the disciplinary habits and practices in both dance and computer science, making them quite well-suited as partners in STEAM education projects.

In the VEnvI project, we explored these parallels between dance choreography and computer programming, beginning with dance activities—a physical warm-up and introduction to the concepts of sequencing (via a dance sequence), loops (repetitions in dance), parallelism/ "do together" (dancing in unison), conditionals (if-then dance scenarios), and programming practices of reusing and iterating (theme and variations in choreography). We purposefully used inclusive dance genres that built on more pedestrian and social line dance movements that all students could explore; we also wove in more technical movements from hip-hop, modern, and ballet genres based on student interests (Figure 3).

Figure 3. Students dancing. Image of students being lead through dance activities and warm-up.

Building on this knowledge, we introduced students to VEnvI, our desktop-based virtual environment, which uses a drag-and-drop interface. Inspired by similar virtual environment learning platforms, including Alice (Conway et al., 1994), Looking Glass (Kelleher, 2009), and Scratch (Resnick et al., 2009), we created VEnvI using Vicon motion-tracking technology and dancers in motion-capture suits to create characters with fluid, humanlike movements. In VEnvI, students customize their character via numerous attributes (gender, height, weight, skin tone, clothing color, eye color, and name; Figure 4). After customizing a character, a character's dancing movements are programmed via the user interface, which includes (1) the virtual environment window at the top left with the customized character, (2) the movement bank and selection area at the bottom left, and (3) the drag-and-drop programming workspace on the right side (Figure 5; Parmar, 2017).

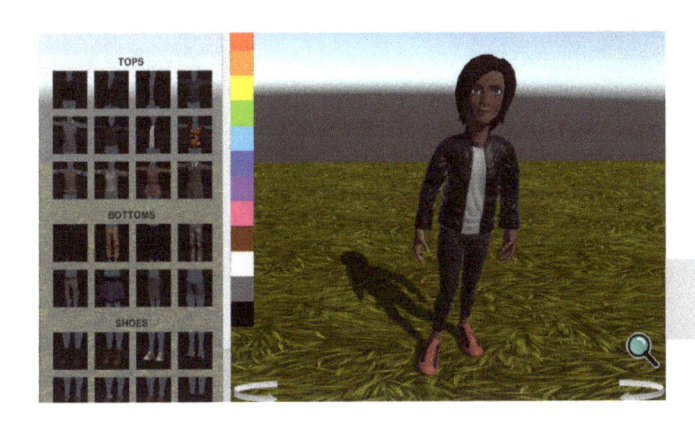

Figure 4. Image of VEnvI character customization screen.

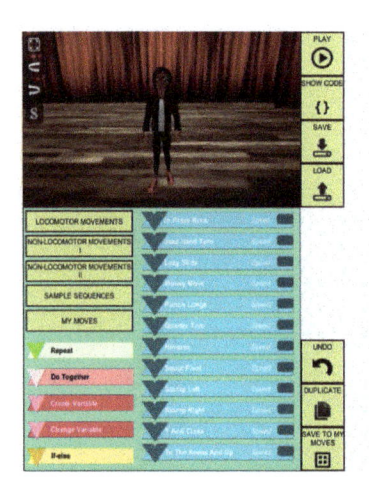

Figure 5. Image of VEnvI interface. Note (1) the virtual environment window at the top left with the customized character, (2) the movement bank and selection area at the bottom left, and (3) the drag-and-drop programming workspace on the right side. Repeat, Do Together, and If-Else blocks have been dragged onto the workspace, along with several movements.

The movement bank contains over 40 unique motion-captured movements or sequences. Based on common dance education designations and the Core Arts Standards (NCCAS, 2015), the movements are categorized into locomotor movements (movements that travel; i.e., step, leap), nonlocomotor movements (movements that stay in place; i.e., jump, turn), and sample sequences. Students can also combine any number of moves and save their combinations as new, customized move blocks under "My Moves." When choosing moves, students also select how many times to loop a particular movement and its performance speed. New moves are added by dragging them from the bank to the workspace and close enough to the existing moves to attach themselves to the closest move by snapping to it, similar to the action of a magnet. The workspace acts like a drafting board so that at any point, there may be multiple connected or disconnected blocks and sequences of move blocks, making it possible for a block or set of blocks to be selected, deselected, duplicated, or deleted at any time in the choreography process (Figure 5).

In the bank and selection area, students choose the building blocks for computational functions used to create their virtual choreography, such as a "Do Together" block that provides the construct to parallelize two different moves and execute them simultaneously. Another construct, "Create Variable," allows students to create "a new Boolean variable, assign a name to it, and set its initial value to either true or false" (Parmar, 2017, p. 27). Then, the "Change Variable" block allows them to be used at multiple points within their sequence choreography to change the value of an already created variable. Finally, the "If-Else" block allows for theme and variation in the choreography by creating two optional sequence scenarios to take place. This block checks for the value of an existing variable—true or false—and then executes the correct branch. The characters perform or stop the dance by pressing the play or stop button. Additionally, a button named "Show Code" generates and displays a pseudo-code based on the move sequences in the programming workspace area.

Assessing our objectives and student engagement, all students filled out a pre- and postbiographical survey to help assess personal student information relevant to our study, such as demographic information, programming and dance experience and perceptions, and attitudes toward school subjects. We also administered a project-specific pre- and posttest based on the computational thinking concepts (e.g., sequences, loops, functions, variables) covered. Depending on the context, we documented other programming and choreographic tasks. For example, students mapped out their programming and choreography on paper, noting the sequences, loops, and variables (Figures 6a and 6b). We also recorded and transcribed exit interviews with students in video- and photo-documented sessions. In one context, we asked students to draw a computer scientist and caption their drawings pre- and post-VEnvI, similar to other research that has been conducted on perceptions in science (Daily et al., 2016; Martin, 2004). Overall, we determined that the students' demonstration of computational thinking concept knowledge increased, they engaged in a myriad of embodied practices, and their perceptions about computer science and dance broadened after participating in VEnvI (Leonard et al., 2021).

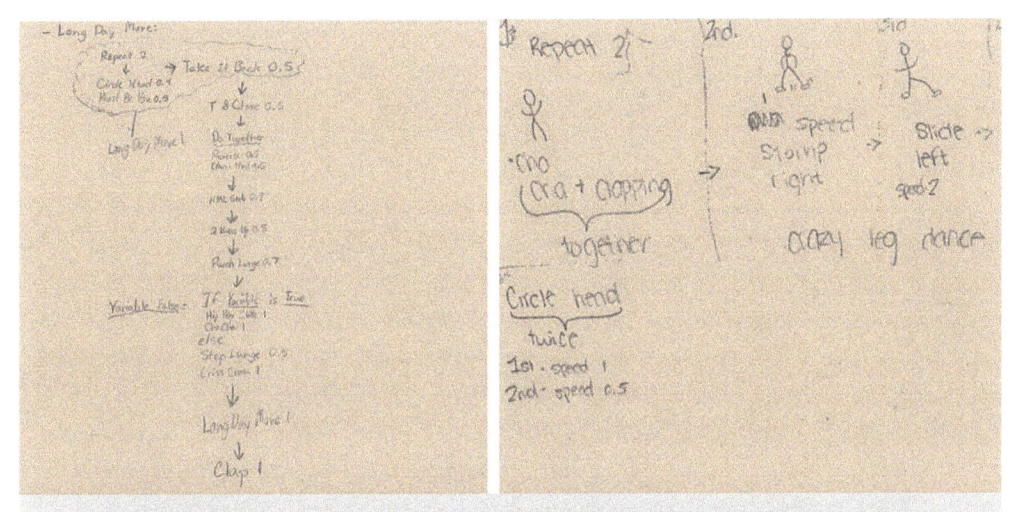

Figures 6a and 6b. Scanned copies of participant's written notes and drawings mapping out dance movements and the sequence of movements (choreography) prior to programming their dancing virtual character.

VEnvI as a Transdisciplinary STEAM Project

VEnvI embodies a transdisciplinary STEAM project by connecting multiple disciplines in a symbiotic way. Although each STEAM letter/discipline plays a distinct role in the VEnvI example, the role that each letter/discipline plays is also inextricably linked to the others. More than an interdisciplinary STEAM project, where disciplines connect and at least a couple play a central role, here all letters/disciplines rely on each other. Specifically, the "S" is represented by computer science and even in one iteration of our project, also by biology. We asked the 5th-grade students to create a physical–virtual choreographic performance inspired by cellular biology (cell, cell membrane, nucleus, cytoplasm, vacuole), which added another STEAM layer to the project (Leonard et al., 2015). The "T" for technology comes in the form of VEnvI as a virtual platform created through virtual reality, human-centered computing, and digital-production arts techniques. Yet, the "T" is also realized in the objectives of learning computational-thinking skills and the process of the students programming to learn and create, along with having their virtual characters perform. Even more, the "T" is also the "S" since the technology is inherently computer science as well.

The "E" has a similar relationship with the "S" and the "T," since computer science can be a form of engineering with the application of the sciences, mathematics, design, and technology essential to the engineering process (NGSS Lead States, 2013). For example, the students also had the opportunity to help in the design and beta phases of our development. As we were developing our virtual platform, we knew students would encounter various bugs; for instance, the drag-and-drop blocks would freeze occasionally, or a character would not repeat a function properly. During one context, we invited the students to try to "break" the program on purpose with the stipulation that they had to be able to reproduce the error to claim they had found a bug. This activity helped us to refine our program's functionality and also exposed the students to the process of debugging, an important practice for computer scientists and engineers.

The "A" is embodied in multiple ways through the use of dance: (1) as a framework for the project in terms of compositional strategy that links with computer programming; (2) as a process of inquiry in exploring programming, and simultaneously as the lens through which programming manifests itself; (3) as the project assignment for students to choreograph both a virtual and physical dance; and (4) as the form of representation via the performance of the physical–virtual dance. Additionally, design also comes into play for the "A," since throughout the development of the VEnvI platform, students gave input along the way; for example, they provided feedback about wanting characters to be more lifelike when we piloted our program using other platforms prior to our launch of our VEnvI platform (Daily et al., 2014; Leonard & Daily, n.d.).

Finally, with the "M," VEnvI might seem to downplay the mathematics component; however, mathematics played a crucial role, particularly since programming code is a form of mathematics. Dance choreography is also innately mathematical, defined by sequences, patterns, timing, rhythm, and spatial relationships. The students often pointed out the relationship of VEnvI and programming to their math classes when we focused on the Boolean logic of creating variables and if-then scenarios. Ultimately, the letters/disciplines of STEAM embodied through VEnvI cannot be separated from each other. Discussing and practicing one discipline through VEnvI invokes and relies on another, exemplifying a transdisciplinary project. If you took one letter out, the entire project would collapse. Quite literally, STEAM fueled VEnvI.

Beyond VEnvI

There have been times when VEnvI was available for download and may be again in the future; however, educators looking to explore a similar project with their students do not necessarily need to use VEnvI. While VEnvI stands as unique, utilizing Vicon motion tracking to create fluid, humanlike dance movements, programs previously mentioned, such as Scratch, Alice, and Looking Glass, do provide narrative and movement-programming capabilities. Moreover, using any online, desktop, or robotic programming platform has potential to work well with dance choreography, utilizing dance standards. I can envision students programming and dancing with robots where the robots and dancers interact and can potentially engage in virtual reality and/or real-time programming-improvisation scenarios. In this case, the embodied interactions take on new layers of meaning-making and possibility with the choreographic and programming process extending into the performance itself. Moreover, students can even engage in programming choreographic tasks without computers, programming or choreographing shorter movement sequences they can expand through looping, combining sequences, if-then scenarios, and other programming or choreographic functions and strategies. Ultimately, the goal becomes creating transdisciplinary STEAM opportunities in which students can engage in embodied ways of inquiry and in representing their knowledge using dance.

Acknowledgments

I would like to acknowledge and thank my VEnvI colleagues for their dedicated and hard work and for collaborating with me on this project: Shaundra B. Daily, Sabarish V. Babu, and Sophie Jörg, and to our "at-the-time graduate student researchers" who made VEnvI possible, including Nikeetha D'Souza, Dhaval Parmar, Kara Gundersen, and Lorraine Lin. A special thank-you to Nikeetha D'Souza for her assistance in preparing this chapter.

The VEnvI project was made possible in part due to a National Science Foundation Grant, Award Abstract #1344228.

IRB approval was used for this research, and permission for photographing participants was granted.

Alison E. Leonard is an associate professor of arts and creativity at Clemson University. She researches and teaches about arts education, primarily utilizing dance, drama, music, and visual arts as a lens for exploring the arts, aesthetics, and design as ways of thinking, inquiry, expression, and communication in schools.

References

American Association for the Advancement of Science & *Science Magazine* (Hosts). (n.d.). *Official rules for Dance Your Ph.D. contest*. http://www.sciencemag.org/projects/dance-your-phd/official-rules

Barsalou, L. W. (2008). Grounded cognition. *Annual Review of Psychology, 59*, 617–645. https://doi.org/10.1146/annurev.psych.59.103006.093639

Brennan, K., & Resnick, M. (2012a, April 13–17). *New frameworks for studying and assessing the development of computational thinking* [Paper presentation]. Annual meeting of the American Educational Research Association, Vancouver, BC, Canada.

Brennan, K., & Resnick, M. (2012b, April 13–17). *Using artifact-based interviews to study the development of computational thinking in interactive media design* [Paper presentation]. Annual American Educational Research Association meeting, Vancouver, BC, Canada.

Conway, M., Pausch, R., Gossweiler, R., & Burnette, T. (1994). Alice: A rapid prototyping system for building virtual environments. In C. Plaisant (Ed.), *Conference Companion on Human Factors in Computing Systems* (pp. 295–296). Association for Computing Machinery. https://doi.org/10.1145/259963.260503

Daily, S. B., Leonard, A. E., Jörg, S., Babu, S., D'Souza, N., Parmar, D., Gundersen, K., Isaac, J., & Acker, S. (2016). Combating perceptions of computer scientists: A short-term intervention. In C. Alphonce, J. Tims, M. Caspersen, & S. Edwards (Eds.), *SIGCSE '16: Proceedings of the 47th ACM Technical Symposium on Computing Science Education* (p. 687). Association for Computing Machinery. https://doi.org/10.1145/2538862.2538917

Daily, S. B., Leonard, A. E., Jörg, S., Babu, S., Gundersen, K. (2014). Dancing Alice: Exploring embodied pedagogical strategies for learning computational thinking. In J. D. Dougherty, K. Nagel, A. Decker, & K. Eiselt (Eds.), *SIGCSE '14: Proceedings of the 45th ACM Technical Symposium on Computer Science Education* (pp. 91–96). Association for Computing Machinery. https://doi.org/10.1145/2538862.2538917

Daily, S. B., Leonard, A. E., Jörg, S., Babu, S., Gundersen, K., & Parmar, D. (2015). Embodying computational thinking: Initial design of an emerging technological learning tool. *Technology, Knowledge, & Learning, 20*(1), 79–84. https://doi.org/10.1007/s10758-014-9237-1

Dils, A. (2007). Why dance literacy? *Journal of the Canadian Association for Curriculum Studies, 5*(2), 95–113. https://jcacs.journals.yorku.ca/index.php/jcacs/article/view/17046

Hanna, J. L. (2014). *Dancing to learn: The brain's cognition, emotion, and movement*. Rowman & Littlefield.

Isaac, J., & Babu, S. V. (2016, March 19–20). *Supporting computational thinking through gamification* [Paper presentation]. 2016 IEEE Symposium on 3D User Interfaces (3DUI), Greenville, SC, USA. https://doi.org/10.1109/3dui.2016.7460062

Jörg, S., Leonard, A. E., Babu, S., Gundersen, K., Parmar, D., Boggs, K., Daily, S. B. (2014, August 10–14). *Character animation and embodiment in teaching computational thinking* [Poster presentation]. SIGGRAPH '14: Special Interest Group on Computer Graphics and Ineractive Techniques Conference, Vancouver, BC, Canada. https://doi.org/10.1145/2614217.2630597

Kaufmann, K. A., & Dehline, J. (2014). *Dance integration: 36 dance lesson plans for science and mathematics*. Human Kinetics.

Kelleher, C. (2009). Supporting storytelling in a programming environment for middle school children. In I. A. Iurgel, N. Zagalo, & P. Petta (Eds.), *Interactive storytelling: Second Joint International Conference on Interactive Digital Storytelling: Proceedings* (pp. 1–4). Springer. https://doi.org/10.1007/978-3-642-10643-9_1

Lakoff, G., & Johnson, M. (1999). *Philosophy in the flesh: The embodied mind and its challenge to Western thought*. Basic Books.

Leonard, A. E., & Bannister, N. A. (2018). Dancing our way to geometric transformations. *Mathematics Teaching in the Middle School, 23*(5), 258–267. https://doi.org/10.5951/mathteacmiddscho.23.5.0258

Leonard, A. E., & Daily, S. B. (n.d.). *The dancing Alice project: Computational and embodied arts research in middle school education*. Voke. http://www.vokeart.org/?p=331&spoke=1

Leonard, A. E., Daily, S. B., Jörg, S., & Babu, S. V. (2021). Coding moves: Design and research on teaching computational thinking through dance choreography and virtual interactions. *Journal of Research in Technology Education, 53*(2), 159–177. https://doi.org/10.1080/15391523.2020.1760754

Leonard, A. E., Dsouza, N., Babu, S. V., Daily, S. B., Jörg, S., Waddell, C., Parmar, D., Gundersen, K., Gestring, J., & Boggs, K. (2015). Embodying and programming a "constellation" of multimodal literacy practices: Computational thinking, creative movement, biology, & virtual environment interactions. *Journal of Language and Literacy Education*, *11*(2), 64–93.

Lin, L., Parmar, D., Babu, S. V., Leonard, A. E., Daily, S. B., & Jörg, S. (2017, September 16–17). How character customization affects learning in computational thinking. In S. N. Spencer (Ed.), *SAP '17: Proceedings of the ACM Symposium on Applied Perception* (pp. 1–8). Association for Computing Machinery. https://doi.org/10.1145/3119881.3119884

Lombana-Bermudez, A. (2016, November 18). Hip-hop coding: Exploring the connections between computational thinking and hip-hop culture. *Berkman Klein Center Collection*. Medium. https://medium.com/berkman-klein-center/hip-hop-coding-exploring-the-connections-between-computational-thinking-and-hip-hop-culture-f7da1ef972e

Martin, C. D. (2004). Draw a computer scientist. *ACM SIGCSE Bulletin*, *36*(4), 11–12. https://doi.org/10.1145/1041624.1041628

Minton, S. C., & Faber, R. (2016). *Thinking with the dancing brain: Embodying neuroscience*. Rowman & Littlefield.

Moore, C., & Linder, S. M. (2012). Using dance to deepen student understanding of geometry. *Journal of Dance Education*, *12*(3), 104–108. https://doi.org/10.1080/15290824.2012.701175

National Coalition for Core Arts Standards. (2015). *National core art standards: A conceptual framework for arts learning*. Rights administered by State Education Agency Directors of Arts Education. http://www.nationalartsstandards.org/content/national-core-arts-standards

NGSS Lead States. (2013). *Next Generation Science Standards: For states, by states* (Vol 2). National Academies Press.

Owen, C. B., Dillon, L., Dobbins, A., Keppers, N., Levinson, M., & Rhodes, M. (2016). Dancing computer: Computer literacy through dance. In B. Abdulrazak, E. Pardede, M. Steinbauer, I. Khalil, & G. Anderst-Kotsis (Eds.), *MoMM '16: Proceedings of the 14th International Conference on Advances in Mobile Computing and Multi Media* (pp. 174–180). Association for Computing Machinery. https://doi.org/10.1145/3007120.3007131

Parmar, D. (2017). *Evaluating the effects of immersive embodied interaction on cognition in virtual reality* (UMI No. 10616288) [Doctoral dissertation, Clemson University]. ProQuest Dissertations and Theses.

Parmar, D., Babu, S. V., Lin, L., Jörg, S., D'Souza, N., Leonard, A. E., & Daily, S. B. (2016, August 11–13). *Can embodied interaction and virtual peer customization in a virtual programming environment enhance computational thinking?* [Paper presentation]. Research on Equity and Sustained Participation in Engineering, Computing, and Technology (RESPECT), Atlanta, GA, USA. https://doi.org/10.1109/respect.2016.7836179

Parmar, D., Isaac, J., Babu, S. V., D'Souza, N., Leonard, A. E., Jörg, S., Gunderson, K., & Daily, S. B. (2016, March 19–23). *Programming moves: Design and evaluation of applying embodied interaction in virtual environments to enhance computational thinking in middle school students* [Paper presentation]. IEEE Annual International Symposium Virtual Reality (IEEE VR), Greenville, SC, USA. https://doi.org/10.1109/vr.2016.7504696

Resnick, M., Maloney, J., Monroy-Hernández, A., Rusk, N., Eastmond, E., Brennan, K., Millner, A., Rosenbaum, E., Silver, J., Silverman, B., & Kafai, Y. (2009). Scratch: Programming for all. *Communications of the ACM*, *52*(11), 60–67. https://doi.org/10.1145/1592761.1592779

Rosenfeld, M. (2016). *Math on the move: Engaging students in whole body learning*. Heinemann.

Schaffer, K., Stern, E., & Kim, S. (2001). *Math dance with Dr. Schaffer and Mr. Stern: Whole-body math and movement activities for the K-12 classroom*. MoveSpeakSpin.

Silveira, J. R. A., Maia, C. O., & Lannes, D. (2014). Cultural and scientific inclusion through dance and science: Lessons from a project in Brazil. *International Journal of Arts & Sciences*, *7*(3), 409–416.

Simpson Steele, J., Fulton, L., & Fanning, L. (2016). Dancing with STEAM: Creative movement generates electricity for young learners. *Journal of Dance Education*, *16*(3), 112–117. https://doi.org/10.1080/15290824.2016.1175570

Sousa, D. A., & Pilecki, T. (2013). *From STEM to STEAM: Using brain-compatible strategies to integrate the arts*. Corwin.

Stapp, A., Chessin, D., & Deason, R. (2018). Dance like a butterfly. *Science and Children*, *55*(6), 54–60. https://doi.org/10.2505/4/sc18_055_06_54

References continued

Stolberg, T. L. (2006). Communicating science through the language of dance: A journey of education and reflection. *Leonardo, 39*(5), 426–432. https://doi.org/10.1162/leon.2006.39.5.426

Sullivan, A., & Bers, M. U. (2018). Dancing robots: Integrating art, music, and robotics in Singapore's early childhood centers. *International Journal of Technology and Design Education, 28*(1), 325–346. doi:10.1007/s10798-017-9397-0

Tay, G. C., & Edwards, K. D. (2015). DanceChemistry: Helping students visualize chemistry concepts through dance videos. *Journal of Chemical Education, 92*(11), 1956–1959. https://doi.org/10.1021/acs.jchemed.5b00315

Warburton, E. C. (2011). Of meanings and movements: Re-languaging embodiment in dance phenomenology and cognition. *Dance Research Journal, 43*(2), 65–84. https://doi.org/10.1017/s0149767711000064

Wilson, A. D., & Golonka, S. (2013). Embodied cognition is not what you think it is. *Frontiers in Psychology, 4,* Article 58. https://doi.org/10.3389/fpsyg.2013.00058

Wilson, M. (2002). Six views of embodied cognition. *Psychonomic Bulletin & Review, 9*(4), 625–636. https://doi.org/10.3758/BF03196322

Wing, J. M. (2006). Computational thinking. *Communications of the ACM, 49*(3), 33–35. https://doi.org/10.1145/1118178.1118215

"But What About the Eyeballs?":
Devised Theatre as Interdisciplinary Knowledge-Generation Tool

Vivian Appler • Emily Pears

I recently found myself in a conversation about astronomy and green screen puppetry with a 10-year-old girl. We were at an informal postshow discussion among artists and audience members for an early performance of *That Which We Call a Rose* (*Rose*), a collaboratively written science, technology, engineering, art, and math (STEAM) play about astronomy, colonialism, and climate change, funded in part by the National Aeronautics and Space Administration's (NASA) South Carolina Space Consortium and the South Carolina Arts Commission. The *Rose* premiere talkback was designed so that artists and actors could mingle with the audience to engage in one-on-one conversations while also giving audience members the chance for hands-on explorations of the performance artifacts. Audience feedback was meant to inform our process as we proceeded with our multifaceted practice-as-research (PaR) project. In this chapter, the conversation about puppetry technique with this inquisitive girl is used as an anecdotal departure point to propose that the theatrical devising process inherent to PaR projects invites interdisciplinary knowledge generation, and that these techniques are well-suited for K–12 learning environments as a precursor to academic and professional theatre pursuits.

As a performance in progress, *Rose* evolved in its utilization of multiple storytelling media (including live action, interactive video, robotics, and puppetry) implemented across several performance platforms, such as a stage, blog, pre- and postshow spaces, and lesson plans. The live performance that provides the primary example of this chapter took place in February 2020, and the digital archive and educational outreach materials are still available at https://blogs.cofc.edu.that-which-we-call-a-rose (Appler, 2019b). Unfortunately, due to the COVID-19 pandemic, our plans for a more extensive version of the project have since been curtailed. Nevertheless, this chapter introduces aspects of the live 2020 performance and proposes that theatrical devising techniques might be implemented as learning methods appropriate for K–12 STEAM curricula. The chapter concludes with sample lesson plans that might be applied by the reader to enhance future arts–science integrative K–12 STEAM education. To begin, the multimodal aspects of the project demand an awareness of how devised theatre can apply to a STEAM knowledge-generation system.

Defining Devised Theatre and PaR

Devised theatre is a term that describes theatre created through democratic methods of movement, text, and other content-generation techniques (Kaufman & McAdams, 2018; Oddey, 1994). The term itself, along with its inherent interdisciplinary potential, has taken hold in Europe and the United States over the past 25 years (Miller, 2016; Zazzali & Klein, 2015). Devised theatre resists the primacy of text that is so highly valued in Euro–American commercial theatrical production, especially since the early 20th century. Non-text-based theatre has a rich history in that its European roots extend at least as far back as the itinerant Italian *commedia dell'arte* troupes of the 16th century (Rudlin, 1994). More recently, Euro–American experiments in alternative approaches to theatre creation have taken shape under various monikers that include (but are not limited to) collective creation, ensemble theatre, physical theatre, dance theatre, site-specific theatre, happenings, multimedia performance, performance art, or live art. To say that a play was devised also means that it was created outside of the hierarchical structure traditionally associated with Euro–American theatre, in which a playwright writes a play; a director interprets that play; actors and designers do their work to realize the director's vision; and a number of wardrobe, scenic, lighting, and sound crew members all work together to make theatre magic happen for an audience to enjoy in a dedicated theatre space. In devised theatre, although each person in the ensemble may have their own strengths, everyone is at the creative table as much as possible to help to achieve a collective theatrical vision that is unique to that group. *Devising* is an umbrella term that references a variety of genres and processes, including PaR.

PaR is a slightly newer, even more contested term than devised theatre, with roots in the Practice as Research in Performance (PARIP) project, a 5-year-long experiment enacted at the University of Bristol under the direction of performance studies scholar Baz Kershaw. The details are described in the University of Bristol report as follows:

> PARIP's objectives were to investigate creative-academic issues raised by practice as research, where performance is defined... as performance media: theatre, dance, film, video and television.... PARIP aimed to develop national frameworks for the encouragement of the highest standards in representing practical-creative research within academic contexts. (*PARIP*, n.d., para. 2).

PaR, as a pedagogical technique in higher education, encourages higher order synthesis of concepts and questions across disciplinary boundaries in ways that transcend intradisciplinary theatrical practices and labor designations.

As PaR has grown, practitioners who enact this kind of creative inquiry have further nuanced their methodologies. In his introduction to *Performance as Research: Knowledge, Methods, Impact*, Bruce Barton (2018), a performing arts scholar, uses the broad term "artistic research in performance (ARP)" and offers a list of the many iterations of this kind of work (pp. 4–5).

Table 1. Iterations of PaR

Performance as research (PAR)	Practice as research (PaR)	Research through practice (RtP)
Research practice (RP)	Practice-based research (PBR)	Studio research (SR)
Research-led practice (RLP)	Practice-led research (PLR)	Research through practice (RtP)
Arts-based research (ABR)	Research-based practice (RBP)	Creative research (CR)

The designations identified in Table 1 are not strict categories, and PaR practitioners may shift among the various emphases designated by each term (see Table 1). I refer to *Rose* as a PaR project because its modalities have evolved from its origins as a scholarly article (RLP) that inspired the creation of a devised play (PAR), to the composition of essays such as this (PLR), to the development of interactive online audience experiences in which the audience and ensemble collaborate in creative inquiry (PBR).

PaR's methods and applicability have reached beyond British pedagogical structures to influence devising processes in professional and academic theatres in the United States, as well as the emergence of academic programs such Columbia University's Digital Storytelling Lab (Columbia DSL); Arizona State University's Pave Arts Incubator Project (Zazzali & Klein, 2015); and Mind Readers, a PaR coalition of PhD students and faculty at University of California, Santa Barbara, attest (Baki et al., 2019). A PaR research model acknowledges theatre creation as a process by which meaning is made, just like the work enacted in astronomical observatories or other scientific laboratories is acknowledged, not purely representational. The lines that divide practice and research are necessarily blurred across PaR distinctions, and this transmodal aspect of PaR unites these diverse approaches under a single heading; the "refusal to accept the bifurcation of research and practice is necessary to future developments in doctoral education in theatre and performance studies" (Baki et al., 2019, p. 128). Here, I suggest it would be productive to extend PaR's practical epistemologies to enhance K–12 STEAM pedagogies.

Interdisciplinary performance studies scholar Lynette Hunter (2015) underscores that the potential of PaR as a knowledge creation process lies in its interdisciplinarity. She argues that "it is precisely the presence of critique that makes practice politically unsettling and can help generate the emergent knowing that leads to creative insight and radical positionalities" (Hunter, 2015, p. 13). Barton adds, "Associated with methodological diversity is the observation that ARP approaches, in both their processes and their resultant knowledge, are inherently *interdisciplinary* and *transdisciplinary*, qualities" (2018, p 11). Ways of knowing are necessarily caught up with ways of doing, and also constitute ways of being (Barton, 2018; Hunter, 2015). The creative processes needed for devised theatre cannot be constrained by intradisciplinary distinctions within the traditional commercial theatre model. For devised PaR projects, the creation process is as valuable to the whole learning process as that of the experience of a "finished" theatrical production. All participants, including the audience, are necessary to the knowledge creation that transpires in a devised PaR work at all phases of the process, and by all of those involved in the performance experience. For instance, the conversation with the girl during the *Rose* talkback is an essential component to the knowledge-generative possibilities embedded in the work of *Rose* as a long-term PaR project.

Rose, the STEAM Play

The theatrical production of *Rose* was developed to encourage a diverse range of audience participants to think creatively about how humans might mindfully encounter planetary bodies in our solar system. The creative ensemble was a mix of College of Charleston faculty, staff, students, and local theatre professionals. After an invited work-in-progress performance at the Women's Theatre Festival in Raleigh, North Carolina, we produced our first full performance for Charleston, South Carolina, area schools in February 2020 at the Cannon Street Arts Center. Audiences were taken on a journey to four planetary bodies that, in 2019–2020, NASA was also studying quite closely: the Moon, Mars, the asteroid Bennu, and Saturn's moon Titan.

Rose asked questions about space exploration through a theatrical treatment of the planetary nomenclature process as it appears in the Gazetteer of Planetary Nomenclature (Gazetteer), a digital product of the International Astronomical Union, maintained by the Planetary Geomatics Group of the United States Geological Survey and NASA. The Gazetteer contains information about every named feature of every planetary body (planet, dwarf planet, asteroid, or moon) in the solar system. It is a vast document that contains a surprising amount of humanities- and arts-based information in its spreadsheet (Appler, 2019a). Using open-access data available through the Gazetteer, we devised an interactive, multimedia play, set upon the terrain of other planetary bodies, using the Earth-cultural sources for those names as our creative starting point. The Gazetteer provided the perfect science content from which to launch our performance-based investigation into Earth's increasingly interplanetary culture.

We incorporated multiple modes of performance in pursuit of our research questions, with results that may yet transpire across different social and temporal trajectories. The performance featured a preshow environment that explained puppetry techniques and science concepts central to the play's plot, characters, and themes. Digitally augmented maps helped audiences explore the histories of planetary topography through QR codes and 3D modeling. On the blog, virtual audiences can still learn about our content and process. *Rose* extends the devising mindset beyond the theatre by inviting audiences to continue to explore the same astronomy content that we found so fascinating *and* our theatrical craft—in classrooms, at home, and online. As artists, we endeavor to be transparent about our performance-creation process so that young audiences may embrace their capacity to learn about themselves and the world through play, imagination, and artmaking. By empowering our diverse and geographically dispersed digital audiences to explore astronomy with and through the arts, young people who represent an array of demographic groups, many of whom have historically been excluded from high-status astronomy professions, may feel empowered to pursue physics and astronomy careers in the future. This is important for the establishment of sustainable science and arts cultures, especially in the United States, where women and people of color represent a disproportionately low number of professionals working in authoritative positions in the science fields of physics and astronomy and also within theatre and film (Erkut & Ceder, 2016; Lauzen, 2020; National Science Foundation, 2019).

Figure 1. "What was that?" Nick Brown, Javaron Conyers, and Jennifer Bettke. Photo by Anna Robertson.

"But What About the Eyeballs?" Devising With STEAM

In the play, the year is 2131. A crew of 22nd-century explorers has been sent on a mission to explore Jupiter's moon Europa as a potential site for human colonization (Figure 1). Humanity has come close to total climate collapse, and Earth can no longer sustain human life or culture. The crew's trip is abruptly interrupted by Dr. Psyche Sutton (Figure 2), the head of the very top secret, and fictional, Consortium of Women Cosmographers (a cosmographer is a person who maps and studies the unknown places of the world using the tools and skills of astronomy, cartography, and geography but not necessarily in a strict sense). Dr. Sutton is named after the real-life, early 20th-century American astronomer, Psyche Rebecca Underwood (Sutton), known for her work on cepheid variables. The fictional Dr. Sutton tasks the crew with "sweeping" the solar system, a job that provides the plot for the rest of the play. "Sweeping the solar system" is a tongue-in-cheek comment on the domestic allusions made regarding other historical women in astronomy—Caroline Herschel (1750–1848), Annie Jump Cannon (1863–1941), Maria Mitchell (1818–1889)— whose observational work was often referred to as "sky-sweeping" (Higgins, 1967; Wright,

1949). In the play, Dr. Sutton lives in an animated space lab populated with a menagerie of organisms that she has collected over the course of her centuries-long quest to clean up the messes left by humanity's exploration of outer space. Her video-interactive scenes create the illusion that the crew, embodied by actors onstage, are engaged in a real-time conversation with Dr. Sutton. In the opening sequence, she is seen observing a pair of disembodied eyeballs that she has collected in her travels—or are they observing her?

As mentioned earlier we held a talkback after the performance. During the talkback, one student was curious about the technical aspects of theatrical production. Referring to Dr. Sutton's interactive video scenes, she asked, "When you were on screen, were you really there?" "No," I replied, and explained that we had pre-recorded those scenes using a green screen. "Oh," she nodded, "I thought so." She paused, "But what about the eyeballs?" This question surprised me. I thought she would want to know more about green screen technology, since this was the part of the process I was most excited about. But she wanted to know about the eyeballs, a throwaway gag and a bit of physical comedy incorporated to introduce Dr. Sutton at work in her observatory. The pair of eyeballs was a cheap prop, purchased out of the Halloween sale bin in a fit of work-shopping. This is a devising technique introduced to me by my teacher Lois Weaver, cofounder of the performance ensemble Split Britches. *Work-shopping* is what happens when you go shopping for your show for inspiration and call it work. In the scene, I stood with my back to the camera, holding the eyeballs just over my head, and used my fingers to rotate the squishy, orbs to move in tandem as if they were looking around the room and at the camera. Animating the eyeball props was a fairly simple task of object manipulation that would have worked just as well onstage as onscreen.

But that's just it. Well-crafted theatricality is essential if devised theatre is to induce audiences to pay attention through the curtain call, and if theatre-integrative STEAM educational efforts are to be effective tools for K–12 learning. In physical theatre, there is no such thing as a throwaway gag, because every moment must work to further engage the audience with the plot, characters, and important themes in the play. Embedding such a simple puppet within the green screen technology worked to hook the audience into thinking more deeply about the play's interdisciplinary content and mechanisms. This savvy 10-year-old already knew enough about video technology to ask intelligent questions about it, but it was the analog puppetry that compelled her to reflect upon and engage with the play even after the curtains closed. This anecdote is by no means a comprehensive study and does not replace a quantitative research effort, but the girl's response suggests that work remains to be done to explore the knowledge-generative connections made across disciplinary boundaries and praxes within PaR devising.

Arts craft should be as integral to K–12 STEAM curricula as science content. Arts-integrative pedagogue Merryl Goldberg (2017) defines her methodology for impactful K–12 education as operating via three modes:

Figure 2. Green screen lab. Vivian Appler (as Dr. Psyche Sutton) and Javaron Conyers (puppeteer). Photo by Jack Wolfe.

- **Learning *with* the arts** occurs when arts are introduced as a way to study about a particular subject.
- **Learning *through* the arts** is a method that encourages students to grapple with and express their understandings of subject matter through an art form.
- **Learning *about* the arts**, by which students gain literacy and skills about and in various arts disciplines. (pp. 36–38)

Within these modes of operation, if the words "cultural domain" are substituted for the phrase "subject matter," it is easy to see how Goldberg's approach—learning *with*, *through*, and *about* the arts—can encourage young learners to mature into adults empowered to actively create the culture they are a part of using the arts across diverse social and cultural divisions, including science. The whole *Rose* PaR project allows all people—K–12 and beyond—who are curious about science and theatre to learn through these different modes. The initial essay that sparked the idea for *Rose*, "Titan's 'Goodbye Kiss': Legacy Rockets and the Conquest of Space," introduced an audience of performance studies scholars to the Gazetteer archives. Throughout the *Rose* devising development period, all creative ensemble members became immersed in the Gazetteer and the histories of planetary nomenclature as a cultural process. We crafted a play for children that was informative, imaginative, and asked questions of those histories. Through pre- and postshow experiences and ongoing digital performance platforms, we encouraged our audiences learning with *Rose* to do the same.

Figure 3. *That Which We Call a Rose*. Osprey over Bennu's Trash Patch. Photo by Anna Robertson.

The entire *Rose* experience offered learning opportunities at all three of Goldberg's proposed modes of engagement. The experience of seeing the play allowed students to learn *about* science *with* the experience of live theatre, that is, learning science *with* the arts, and that experience may inspire young audience members to become theatre and science enthusiasts in the future. Our educational outreach specialist, Emily Pears, developed arts-integrative lesson plans in which students learned *about* theatre using science as the catalyst and content. For example, in the lesson plan Shadow Puppets, Storytelling, and Phases of the Moon, students learned *about* mythological explanations for the phases of the moon, created their own stories to explain the phases of the moon, and made their own phases of the moon shadow puppets; they learned *about* astronomy *through* theatrical devising.

The following Grade 1 lesson plans are available on our blog: (https://blogs.cofc.edu/that-which-we-call-a-rose/about-us/educational-outreach/first-grade-lessons-shadow-puppets-storytelling-and-phases-of-the-moon). The K–4 version of *Rose* explored Earth's Moon and the asteroid Bennu (see Figure 3). These lessons specifically address the content in the *Rose* scene, "Monsters on the Moon." On the Moon, the crew lands near the Camelot Crater, which was the landing site for NASA's Apollo 17 lunar mission. In the scene, Javaron, the mission's science historian and cultural anthropologist, frightens his crewmates when introducing the abandoned site by whispering, "Here be dragons," a phrase once used on the Hunt-Lenox Globe (1510), but which has been misremembered as a common cartographical phrase in subsequent centuries (Meyer, 2013). Javaron proceeds to tell tales of dragons, King Arthur's court, the Indian myth of Rahu (a disembodied head that repeatedly tried to eat the moon, but always unsuccessfully), and the Norse myth of the wolf gods Skoll and Hati, who "were always trying to plunge the earth into darkness by eating the Sun and the Moon" (*Rose*, February 2020, "Monsters" scene). The STEAM lessons discussed here reinforce the science and humanities concepts and plot points from this scene while teaching 1st graders skills in shadow puppetry and storytelling.

The STEAM Lesson Plans for *Rose*

Pears created pre- and postperformance arts-integrative lessons for kindergarten, 1st, 6th, and 8th grades. The play itself encompassed the STEAM subject areas of astronomy and physical science, so it was decided that the lessons should teach theatre skills while supporting both theatre and science standards. The lessons were created to help teachers facilitate experiences in which students would collaboratively create puppets and devise original stories to explain astronomical phenomena while encouraging them to ask questions and synthesize knowledge about both the arts and the natural world. In short, the K–12 lessons mimic the *Rose* PaR-devising process by providing science content *about* which students are free to follow their own curiosities *through* theatre. The preshow lessons prepare students for the experience of seeing the play, and the postshow lessons should allow students an opportunity to think through some of the play's content using theatrical devising techniques. All of the lessons were originally distributed to school groups who came to the show. They remain on the *Rose* blog so that educators may continue to learn *about* astronomy *with* these arts techniques in the future, even without the experience of seeing the live play.

Preshow Lesson: Phases of the Moon Shadow Puppets (Grade 1)

In the preshow lesson, students are instructed in shadow puppetry (a mode of performance that appears in the play). The puppets described in the lesson plan represent the phases of the moon, and they address the Grade 1 South Carolina state science standards on light and shadows. Some basic information on Indian and Chinese shadow puppets brings focus to the Theatre Anchor Standard 7: "I can examine the role of theatre through history and culture" (South Carolina Department of Education, 2017, p. 469). In this lesson, students will construct their own knowledge and understanding of physical science concepts through exploration and guided questions, first in a small group or one-on-one setting, then in a whole-group setting. Thinking about how the Moon is sometimes obscured from our vision by the Earth's shadow prepares students to understand the science behind the myths performed in the play. In this lesson, students learn how light and shadows work, and how these concepts also apply to the phases of the Moon, and they can see these concepts at work *through* construction and play with their phases of the Moon shadow puppets. This lesson is also *about* theatre, as it introduces shadow puppet traditions from around the world. Students have multiple opportunities to develop their understanding of and ask questions about the arts, culture, and the natural world. For students who attended the 2020 event, following this lesson with the live theatrical production would have further enhanced students' understanding of light, shadows, and the moon's phases.

Postshow Lesson: Lunar Storytelling (Grade 1)

The postshow lesson was originally designed to be conducted after seeing the play, although it, too, may now be taught independently of the live theatre experience. This lesson delves into the cultural histories that appear in the play's dialogue. Because the play incorporates the mythologies of many cultures, the postshow lesson also includes a mythology element. This lesson addresses the Grade 1 South Carolina state science standards about predicting how the appearance of the moon changes while also supporting theatre-writing standards. This lesson encourages students to create new knowledge as they make up their own stories to explain the phenomena of lunar phases and eclipses. The lesson's motivational narrative reviews the mythology introduced in the play and qualifies this module as learning science and culture *with* theatre. Students synthesize what they learned *about* eclipses *through* the preshow activity and *with* the play, and again build on these cumulative learning experiences *through* a culminating storytelling exercise. Group writing activities for students of this age range can be challenging due to a heterogeneous mix of skill levels in any classroom. Therefore, to consider adaptations for this lesson, teachers have the option to use whatever recording technology the school provides to document the students' original stories. Students can record their stories rather than write them, physically improvise their story after brainstorming, or draw a picture of their story and then explain it to the class. Students construct their own knowledge of these concepts by asking questions and creative means.

Conclusion

The "A" at the heart of STEAM necessarily demands an arts-learning process that is equivalent to the disciplines represented by the other letters in the acronym. This applies to the quality of arts instruction in the classroom and the value placed on the arts within the broader context of K–12 STEAM curricula. Too often, K–12 teachers are not offered adequate training to lead arts processes for their students (often because students of education themselves have been denied authentic creative experiences in their own K–12 educations). Creative arts practices are often obscured when audiences enter a professional theatre or walk through an art gallery, and this can make the creative arts seem somehow separate from the rest of culture, and intimidating in its seemingly esoteric processes. However, just as there is a scientific process that can be taught, artists adhere to creative processes that are unique to each genre, whether it be visual, musical, or performance oriented. These are skills that can be developed in all students, and that should therefore be rigorously deployed within STEAM curricula. Arts processes do not merely enhance the learning of other topics such as physics and math; they are valuable tools for individual students' intrapersonal processes for understanding, questioning, and knowing the world.

Of all the multimedia elements of *That Which We Call a Rose*, the most powerful storytelling techniques were analogic: live acting, puppetry, and storytelling. "But what about the eyeballs?" is a question rooted in curiosity about theatre enacted within a science context. The more arts-integrative modes of asking questions and processing knowledge we can offer K–12 students, the better they will be able to engage authentically with any subject matter. Instruction about theatre making, using astronomy as the core theme, allows inquiry about the natural world and the night sky to transcend traditionally delineated disciplinary boundaries. Students learn about light and shadow through an arts project. They learn it again as they create and perform their own mythologies, and again when they see these concepts performed in a play. With each activity, whether in the classroom or at a live theatre event, students are challenged to ask their own questions and create their own interdisciplinary connections among the arts and sciences. A devised theatre approach modeled after the PaR techniques used in higher education and professional arts research allows for the development of shared authorship and authority among collaborative groups of curious students engaged in understanding their place in the universe.

Vivian Appler *is an associate professor of performance studies at the University of Georgia. She has published in* Global Performance Studies, Theatre History Studies, *and other journals. She is coeditor of* Identity, Culture, and the Science Performance, Volume 1: From the Lab to the Streets *(2022) and its sister volume* From the Curious to the Quantum *(2023). She is a former fellow of Fulbright and the Huntington Library.* That Which We Call a Rose *was developed with funding from NASA's SC Space Consortium and SC Arts.*

Emily Pears *is an elementary school theatre teacher in Moncks Corner, South Carolina. She holds an MAT in K–12 Theatre from College of Charleston and a BFA in Musical Theatre. She also serves as the educational outreach coordinator for the STEAM theatre project,* That Which We Call a Rose.

References

Appler, V. (2019a). Titan's "Goodbye Kiss": Legacy rockets and the conquest of space. *Global Performance Studies, 2*(2). https://doi.org/10.33303/gpsv2n2a5

Appler, V. (2019b, September 30). "That Which We Call a Rose": A true STEAM project. *That Which We Call a Rose*. http://blogs.cofc.edu/that-which-we-call-a-rose/2019/09/30/that-which-we-call-a-rose-a-true-steam-project

Baki, H., Ball, J., Jahanmir, Y., Kreie, H. (2019). Mind Readers: Imagining research-led practice in doctoral education. *Theatre Topics, 29*(2), 127–139. https://doi.org/10.1353/tt.2019.0019

Barton, B. (2018). Wherefore PAR? Discussions on "a line of flight." In A. Arlander, B. Barton, M. Dreyer-Lude, & B. Spatz (Eds.), *Performance as research: Knowledge, methods, impact* (pp. 1–19). Routledge. https://doi.org/10.4324/9781315157672-1

Erkut, S., & Ceder, I. (2016, December). *Women's leadership in resident theaters: Final report*. Wellesley Centers for Women, Wellesley College. https://www.wcwonline.org/Active-Projects/womens-leadership-in-resident-theaters

Goldberg, M. (2017). *Arts integration: Teaching the subject matter through the arts in multicultural settings* (5th ed.). Routledge.

Higgins, F. L. (1967). *Sweeper of the skies: A story of the life of Caroline Herschel, astronomer*. Follett.

Hunter, L. (2015). Being in-between: Performance studies and processes for sustaining interdisciplinarity. *Cogent Arts & Humanities, 2*, 1124481. https://doi.org/10.1080/23311983.2015.1124481

Kaufman, M., & McAdams, B. P. (with Fondakowski, L., Paris, A., Pierotti, G., Simpkins, K., Maize, J., & Barrow, S.). (2018). *Moment work: Tectonic Theater Project's process of devising theater*. Vintage Books.

Lauzen, M. M. (2020). *Living archive: The celluloid ceiling: Documenting two decades of women's employment in film*. Center for the Study of Women in Television and Film, San Diego State University. https://womenintvfilm.sdsu.edu/research

Meyer, R. (2013, December 12). No old maps actually say "here be dragons." *The Atlantic*. https://www.theatlantic.com/technology/archive/2013/12/no-old-maps-actually-say-here-be-dragons/282267

Miller, R. (2016). The courage to teach and the courage to lead: Considerations for theatre and dance in higher education. *Theatre Topics, 26*(1), E-1–E-7. https://doi.org/10.1353/tt.2016.0001

National Science Foundation. (2019). *Women, minorities, and persons with disabilities in science and engineering*. National Center for Science and Engineering Statistics. https://ncses.nsf.gov/pubs/nsf19304

Oddey, A. (1994). *Devising theatre: A practical and theoretical handbook*. Routledge.

Practice as Research in Performance. (n.d.). http://www.bris.ac.uk/parip/introduction.htm

Rudlin, J. (1994). *Commedia dell'arte: An actor's handbook*. Routledge.

South Carolina Department of Education. (2017). *South Carolina college- and career-ready standards for theatre proficiency*. https://ed.sc.gov/instruction/standards/visual-and-performing-arts/standards/theatre-design-and-media-arts-standards

Wright, H. (1949). *Sweeper in the sky: The life of Maria Mitchell, first woman astronomer in America*. Macmillan.

Zazzali, P., & Klein, J. (2015). Toward revising undergraduate theatre education. *Theatre Topics, 25*(3), 261–276. https://doi.org/10.1353/tt.2015.0034

SECTION VI
Mathematics

This section begins with a powerful opening chapter that connects the visual ways of writing words to express mathematical symmetry in "Connecting Mathematics to Verbal–Visual Art." Rather than the normal mathematics class, the authors of "Guitar Makers on the Border: Bilingual Elementary Students Learning Math by Designing and Building Guitars" used STEAM education to break the language barrier as they created and designed guitars. "Providing a Compass for STEAM With M.C. Escher and Tessellations" teaches students how to use mathematical tools and concepts to create works of art. "Imagination, Color Theory, and Symmetry" brings complex concepts to an early childhood level. Each chapter links math with visual arts, among other disciplines, and delves into the research found in each lesson.

Connecting Mathematics to Verbal–Visual Art

Punya Mishra • Danah Henriksen

> *The desire for symmetry, for balance, for rhythm in form... is one of the most inveterate of human instincts.*
>
> —Edith Wharton, *Complete Works of Edith Wharton*

> *By all means break the rules, and break them beautifully, deliberately and well.*
>
> —Robert Bringhurst, *The Elements of Typographic Style*

Distorting visual letterforms and writing words to express mathematical symmetries may appear to be a strange way of engaging with math learning. But this is precisely the type of creative approach that high school students applied at a local school in Phoenix during a creative math–art lesson with the first author. Working individually or collectively, students grappled with the task of exploring the perceptual flexibility of shape perception and pattern formation through creative visual wordplay.

In this piece, we will discuss the use of "ambigrams"—a neologism created by the cognitive scientist Douglas Hofstadter (Polster, 2000)—for exploring and learning about mathematical symmetry. Ambigrams are a form of visual wordplay focused on writing words as an art form that allows them to be read in multiple ways. We situate this in a real-world math lesson done with high school students of multiple ages, where they created new and surprising ways of writing words such that they could be read when rotated 180 degrees, or when reflected in a mirror or as a fractal. These activities required learners to see words both as carriers of meaning *and* as geometric shapes that can be artfully manipulated and played with. For the students, the process was at times frustrating and challenging yet fun, and it connected visual artistry with mathematical concepts for a unique, creative learning activity.

Creativity is a driving force in mathematics. As Manjul Bhargava, Fields Medal winner in mathematics, wrote:

> For mathematicians, mathematics—like music, poetry, or painting—is a creative art. All these arts involve—and indeed require—a certain creative fire. They all strive to express truths that cannot be expressed in ordinary everyday language. And they all strive towards beauty (as cited in Rajghatta, 2014, para. 26).

It can be challenging, however, to find approaches that blend math and visual arts to help students recognize the inherent creative connection between the disciplines. Research demonstrates that creativity is not "magical"; instead, creative ideas emerge from combining or recombining preexisting ideas and concepts in unique and new ways (Ferguson, 2011). We suggest that math lessons can draw upon three principles of artistic creativity to help teachers integrate mathematics and the arts in science, technology, engineering, the arts, and math (STEAM) approaches.

The ambigram lesson we will share later is grounded in these creative principles: (1) learning to see, (2) creativity through constraints, and (3) the importance of play. Despite our specific focus on ambigram lessons, these can be useful to teachers in designing any STEAM-based lesson. Therefore, we begin with an overview of the principles before discussing how they played out in the ambigram lesson.

Creative Foundations for STEAM Lessons

Each of the principles used in this lesson, of learning to see, creativity through constraints, and the importance of play, are central to the work of creativity across disciplines. *Learning to see* is important because in creative practices (whether in math, art, or any discipline) students must learn to see the world to notice details and identify existing patterns—and then go beyond that to imagine new and interesting possibilities. Root-Bernstein and Root-Bernstein (2013) describe this ability to observe the world and identify existing patterns (then to create new ones) as a big-picture thinking skill for creativity across disciplines. This skill is foregrounded in the visual arts. Visual artists experience the world through observant fascination. Christensen (2019) notes that a painter might be enchanted by the color of a shadow, or marvel at shapes in a flower's petal. Trained artists view seemingly mundane sights as compelling. Rather than seeing an apple as an apple, they might scrutinize its form and shifting shades of color, or examine the curving shape, texture, and the play of light and dark or the shape of the shadows. By seeing what is actually there, rather than what the mind assumes is there, an artist learns to truly see (Thomas et al., 2008), which allows for a new creation. Anyone can develop this skill.

Importantly, *creativity occurs through constraints*. While creative people are open-minded, creativity is best expressed by bringing imagination to the constraints of the task at hand. Without constraints, a project or task becomes too open and potentially chaotic to produce something new and effective (Onarheim, 2012). Research reveals that creative work benefits from *appropriate* proportions of constraint to offer some guides or expectations for the task at hand (Rosso, 2014). The meaning of "appropriate" varies—but in general it is best to avoid task designs that are so open they are unlimited and undirected, but also not be so constrained as to impede fresh possibilities and new ideas. Discovering or inventing solutions within constraints is crucial to creativity.

Finally, the *importance of play* in creativity is essential. "Play" is often thought of as a childhood activity—something for fun, like games or sports. This just-for-fun view of play sometimes precludes it from classroom learning (i.e., it is seen as being for recess or outside of lessons). But play is critical in the creative process for people of any age (Conklin, 2014). Play brings joy, fun, and meaning and is foundational to how students learn and develop creatively. Mishra et al. (2011) state that "deep" or transformational learning play is open-ended—it involves toying with ideas to inspire creative, boundary-breaking thinking. It is a cognitive skill that develops whenever students get to play with ideas, signs, symbols, or artifacts in an open-ended way, to see what comes of it. Play is essential to creative learning, letting students extend their thinking and trial ideas.

STEAM education involves developing learning approaches that cut across disciplinary lines, and we share these three principles as a frame to structure lessons using mathematics and art, which are part of the ambigram examples, below. These ideas are also applicable and transferable to other types of STEAM lessons that teachers might create.

Working With Ambigrams

Ambigrams are a way of writing words (in artistic rendering) such that they can be read or interpreted multiple ways. Ambigrams exploit *how* words are written. In doing so, they bring together the mathematics of symmetry, the elegance of typography, *and* the psychology of visual perception to create surprising, artistic designs.

Figures 1 and 2 provide examples of words written such that they can be read the same when rotated 180 degrees.

Figure 1. Ambigram for "wordplay"—invariant under rotation (i.e., flip it 180 degrees vertically or horizontally and it reads the same).

Figure 2. Ambigram for "ambigram"—invariant under rotation (i.e., flip it 180 degrees vertically or horizontally and it reads the same).

STEAM Education: An Interdisciplinary Look at Art in the Curriculum

Ambigrams come in many styles. Consider Figure 3, where the word "right," when reflected across the 45-degree axis, reads "angle." Ambigrams can also come in chains, such as this design for the word "infinity," mapped into the infinity symbol (Figure 4). Ambigrams can also be similar to tessellations (akin to the graphic art of M.C. Escher). See, for instance, the design for the word "space" (Figure 5), where replications of the word map on to the surface of a sphere.

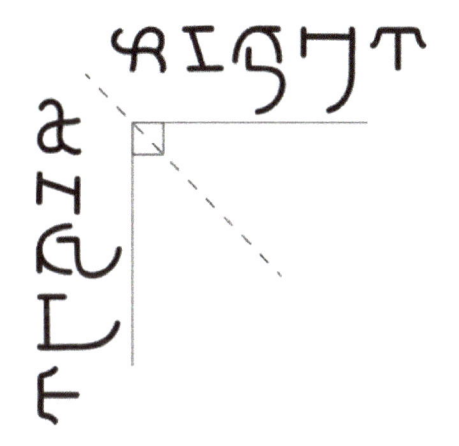

Figure 3. The word "right" becomes "angle" when reflected 45 degrees. Inspired by a solution first put forth by Bryce Herdt.

Figure 4. The word "infinity" written such that it can be read when rotated, and also makes the symbol for infinity.

Figure 5. A space-filling design for the word "space"—a verbal–visual tessellation similar to M.C. Escher's tessellations.

Connecting Mathematics to Verbal–Visual Art

At heart, ambigrams are about symmetry, a critical concept in geometry, science, and art. In this context, ambigrams can speak to specific mathematical transformations and relationships. For instance, mathematicians speak of four specific transformations we can use to manipulate a geometrical shape: rotation (Figure 6), reflection (Figures 7 and 8), translation (Figure 9), and dilation/resizing (Figure 10).

Figure 6. A 180-degree rotational ambigram for the word "rotate."

Figure 7. A vertical-reflection ambigram for the word "algebra," symmetric around the vertical axis.

Figure 8. A "lake" reflection for the world "Chicago," symmetric around the horizontal axis.

Figure 9. A set of shapes that reads the word "translate" when moved horizontally.

Figure 10. A dilation ambigram for the word "zoom," which reads the same when resized.

Mathematicians are not satisfied with just these four moves. For instance, they like to combine two or more transformations (such as a reflection *followed by* a translation or rotation) on the same object. For instance, see the rich design for the word "fractal" (Figure 11). A fractal is a geometric pattern that recursively repeats itself at ever-smaller (or ever-larger) scales. Similarly, here is a design for the "sine curve" (Figure 12) showing both rotational and translation symmetry (a property of the mathematical idea of the sine curve).

These examples situate and ground the abstractions of mathematics within the words and are a form of artistic wordplay. These explorations allow learners to grasp, in an aesthetic and fun manner, ideas related to symmetry, paradox, limits, and infinity. The act of appreciating ambigrams and creating them could allow learners to see these deeper patterns and to experience these ideas.

Figure 11. Fractal ambigram for the word "fractal," which reads the same when you rotate and zoom into or away from the design.

The process of creating ambigrams connects deeply to the three themes we described above. Taking each in turn:

Figure 12. A design for the word "sine" that captures the rotational, translational symmetry of the sine curve.

1. *Learning to see*: We can all read, but we often do not "see" letterforms and shapes. Creating ambigrams requires a dual sensitivity, to see letters and words as both symbolic conveyers of meaning and as complex geometric shapes that can be manipulated. Considering the "right-angle" reflection ambigram, creating it requires one to see how the letter "a," *if written the right way*, could be reflected to the letter "r"—something that is not obvious at first glance.

2. *Creativity through constraints*: There are tight constraints to creating ambigrams. For instance, to create a reflection design (such as the one for "reflect") requires distorting letterforms so they can be symmetric on reflection and remain legible. Essentially, every ambigram has a tight walk between legibility and conveying multiple readings.

3. *The importance of play*: The only way to create ambigrams is to doodle and play with words and letters, and most importantly their shapes. Solutions are not preordained but have to be discovered but sketching out possibilities and just being open to possibilities that emerge.

Underneath the fun exterior, there are deeper discussions on mathematics, language, and human perception. To create ambigrams, one must *play* with words and letters as carriers of meaning but also as abstract shapes that can be manipulated. The act of creating ambigrams pushes the creator to attempt to distort the visual shape of a letterform even while maintaining its "essence," as it were. There is intentionality and serendipity—where solutions can be both surprising and elegant. Douglas Hofstadter, the cognitive scientist, described creating ambigrams as being a "microworld" for the creative process.

Exploring Ambigrams and Mathematics

The first author taught a series of ambigram activities created for students to become creative and flexible in connecting the mathematics and aesthetics of words. Although these activities were done with students in upper middle and high school, variations of these tasks could be given to younger and older learners as well. These are scaffolded exercises that allow students to (1) learn to see the world of letterforms differently, (2) help them understand the constraints inherent in the "game," and (3) provide them structured opportunities to play with shapes and meaning.

The goal for a teacher is to help students learn to play with ideas of symmetry, representation, visual manipulation, and artistic design. Students must be scaffolded into the process. It is not easy to see letterforms as perceptual shapes that can be visually manipulated to convey meaning. Thus, providing examples of ambigrams is important. There are some books (Kim, 1996; Langdon, 2005; Polster, 2008; Prokhorov, 2013) and a range of online resources available that provide examples to inspire students.

Ultimately, there is no shortcut to jumping in and playing with writing words in interesting ways. Our experience has shown that these are deeply engaging activities—and students will jump in immediately. The tasks appear to be intrinsically motivating as students start playing with words and shapes, tweaking them, rotating their writing pads (in which they have been sketching) to see how the words look and whether they are legible. There are also activities and games that can help scaffold students to see letterforms in new ways, as making meaning from geometrical shapes that can be played with in creative ways. Incorporating some collective or individual discussion can be helpful for making connections between students' artistic choices and geometric concepts—strengthening both areas of knowledge.

Figure 13. The first image above is a scanned image of a rotational ambigram for "Jason," created by a student. Below is a cleaned-up version of the same design. The second image highlights the rotational symmetry that the student noticed and manipulated.

Here, we showcase a few student examples and highlight the mathematical properties of their solutions. With just a few minutes of open exploration, students can often come up with some original designs and in certain cases exploit the mathematical dimensions of this art form. Perhaps unsurprisingly, the students often started by writing out their own names, playing with the letters in their names, tweaking shapes to seek patterns and symmetries—to identify visually interesting solutions that work with basic geometrical transformations.

The first few examples, below, focus on constructing rotational symmetric designs of their names. In each, the students tried to find ways to capture half of their name in such a way that when rotated it would make the other half. For instance, the eponymous design for "Jason" can essentially be seen as being constituted in two parts—each a rotational identical of the other, as shown in Figure 13.

The next two examples are similar (and subtly different). Figure 14 shows a design by a student for his name—"Andrew." It has the same rotational symmetry as "Jason" above, with an additional insight involving combining letters to create a compound shape that reads one letter one way and two letters the other way. For instance, consider the manner in which the "An" maps onto "w." The previous example ("Jason"), on the other hand, had a one-to-one mapping of better letters.

Figure 14. The first image is a scan of a rotational ambigram for "Andrew" as sketched by a student. The image below has been cleaned up and colored to highlight (1) the rotational symmetry of the design and (2) the manner in which TWO different letter shapes map into a single letter shape (the "a-n" mapping into "w" in this example).

In the next eponymous design, "Meredith" (Figure 15), the student took this idea of collapsing multiple letters to create one letter to another extreme. In this design, the letter "M" maps onto not one, or two, but rather to *three* different letters, i.e., "M" maps onto "i," "t," and "h." This is a sophisticated way of looking and thinking about letterforms and symmetry, especially for a high schooler who had never heard of this particular art form before.

Figure 15. Scanned image of a rotationally symmetric design for "Meredith" as sketched by a student. Below is the cleaned-up version of the design, highlighting both the rotational symmetry of the design and the manner in which THREE different letters map into a single letter shape (the "m" mapping onto "ith").

The next two designs demonstrate just how creative even beginners in the art of ambigrams can be, with minimal introduction. Figure 16 shows an attempt by a student to create a 90-degree rotational design that reads "fire" one way and "water" the other. Though not entirely successful, the attempt itself demonstrates a willingness to experiment and take creative risk, to see letters both as shapes and carriers of meaning, and to perceive rotational symmetries in the letterforms.

Figure 16. A 90-degree rotational design created by a student where the word "fire" maps onto the word "water," and a cleaned-up version of the same.

Figure 17. Scanned image of a pentagonal design for the name "Alexa," where the student took advantage of the manipulating the letter "l" so that it would work as an "x" when rotated 72 degrees. The lines she drew demonstrate that she thought not just of the words but also of the underlying mathematical symmetries. This can be more clearly seen in the cleaned-up version of the image.

Figure 17 is another geometrically ambitious attempt by a student to create an eponymous design for her name, "Alexa." The student manipulated the letters "l" and "x" so "l" could be read as "x" and vice versa when rotated by 72 degrees. And that is what gives the design its fivefold (pentagonal) symmetry!

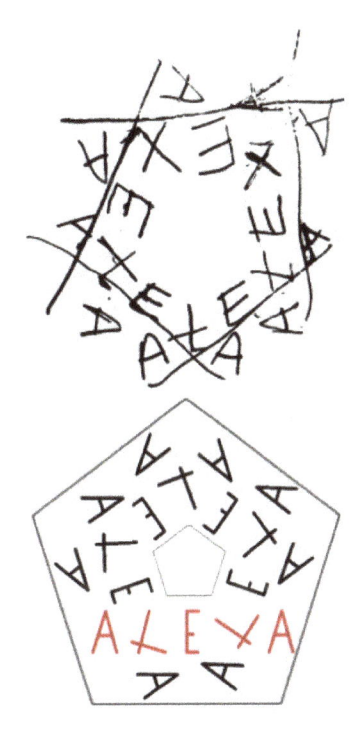

How Do Teachers Introduce These Ideas to Students?

An important part of getting students to create ambigrams is to provide them with concrete examples, either from books or websites. Ambigrams are hard to describe but easy to grasp visually. That said, there are activities that can scaffold students' experiments with ambigrams. We provide some examples of these activities below, as well as some insights into how teachers can create their own activities. We suggest the following ambigram activities, lessons, or play can be used alongside discussion to help students make connections between what they create and math concepts.

The activities start with relatively easy problems that push students to see letter and number shapes in new ways and gradually become more complex. These activities then prompt them to manipulate letterforms and shapes to create coherent designs. Thus, the first few activities appear simple and almost as visual puzzles—but they hide deeper insights and ways of looking at letterforms.

Digital Conversion

Figure 18 demonstrates an activity where the students have to see numbers as letter shapes. They have to use all the numbers (0–9) in the top row to spell the names of all the numbers in the boxes below. Basic geometric transformations (rotation and reflection) are allowed. The first example has been completed for them—where the word "zero" has been created by rotating or reflecting the numbers 2, 3, 7 and 0. This activity prepares them for seeing numbers as being shapes that can be "seen" in new ways.

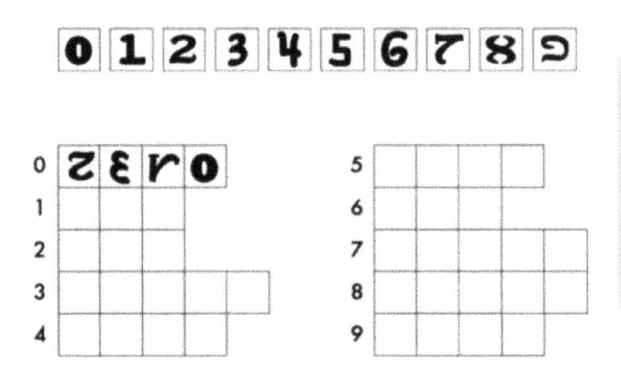

Figure 18. The digital conversion activity (inspired by Scott Kim) is a structured activity that encourages looking at numbers and letterforms as shapes that can take on multiple meanings depending on how they are perceived.

Half-a-Bet. The activity shown in Figure 19 is similar to the previous one, but here the students are asked to rotate and reflect the 13 letters provided to create the rest of the alphabet. The constraint is that you can use each shape just once. This activity allows students, within constraints, to see shapes in new and meaningful ways.

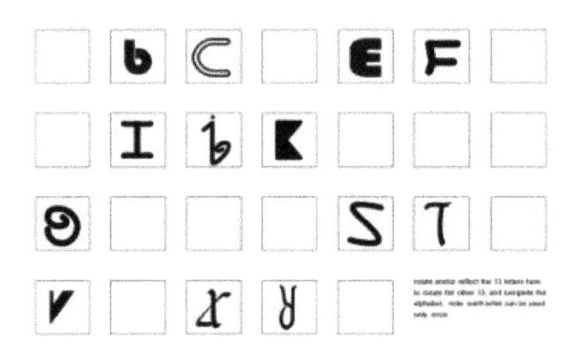

Figure 19. The half-a-bet activity (inspired by Scott Kim) undermines an essentialist reading of the alphabet and encourages constrained yet flexible interpretations of their shapes that can take on alternative meanings depending on how they are perceived.

Split-Personalities I and II. In Figure 20, the goal is to fill in the box with a letter written to have two different meanings, depending on context (e.g., the shape at the center can be seen as both "B" and "13."). The activity that follows goes further, except that it requires rotation by 180 degrees. Again, the goal is to have students drawing and playing with shapes to see how they change meaning in context.

In Conclusion: Aesthetics, Ambigrams, and Mathematics

One of the challenges of mathematics as taught in schools today is how dryly it is approached, and how often it feels divorced from artistic, visual, or captivating abstractions that geometry, puzzles, and problem solving allow for. The pleasure and beauty of playing with ideas, visuals, representations, and symmetries sometimes gets lost in dry curricula, where students do not get to creatively play in hands-on ways. As Bertrand Russell said, speaking of art and mathematics, the "true spirit of delight" can be found in both mathematics and poetry (Russell, 1961/2009, p. 229). Figure 21 captures this idea; that is, "math" becomes "poetry" (and vice versa) when rotated.

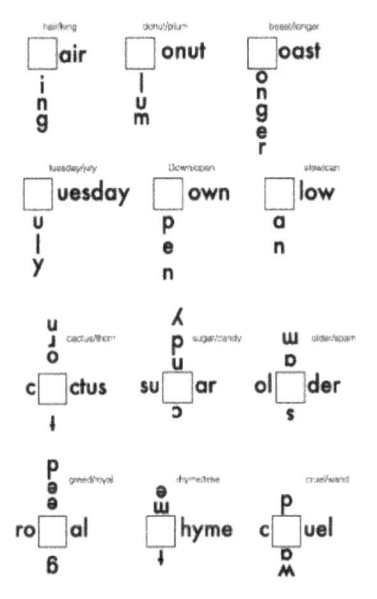

Figure 20. Split-Personalities I and II. These two activities are stepping stones to creating ambigrams. Solving these open-ended visual puzzles requires looking at the shapes of alphabets as being flexible and allowing for multiple readings, depending on context.

The creation of ambigrams can be a highly engaging activity that can lead to seemingly inevitable and yet surprising and elegant solutions, solutions that either take advantage of inherent asymmetries or reveal hidden symmetries. A big part of the learning can come in opportunities to "debrief" with students, getting them to reflect (no pun intended) on their thinking. So, after engaging in these or other ambigram activities, it helps to have a guided discussion where the teacher asks students to share their work and thinking, to connect to deeper ideas of symmetry and meaning-making.

Both mathematicians and artists engage in creative, open-ended play with ideas through manipulating abstract symbols. Ambigrams allow learners across the board to genuinely experience some of these pleasures that playing with ideas can bring and through that develop a deeper appreciation of both mathematics and art.

Figure 21. Rotational ambigram that reads "math" one way, and "poetry" when rotated by 180 degrees.

Author's Note: All designs in this article have been created by Punya Mishra. ©Punya Mishra unless indicated otherwise.

Punya Mishra (https://punyamishra.com) *juggles between being associate dean, professor, educator, researcher, author, and designer at the Mary Lou Fulton Teachers College at Arizona State University.*

Danah Henriksen (http://danah-henriksen.com) *is an associate professor at the Mary Lou Fulton Teachers College at Arizona State University, and she studies creativity in education.*

References

Christensen, I. (2019, April 23). *How to train your eyes to see like an artist.* Artsy. https://www.artsy.net/article/artsy-editorial-5-ways-train-eyes-artist

Conklin, H. G. (2014). Toward more joyful learning: Integrating play into frameworks of middle grades teaching. *American Educational Research Journal, 51*(6), 1227–1255. https://doi.org/10.3102/0002831214549451

Ferguson, K. (2011, June 20). *Everything is a remix, part 3: The elements of creativity* [Video]. Internet Archive. https://archive.org/details/EverythingIsARemix3

Kim, S. (1996). *Inversions: A catalog of calligraphic cartwheels.* Key Curriculum Press.

Langdon, J. (2005). *Wordplay: The philosophy, art, and science of ambigrams.* Broadway Books.

Mishra, P., Koehler, M. J., & Henriksen, D. (2011). The seven trans-disciplinary habits of mind: Extending the TPACK framework towards 21st century learning. *Educational Technology, 51*(2), 22–28.

Onarheim, B. (2012). Creativity from constraints in engineering design: Lessons learned at Coloplast. *Journal of Engineering Design, 23*(4), 323–336. https://doi.org/10.1080/09544828.2011.631904

Polster, B. (2000). Mathematical ambigrams. In *Proceedings of the Mathematics and Art Conference* (pp. 10–12). Bond University.

Polster, B. (2008). *Eye twisters: Ambigrams & other visual puzzles to amaze and entertain.* Allen & Unwin.

Prokhorov, N. (2013). *Ambigrams revealed: A graphic designer's guide to creating typographic art using optical illusions, symmetry, and visual perception.* New Riders.

Rajghatta, C. (2014, August 17). Math teaching in India is robotic, make it creative: Manjul Bhargava. *The Times of India.* http://timesofindia.indiatimes.com/home/sunday-times/deep-focus/Math-teaching-in-India-is-robotic-make-it-creative-Manjul-Bhargava/articleshow/40321279.cms

Root-Bernstein, R., & Root-Bernstein, M. (2013). *Sparks of genius: The thirteen thinking tools of the world's most creative people.* Houghton Mifflin Harcourt.

Rosso, B. D. (2014). Creativity and constraints: Exploring the role of constraints in the creative processes of research and development teams. *Organization Studies, 35*(4), 551–585. https://doi.org/10.1177/0170840613517600

Russell, B. (2009). *The basic writings of Bertrand Russell* (R. E. Egner & L. E. Denonn, Eds.). Routledge. (Original work published 1961)

Thomas, E., Place, N., & Hillyard, C. (2008). Students and teachers learning to see: Part 1: Using visual images in the college classroom to promote students' capacities and skills. *College Teaching, 56*(1), 23–27. https://doi.org/10.3200/ctch.56.1.23-27

Guitar Makers on the Border:
Bilingual Elementary Students Learning Math by Designing and Building Guitars

Daniel A. Tillman • Song A. An

During the 2019–2020 academic school year, a classroom of bilingual elementary students on the El Paso border learned that instead of the normal 3rd-grade math curriculum to which they were accustomed, every other Wednesday they would be working with a volunteer professor from the local university. He would be teaching them math, but not with books or worksheets or calculators—instead they would be designing and building their own guitars. Despite some unforeseen obstacles, the students built working acoustic guitars and demonstrated in the process that guitar making can serve as a lively and rewarding context for creating math pedagogy that is both memorable and effective. As an illustrative example, Figure 1 displays one of the guitars that was designed and built by the participating 3rd-grade students.

Figure 1. One of the guitars designed and built by the participating 3rd-grade students.

Design Activities as a Context for Math Education

The guitar-making activities were created for the purpose of educating students who were struggling with learning math because of, at least in part, the language barriers involved in learning a challenging subject like math in a secondary language. The bilingual students who participated in the guitar-making activities were from homes where the spoken language was predominantly or completely Spanish, but at school they were learning math in English every other class day. The guitar-making activities were intended to provide an engaging, real-world context for the math concepts the students were learning, so that language barriers would become less detrimental to their learning. The entertainment–education (also called edutainment or E-E) model of instruction provided a theoretical framework for integrating the selected school subject—math in this case—with a topic the students found authentically engaging, for which making and playing guitars was selected.

The entertainment–education model is a learning strategy that aims to combine the genuine engagement arising during informal education activities with the clearly defined and quantitatively evaluated learning goals that are the hallmark of formal education (Tillman, 2016). This strategy relies on learning theories garnered from numerous academic fields, including social learning theory, social constructivism, social cognitive theory, diffusion of innovations, and dramatic theories (Robertson & Lesser, 2013; Singhal, 2007). More generally speaking, at the level of grand theory, Bruner's constructivism has provided a foundational justification for introducing entertainment–education within formal schooling (Brooks & Brooks, 1993; Bruner, 1960). Simultaneously, the modern movement toward democratization of production—both for physical production like manufacturing and digital production like video game creation—has provided a plethora of real-world contexts for students to partake in meaningful problem solving (Bull & Groves, 2009; Hill, 1998).

Within math education, the entertainment–education model has resulted in both pedagogy and research covering a wide gamut of topics, from the quantification of skateboarding (Robertson & Lesser, 2013) to students creating geometrical wind turbines using 3D printers (Tillman et al., 2014). For almost a decade, research about students learning math during music-themed activities has been a prominent focus for the authors of this chapter (e.g., An et al., 2013, 2014; An & Tillman, 2015; An, Tillman, & Paez, 2015). Our goal has been to help students develop conceptual connections between their experiences with music, which are often deeply meaningful and personal to each student, and their understanding of math and the mathematical nature of the world in which they live (Tillman et al., 2015).

During this research, students participated in learning activities that included musical composition, musical performances, producing music videos, and attending professional music concerts. As a collective body of research, these entertainment–education studies indicate the instructional potential for interdisciplinary pedagogy, particularly within a classroom environment designed for minimizing language and cultural barriers faced by English-language learners (An, Zhang, et al., 2015). Further, these previous interdisciplinary activities formed a theoretical and pedagogical foundation for the guitar-making activities, which this chapter now examines in detail.

Making Guitars

The guitar-making activities began several weeks after the fall semester had commenced. The students were already familiar with their teacher, their classroom, and the specialized routine that formed the foundation of the school's bilingual mission—every other day was conducted fully in Spanish, with students in each grade divided into two groups that would alternate between the English-speaking and Spanish-speaking 3rd-grade teachers. One of the groups was selected by the teachers to serve as the initial participants in the guitar-making activities, and the other group participated in normal math instruction with the understanding that they would be making guitars the following year.

The students were introduced to guitar making with a design activity wherein they each created a custom guitar plectrum (commonly called a "pick") with their name on one side and a selected animal on the other side. Both sides had to be designed—meaning the name was legible and the animal was recognizable, while also ensuring that the name and animal created went beyond mere functionality. Instead, the picks journeyed into the realm of the interesting, and in the process the students formed a shared aesthetic theme for guiding the more complex guitar-making activities to follow. Both the name and animal on the plectrum design also had to scale, in that each student created a much-enlarged version on cardstock paper first and then a properly scaled cardboard model followed. This type of geometric transformation, known as dilation, was an important but a challenging math topic for many students, and perhaps early exposure with memorable hands-on learning can facilitate future encounters with this universally pervasive mathematical topic. When scaling is encountered in algebra, it is generally analyzed alongside the study of proportion—and similarly to geometric dilation, this topic can be quite challenging for many students. The empirical study of how early exposure to learning about algebraic proportion and geometric dilation can improve students' performance later on during middle and high school is a topic worthy of further research.

Figure 2. Initial sketch and final concept for *Teddy Guitar* created by 3rd-grade student.

During the plectrum design process, the students were introduced to the concept of *initial sketching* and given the opportunity to make "throwaway" drawings that would later become the conceptual basis for their actual design drawings. Figure 2 shows an example of a student's initial sketch for a "Teddy Guitar" that was later more fully developed into both a final concept (shown on the right side of Figure 2) and then an actual guitar.

After the students had completed the initial guitar plectrum activities, they progressed to designing monochords—single string instruments that replicate the basic functionality of a guitar, while maintaining a much-decreased level of complexity. The monochords that the students created used a 12-inch wooden ruler as the base, and a large rubber band wrapped the long way around the ruler served as the string. A small piece of cardboard or something similar was placed between the rubber band and one side of the ruler, resulting in a monochord that functioned by sliding the cardboard up and down the ruler while simultaneously plucking the rubber band with a finger or the plectrum created earlier.

When the students had advanced beyond simple monochord designing, they progressed to creating monochords that also had a sound box, which were created by attaching a cardboard box to a monochord's ruler such that it amplified the rubber band being played. This sound-amplification process is technically a science topic, and while the chosen pedagogical goals of the guitar-making activities did not emphasize learning science, the pedagogy certainly did aim to highlight the connections between math and science, as well as the potential role for design activities to make the math–science connection tangible for students. For example, during this stage of the activities the students explored the differences between their stringed instrument with a sound box and the same stringed instrument without a sound box.

The students next tried to express their understanding of the amplified loudness using numbers, with some including percentages in their attempts. If any of the students chose to continue learning in greater depth about the design of acoustics, they would eventually encounter a class (most likely in college) that discussed how the size of the guitar's hole impacts the loudness of the sound in a parabolic relationship—this was of course much too advanced for the participating 3rd graders, but again it would be interesting to learn how these early educational experiences might catalyze the growth of future advanced understanding.

The design of each student's sound hole (enabling the amplification effect from the sound box) was a custom process, and many of the designs incorporated the sound hole into the design itself by having it represent, for example, Saturn and its rings, or a popular video game character. The remainder of the sound box was also designed elaborately and thematically to coincide with the earlier plectrum design aesthetic that had been individually chosen by each student. The students were encouraged to make their guitar

Figure 3. Guitar tuners on heads designed by 3rd-grade students.

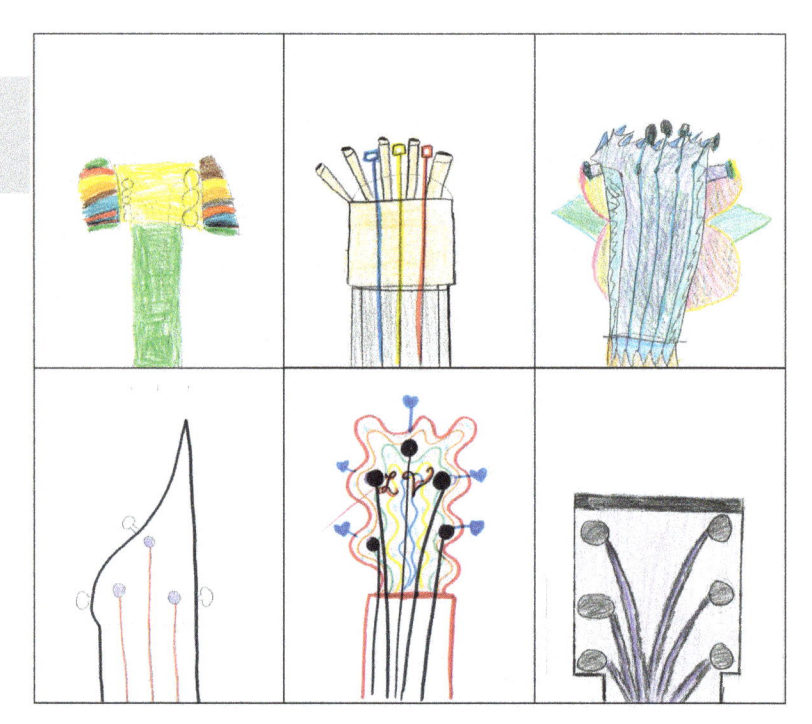

recognizable and memorable as being a designed object with its own personality and presentation—in other words, don't try to imitate your idea of a classical guitar or an electrified Fender, but instead strive to create something meaningful and original to yourself.

Paper-based activities included having each student design a custom head for placing their guitar's tuners. Figure 3 presents some examples of how the students solved the geometrical problem of placing three to six strings, while avoiding having any of the strings crossing over each other. Appreciating the basic properties of parallel lines in a hypothetically infinite two-dimensional space is an essential topic to the understanding of Euclidean geometry. Further, it was one of the topics with which Euclid himself was deeply obsessed, in that he saw within the behavior of parallel lines a simple but fascinating concept: Even if placed a mere single hair's width apart from each other, the two lines will run forever in each direction without ever crossing or even touching each other. Within this unpretentious yet still formidable idea, Euclid's infamous parallel lines presented the world with a glimpse of the striking power inherent within mathematics.

Because of the mathematical principles that were naturally embedded within the design of the guitar heads, the instructors did not have to search for and artificially add mathematics-themed tasks to the guitar designing activities—instead, the inherently mathematical nature of the guitars the students were designing rose to prominence of its own accord.

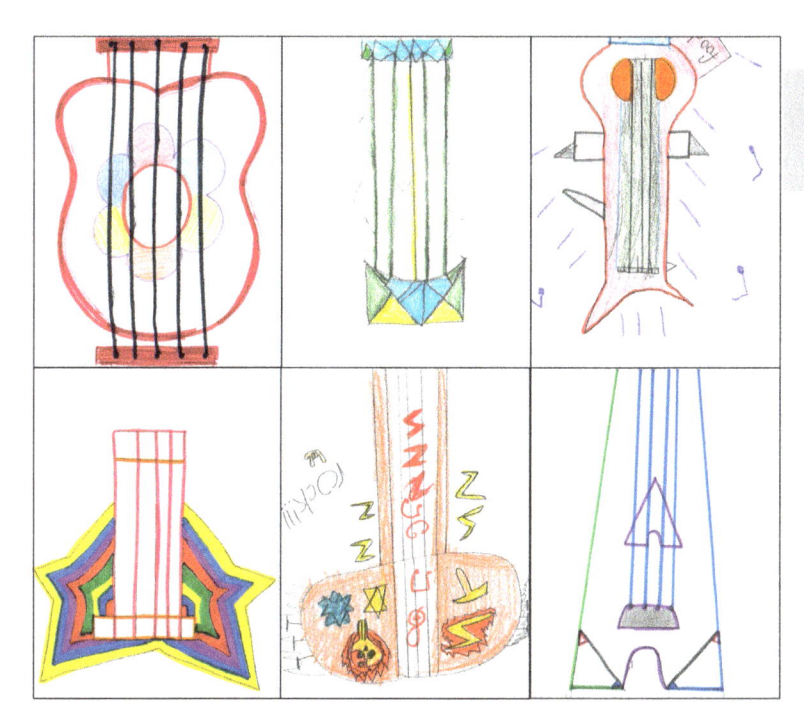

Figure 4. Guitar bodies designed by 3rd-grade students.

Figure 4 shows the inherently geometrical nature of guitar-body design, wherein the strings must run parallel and equidistant, culminating in a shared bridge. It is also important for playability that the student consider the spacing between each string as well as the string to fingerboard distance. If the spacing is not large enough, the strings might hit each other or the guitar's neck when they vibrate; if the spacing is too large, then it will cause problems during the finger pressing that is necessary to play the guitar.

These geometrical criteria remain consistent regardless of the aesthetic or theme chosen by the guitar's designer, and thus a viewing of the infinitely variable designs (as shown in Figures 3 and 4) simultaneously reveals both the complexity and the simplicity intrinsic to mathematics.

After building their designs for sound box amplified monochords, the students progressed to creating multistring guitars with the option of having three, four, five, or six strings on their final design, which they would later amplify with an attachable pickup built for use with acoustic guitars. The designs now required more structural stability, more ingenious solutions to placement of the strings (i.e., rubber bands), as well as creative solutions to a variety of other real-world design dilemmas presented by their guitar-making activities and goals. Guitar-making activities that involved solving mathematics-themed obstacles were intentionally selected by the professor and participating teachers wherever possible, as the chief pedagogical goal for all of the students' design experiences was to connect math and math-themed problem solving with real-world challenges that were meaningful and memorable to the individual students.

Figure 5. Guitars with heads and bodies designed by 3rd-grade students.

Figure 5 shows a sampling of some of the final guitar concepts developed by the participating 3rd-grade students. Varying from a "Teddy Guitar" to "The Flower Guitar" to "The Super Star" with other options in between, such as "Guitarra de Colores" and "The Super Electric Canon," it seems these students were not lacking for ideas.

During all of these guitar-making activities, the students participated in numerous design challenges that had an overt math theme, such as when they built customized guitar heads with mathematized criteria pertaining to the placement of the strings. The students were supposed to end the guitar-making activities with an opportunity to electrify the guitars using a portable electric amplifier and acoustic guitar pickup, followed by a performance showing the rest of their school the guitars that they had created, but outside circumstances interfered. Nevertheless, the learning activities that were completed did demonstrate the plausibility of guitar making as an affordable and credible context for math education.

Figure 6. Some of the guitars designed and built by the participating 3rd-grade students.

During the musical instrument design activities, the participating students became genuine junior *luthiers*—perhaps not on par with Les Paul or Leo Fender, but with a personal design sensibility and aesthetic nonetheless. Figure 6 shows just a sample of the wide-ranging designs the participating 3rd-grade students created. To improve the quality of the guitars during future learning activities, it is recommended that more professional-grade materials be obtained before the design activities take place—including actual guitar strings (instead of rubber bands), wooden sound boxes (instead of cardboard), and other similar resources that will lend authenticity to the look and sound of the musical instruments students create. And while their guitars will never sound or harmonize like those created by the masters, there is an unmistakable self-respect experienced each time you play a musical instrument that was created with your own hands and heart; and it is the hope of this chapter's authors that each person, whether child or adult, should get to experience that pride at least once.

Daniel Tillman *is an associate professor in educational technology within the Teacher Education Department of The University of Texas at El Paso's College of Education.*

Song An *is an associate professor in mathematics education within the Teacher Education Department of The University of Texas at El Paso's College of Education.*

References

An, S., Capraro, M. M., & Tillman, D. A. (2013). Elementary teachers integrate music activities into regular mathematics lessons: Effects on students' mathematical abilities. *Journal for Learning Through the Arts, 9*(1). https://doi.org/10.21977/D99112867

An, S. A., & Tillman, D. A. (2015). Music activities as a meaningful context for teaching elementary students mathematics: A quasi-experiment time series design with random assigned control group. *European Journal of Science and Mathematics Education, 3*(1), 45–60. https://doi.org/10.30935/scimath/9420

An, S. A., Tillman, D. A., Boren, R., & Wang, J. (2014). Fostering elementary students' mathematics disposition through music-mathematics integrated lessons. *International Journal for Mathematics Teaching and Learning, 15*(3), 1–18.

An, S. A., Tillman, D. A., & Paez, C. R. (2015). Music-themed mathematics education as a strategy for improving elementary preservice teachers' mathematics pedagogy and teaching self-efficacy. *Journal of Mathematics Education at Teachers College, 6*(1), 9–24.

An, S. A., Zhang, M., Flores, M., Chapman, J. R., Tillman, D. A., & Serna, L. (2015). Music activities as an impetus for Hispanic elementary students' mathematical disposition. *Journal of Mathematics Education, 8*(2), 39–55.

Brooks, J. G., & Brooks, M. G. (1993). In search of understanding: *The case for constructivist classrooms*. ASCD.

Bruner, J. S. (1960). *The process of education*. Harvard University Press.

Bull, G., & Groves, J. (2009). The democratization of production. *Learning & Leading With Technology, 37*(3), 36–37.

Hill, A. M. (1998). Problem solving in real-life contexts: An alternative for design in technology education. International *Journal of Technology and Design Education, 8*(3), 203–220. https://doi.org/10.1023/a:1008854926028

Robertson, W., & Lesser, L. M. (2013). Scientific skateboarding and mathematical music: Edutainment that actively engages middle school students. *European Journal of Science and Mathematics Education, 1*(2), 60–68. https://doi.org/10.30935/scimath/9388

Singhal, A. (2007). Popular media and social change: Lessons from Peru, Mexico, and South Africa. *Brown Journal of World Affairs, 13*(2), 259–269.

Tillman, D. A. (2016). Not just consumers: Finding space for student creativity during mathematics instruction. *Journal of Mathematics Education, 9*(2), 1–3.

Tillman, D. A., An, S. A., Cohen, J. D., Kjellstrom, W., & Boren, R. L. (2014). Exploring wind power: Improving mathematical thinking through digital fabrication. *Journal of Educational Multimedia and Hypermedia, 23*(4), 401–421. https://www.learntechlib.org/primary/p/42079

Tillman, D. A., Zhang, M., An, S. A., Boren, R., & Paez-Paez, C. (2015). Employing rapid prototyping design technologies to support contextualized mathematics education. *Journal of Computers in Mathematics and Science Teaching, 34*(4), 455–483. https://www.learntechlib.org/primary/p/129901

Providing a Compass for STEAM With M.C. Escher and Tessellations

Melody Weintraub

The artist Maurits Cornelis Escher (M.C. Escher), once wrote regarding an example of his work, "It remains for me an open question whether the game with little white and black figures, as revealed in the six woodcuts of this book, belongs to the domain of mathematics or to that of art" (1989, p. 92). The work to which Escher was referring is a series of tessellations, or mathematically speaking, "regular divisions of the plane."

Escher also said, "He who wonders discovers that this in itself is wonder" (n.d., sec. 1). It was that sense of wonder that drew artist M.C. Escher's fascination with the connection between mathematics and art. He was inspired by reading mathematical ideas and developing his art from explorations of plane and projective geometry. It is also notable that (to his own admission) as a student, he did not receive high marks in math. He once declared,

> In school in Arnhem I was a particularly poor student in arithmetic and algebra because I had, and still have, great trouble with the abstractions of numbers and letters. Things went a little better in geometry when I was called upon to use my imagination, but I never excelled in this subject either while I was in school. (Escher, 1989, p. 21)

Perhaps, had Escher been able to connect math to art at an earlier age, he would have had a different assessment. In any event, he seemed humored by the fact that mathematicians have prolifically used his illustrations as examples in textbooks in the study of the geometry of space (Smith, 2014).

As Ana Brezovnik (2015) observes, the weaving of mathematical and artistic components has been historically evident in design throughout Eastern and Western cultures for thousands of years. Mathematics has been used to create art, and art has been used to demonstrate mathematical concepts. From the patterns found in textiles to the tilework found in architecture, art and math have harmoniously coexisted. Math has also been used in art to demonstrate everything from linear perspective and the golden ratio to proportional life drawing. This relationship has also been evident in the natural world, arousing a sense of wonder in not only mathematicians and artists, but also in children. The inquisitive imagination of a child is perhaps the first to notice the symmetry of a butterfly's wings or the hexagonal shape of a honeycomb. Brezovnik further states, "Fine art is what brings creative thinking into mathematics" (2015, p. 14).

In 1999 the Kennedy Center began an initiative with schools in the Washington, DC, area to help teachers implement arts integration. The program that resulted, Changing Education Through the Arts, was established. The program first sought to carefully define the differing nature of arts integration at length. The three areas the program focused on were (1) Arts as Curriculum, (2) Arts Enhanced Curriculum, and (3) Arts Integrated Curriculum. An example of *Arts as Curriculum* is when one of the arts is an actual class at school. Examples are visual arts, vocal music, instrumental music, theatre, and dance. *Arts Enhanced Curriculum* is when one of these art forms is used primarily to teach another discipline, to check for understanding, or to make the lesson more engaging for students. An example of this is when a science teacher instructs students to make a diorama of an environment in an animal study. The objective of the lesson is not to learn how to make an assemblage or installation, or even the history of installation and assemblage. Rather, the objective is for students to understand that certain animals' survival depends on the environment. Making the diorama makes the lesson more engaging or fun. *Arts Enhanced Curriculum* is sometimes confused for *Arts Integration*. The primary difference is the goal of the implementation. In *Arts Integration*, the object is for the student to learn about a particular discipline, such as math, science, history, or writing , while equally learning about a particular visual arts period, skill, media, method, or artist (Silverstein & Layne, 2020).

The following lesson is one I designed for a middle school art classroom. This is an example of *Arts Integration* as defined by the Changing Education Through the Arts program. This lesson connects mathematics and technology to visual art. In this lesson students learn not only how to make a tessellation, but also how to make a geometrical shape using a compass while connecting the project to the artwork of M.C. Escher and the study of mathematics.

Lesson

My lesson began with an introduction to M.C. Escher and his work with tessellations. A *tessellation* is a pattern of shapes that interlock on a flat surface, meaning they fit together with no spaces or gaps between the shapes, similar to a puzzle. Another characteristic of a tessellation is that this pattern of interlocking shapes seems to repeat indefinitely. Although some examples of tessellations are more intricate, a more common example of this can be found in domestic tile work. So, sometimes tessellations are referred to as "tilings." Escher was first inspired to explore tessellations after a trip to Spain in 1922, where he saw an intricate but abstract type of tile work at the 14th-century palace, Alhambra. These Moorish tiles created a sense of wonder in the artist, and Escher began to explore the idea of creating similar nonabstract designs. These images included recognizable objects within the patterns. However, it was not until his second trip to Alhambra 10 years later that Escher was able to begin to develop a more congruous method for drawing these "periodic space-fill[ers]" (as cited in Ernst, 1976, p. 13). Later he would describe the process of drawing these in terms of an addiction; Escher writes, "this [periodic space-filling] has remained a very strenuous occupation, a real mania to which I became enslaved and from which I can only with greater difficulty free myself" (as cited in Ernst, 1976, p. 41).

My goal in teaching students not only about the challenges that Escher faced in understanding mathematics in school, but also how he later used math to make art that continues to mesmerize both mathematicians and artists alike, would hopefully result in students making a lasting connection between art and math.

After learning about Escher and his history with tessellations, students were exposed to the use of a mathematical tool that dates back to ancient Rome: the compass. The lesson ended with the use of 3D technology. My motivation for this class was to show students another example of how mathematics can be used when creating art.

Vocabulary

- tessellation: A shape that can be repeated without gaps or overlaps on a surface.
- plane: A flat two-dimensional surface that has no thickness.
- hexagon: An equally sided shape with six sides.
- compass: A tool used for drawing circles.
- arc: Part of the distance of a circle or a curve.
- vertex: The corner where lines meet.
- vertices: Plural of "vertex."
- pattern: A series, sequence, or design that repeats.

Materials

Pencil, paper, compass, straight-edge ruler or protractor, scissors, tape, cardstock or index card, drawing paper (12 x 18 inches), markers, access to internet, technology (e.g., laptop), and 3D printer (optional).

Components

This lesson was designed for a class of 7th-grade art students who came to art every weekday throughout the school year. They submitted an application to attend visual arts class, so they had a vested interest in visual arts, which facilitated their engagement in the art lessons. Since most of them do not take a formal geometry class until 8th or 9th grade, most students didn't know how to use a compass.

I began the lesson by teaching them how to draw a circle of any size using a compass. We also discussed ways to draw larger scale circles using the principles of a compass. I shared

Figure 1. Teacher drawing line segment and arc with a compass.

with them how I once used this principle (a pencil tied to a string and tethered to a nail) to draw a large moon for stage scenery.

The purpose of learning to draw a circle with a compass was for them to transform that circle into a hexagon. First students practiced with the compass in their sketchbooks, so they saw the importance of keeping the angle of the compass fixed and the point maintained in order to draw a circle. Students then viewed a simple video tutorial that demonstrated how to make a hexagon by using a compass. In the video, they learned that a hexagon is the only regular polygon where the sides are equal to the radius of the circle.

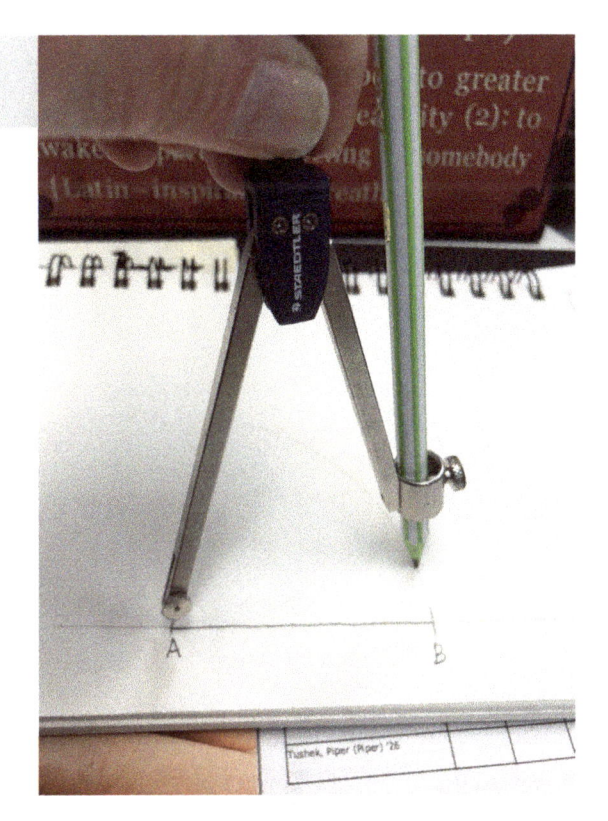

Steps to Drawing a Hexagon With a Compass

1. Draw a straight line at the bottom of the page.
2. Fix the compass on a segment of the line. This will determine the radius of the circle and the length of the sides of the hexagon.
3. Mark the compass point "A" and the end of the segment "B" (See Figure 1).
4. With the compass set on Point A, draw an arc to the left.
5. Set compass point on Point B and draw another arc to the left.
6. Set compass point where these two arcs intersect and draw a circle (See Figure 2).
7. Set compass point on B and make an arc to the right on the circle. This intersecting arc will be one of the vertices of the hexagon.
8. Next, set compass on that arc or vertex and draw the next arc to the right.
9. Continue marking the vertices around the circumference of the circle until it meets back at Point A.
10. Now, using a straight edge or ruler, connect the vertices with a straight line (See Figure 3).

Providing a Compass for STEAM With M.C. Escher and Tessellations

Figure 2. Student using compass in art.

Figure 3. Student connecting vertices with a straight line.

After watching the video, I demonstrated it again for them as they drew along with me. Then I asked them to draw hexagons independently while I observed. Next, they learned more about tessellations. They experimented with the use of a square shape to design a tessellation that filled a page in their sketchbooks. To make a shape tessellate, the square shape had to have something removed from one side that was added to the opposite side of the square. That way the negative space of the shape fits into the positive space removed.

Figure 4. Student with drawing of completed hexagon.

STEAM Education: An Interdisciplinary Look at Art in the Curriculum

Figure 5. Student connecting subtracted shape to opposite side of the hexagon.

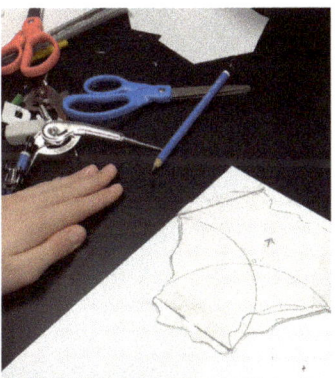

Figure 6. Two-dimensional tessellation shape complete.

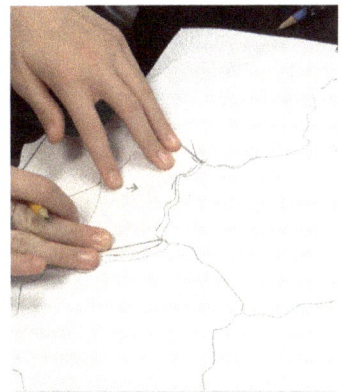

Figure 7. Student tracing a paper template to make a tessellation.

Then, students learned how to make a tessellation using a hexagon (Figure 4). The same principle applied. Whatever was removed from one side of the hexagon had to be taped to the opposite side (Figures 5 and 6). Next, students traced the shapes they made onto larger pieces of paper multiple times to fill the pages, with no spaces between the shapes and nothing overlapping (Figure 7). Students studied their shapes, and when they found something the shape resembled, they looked for visual references and added details. Students had previous experience in recognizing objects in nonobjective art with a collage project in an earlier lesson. In the collage project, students printed decorative papers on deli wrap using acrylic paint, a gel plate, and stencils. These multicolored papers were torn and collaged randomly onto canvases (Figure 8). Students were reminded to try to compositionally balance the colors and textures but not intentionally create recognizable images. When they had completely covered their canvases, students rotated them and looked for objects or scenes that emerged, much like seeing images by observing cloud shapes in the sky (Figures 9 and 10).

Figure 8. Student working on nonobjective collage of decorative papers.

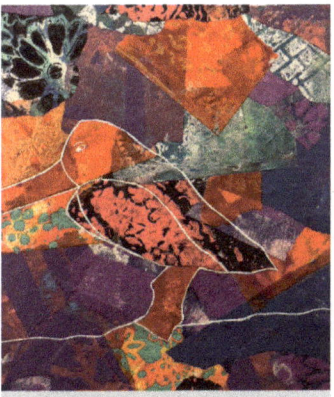

Figure 9. Student-outlined image of a duck in collage.

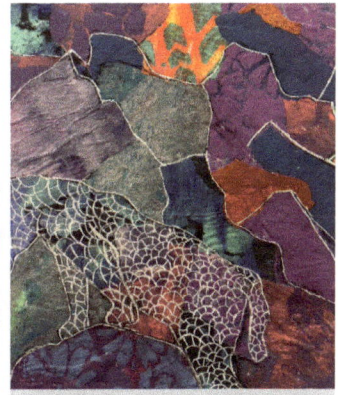

Figure 10. Student-outlined image of a mountain lion in collage.

Providing a Compass for STEAM With M.C. Escher and Tessellations

Figure 11. Owl tessellation in progress.

This activity is also related to Escher's identifying objects in tessellations or manipulating the shape in order to make artwork such as his lithograph, *Reptiles 1943*. Some students also experimented with their shapes once they saw how the shapes tessellated to create more intentional designs. These drawings were finished by adding outlines and color with markers or color pencils. Some students chose to use color to add variety to each object in the pattern while the shape remained the same (see Figures 11–17).

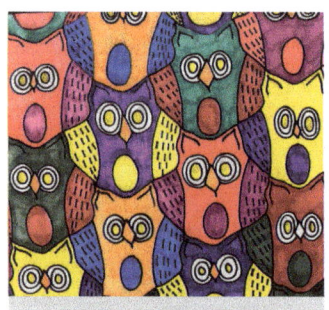

Figure 12. Owl tessellation complete.

Figure 13. Rose tessellation in progress.

Figure 14. Pony tessellation in progress.

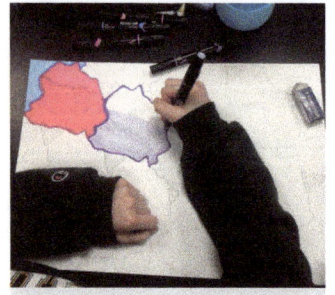

Figure 15. Ice cream cone tessellation in progress.

Figure 16. Ice cream cone tessellation complete.

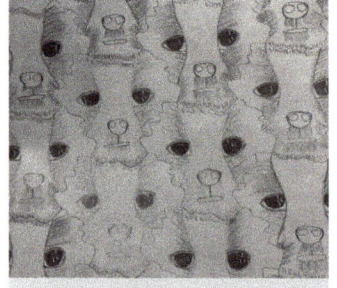

Figure 17. Dog-face tessellation.

Once students were satisfied with the shape of their tessellations, they uploaded the designs to the school's 3D printer for the final step. The first step in this process was to scan an image of the original shape and upload it into an image converter, changing the image to an scalable vector graphic (svg) file. I located a free website to make the conversion, https://image.online-convert.com/convert-to-svg, which I shared with students so they could follow the easy steps to complete this process. The first student who successfully converted an image of his tessellation shape to an svg file and sent it to the 3D printer became a peer mentor for the other students. The svg conversion was required for students to upload their images to Tinkercad (https://www.tinkercad.com), which converts designs for printing with the 3D printer located in our school library. After students printed their forms, they used these forms as templates for tessellations (see Figures 18 and 19). They also were able to share their tessellation templates with their peers.

Figure 18. Bulls-in-dust tessellation.

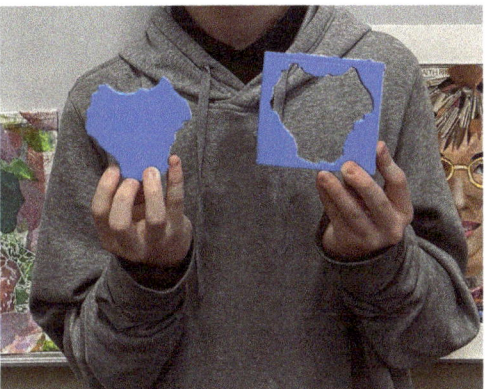

Figure 19. Student holding his original 3D printed template.

Findings

I observed that, just as in the collage lesson, some students had difficulty finding or imagining objects to embellish in the tessellations, while others identified shapes and began to immediately refine details in the shapes. If a student continued to have difficulty in this search, I allowed them to collaborate with peers to help them identify an image. If, after collaborating, some students were still unable to find something to design, I modified the criteria and allowed them to simply fill in the shapes using contrasting colors.

Engagement

I also noticed that although students seemed engaged in the lesson, some oversimplified their tessellations and details of their drawings, while others made more intricately designed details in their tessellations. Some students were so engaged in the lesson that they made multiple templates for multiple tessellation options and even voluntarily took their art home to complete it.

By giving the students the opportunity to make their tessellation shapes on the 3D printer, they were able to experience the extension of technology and functional design. This experience allowed students who learn better kinetically to connect to art and design in a tangible way.

Improvements

Overall, students seemed empowered by learning to draw a hexagon in this manner and when seeing the shapes they made successfully tessellate. In fact, when students from the upper grades came to art and saw what the class had been doing, they wanted to learn the process as well. The 7th-grade students also learned the importance of starting with an accurately drawn hexagon for a successful tessellation. Students independently learned to adjust the size of their hexagons to allow the pattern to be repeated multiple times on the page. Advanced learners discovered how to alter the design of the template to conform to an object they desired to tessellate. One student found multiple ways to create details in her tessellation before finally completing her design. Figure 20 demonstrates a detailed tessellation design in progress.

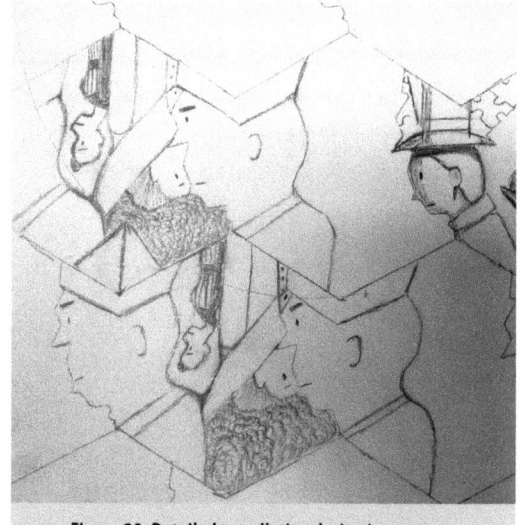

Figure 20. Detailed tessellation design in progress.

Others discovered that if they did not correctly tape the cutout to the opposite side of the hexagon or trace the template accurately, it would not tessellate.

As far as the application of the 3D template, students realized the svg scanned image would print better when outlined with a thick line. For the printer we used, a thin outline resulted in a 3D form that had to be trimmed.

Modifications for Diverse Learners

This lesson shows the importance of skillfully drawing the details so objects can readily be identified. However, this lesson could be adapted in a nonobjective art lesson, where contrasting colors are added to the tessellated shapes instead of identifiable images—much like the Moorish tiles observed by Escher.

If the drawing of the hexagon is too challenging for some students, they could make tessellations simply using a square, which is modified, taped, and traced in the same fashion as the hexagon. The same geometrical principles can be emphasized in both the square and the hexagon. Basically, whatever shape is removed from one side has to be added to the opposite side so the designs will tessellate, or fit together with no gaps or overlaps as mentioned previously.

Discussion

In practice, this lesson began with the introduction of an artist, M.C. Escher, who is known for his mathematically influenced designs called tessellations. The lesson proceeded by teaching students the mathematical process used to make similar designs. It continued by showing students an application of this skill to make art. Finally, this lesson is extended with the use of technology to make a 3D model that can, in turn, facilitate the production process.

Modifications need to be considered for students with different learning styles and grade levels. One such modification would be to offer some students a shape on which to begin designing a tessellation, instead of requiring them to make it by first drawing a hexagon. However, by demonstrating the use of a mathematical tool like a compass in drawing a circle and then converting the circle to a hexagon in order to make the tessellated work of art, students may be better able to make the art–math connection.

Implementing the Steps of Engineering Design in Art

Six magnetic posters were always visible in my art room. They are the Steps of Design Engineering: *Ask, Imagine, Plan, Create, Experiment, Improve*. These steps were applicable in this lesson on tessellations. After learning that a shape would not tessellate, students could *Ask* themselves why. The reason could be because it was inaccurately measured, not taped correctly, or inaccurately traced. Students then could *Imagine* a solution to the problem, as well as consider what the final image could look like, which also involves the need to *Plan*. Next, students *Create* by applying template to paper. Some students found they could *Experiment* by manipulating the template to *Improve* their designs. Students discovered the importance of geometric principles in making this type of technical art. They were also hopefully able to identify other ways that this skill can be used (real-life examples: architecture, design), as well as ways it can be implemented into future art projects. During free periods of working independently in their sketchbooks, I noticed that several of them reached for compasses.

Strategies

In reflecting on this lesson, I realized it might have been a good idea to open the lesson by asking students (without prior knowledge) to make a design tessellate (no gaps, no overlaps) on a page without first showing them the geometrical process. Making an inquiry-based lesson like this and eventually guiding them to the solution could have made an even greater impact. However, by showing students everyday examples of tessellations, I was able to draw them into the lesson and by connecting the art and math of tessellations to real life (e.g., tile floors, beehives, quilts, brick walls).

Benefits of Art–Math Integration

This lesson supported the importance of quality art education through an interdisciplinary approach. It reinforced an interdisciplinary approach to learning by demonstrating to students not only how a mathematical principle can be used pragmatically in a work of art, but also how art can be used to enhance applied geometry. Students also learned how valuable a simple mathematical tool like a compass can be when creating shapes, and how those shapes can be transformed into meaningful art.

Ideas for Implementation

Before introducing this lesson, art educators should definitely make several tessellations using both a square and polygons (such as the hexagon) to be comfortable with the process before teaching it. Independent research using the resources listed at the end of this chapter will also help.

One should always include a description of the lesson when displaying student work. With this lesson, it might be wise to explain the tessellation's relationship to math and to art. The 3D printed template could also be displayed with the finished tessellation artwork to show the use of technology. In addition, an art teacher could take a group of students with their 3D printed templates to their elementary STEM lab or math class and allow them to help those students make tessellations, or show them how to make a hexagon by starting with a compass. This project is an excellent way to collaborate with the math teacher, who can be asked to present part of the lesson, or to explain how this art relates to math. It might also help to ask the math teacher to review your lesson in advance to see if they have any suggestions on how to present it in respect to the students' prior mathematical knowledge. It might also be a good idea to offer in exchange to do the same in math class for the art component of one of their project-based lessons. It is never too early for art students and art teachers to become enraptured with a sense of wonder by the connection between art and math. Escher's *Drawing Hands, 1948* is a mesmerizing print of two hands, each drawing the cuff of the other hand. In this cyclical way, each is making the other visible. If either hand stopped drawing, the other would not exist. This is also an illustration of how art should coexist with all the other disciplines, comprehensively creating both a sense of wonder and educational harmony for the learner. And just as a repeated pattern in a tessellation, the possibilities of this type of education seem endless.

Conclusion

By introducing the art of M.C. Escher and his work with tessellations as well as his lifelong interest in mathematics, I was able to help students anticipate learning how tessellations are made, and to show them the connection this form of art has to mathematics. By starting with the square tessellation as practice, I was able to prove to them that this principle works before proceeding to the more complicated drawing of the hexagon. Demonstrating how to draw the hexagon with a compass not only fascinated the students, but by successfully drawing it, they experienced a sense of accomplishment even before the project began. By including an application of technology using 3D printing, students were able to see tangible results, as well as a function for their designs. Finally, the art of the tessellation gave students a way to individually and creatively express their learning.

Numerous connections exist between art and mathematics. Tessellations explore the use of space on a plane, which is mathematical, while art explores the use of space in composition as one of the elements of design. The golden ratio is explored by both mathematicians and artists. The principles of symmetry and balance are used in both art and in math. The concept of the pattern is a visible factor in math and a design element used in art. Geometrical patterns and shapes are found in the work of many artists besides M.C. Escher, including Piet Mondrian.

Melody Weintraub is a retired visual arts teacher. She has taught art classes from preK through the graduate level, both as an adjunct and full-time instructor. She has a master's degree in teaching from The University of Memphis (2007) and is a regular contributor to SchoolArts magazine. Her article, "Proofs and Spoofs," appears in SchoolArts Collection: STEAM (Davis, 2020). She has presented workshops and lectures both on the state and national level. Her awards include the 2014 Tennessee Middle School Art Educator of the Year. She served as the President of the Tennessee Art Education Association from 2020 to 2022. Website: http://www.melodyweintraub.com

Resources

National Standards for Geometry:
https://www.nctm.org/Standards-and-Positions/Principles-and-Standards/Geometry

How to draw a hexagon with a compass:
https://youtu.be/ZfZzlN_5cgQ

Image converter:
https://image.online-convert.com/convert-to-svg

Tinkercad (app for 3D design):
https://www.tinkercad.com

How to import an image into Tinkercad:
https://youtu.be/l69679n_KEQ

References

Brezovnik, A. (2015). The benefits of fine art integration into mathematics in primary school. *Center for Educational Policy Studies Journal, 5*(3), 11–32. https://cepsj.si/index.php/cepsj/article/view/125

Ernst, B. (1976). *The magic mirror of M.C. Escher* (J. E. Brigham, Trans.). Ballentine.

Escher, M. C. (n.d.). *Quotes M.C. Escher.* https://mcescher.com/about/quotes

Escher, M. C. (1989). *Escher on Escher: Exploring the infinite.* Abrams. https://www.escherinhetpaleis.nl/story-of-escher/metamorphosis-i-ii-iii/?lang=en

Silverstein, L. B., & Layne, S. (2020, January 14). *What is arts integration? Explore the Kennedy Center's comprehensive definition.* Kennedy Center. https://www.kennedy-center.org/education/resources-for-educators/classroom-resources/articles-and-how-tos/articles/collections/arts-integration-resources/what-is-arts-integration

Smith, B. S. (2014, February 12). *The mathematical art of M.C. Escher.* Platonic Realms. https://platonicrealms.com/minitexts/Mathematical-Art-Of-M-C-Escher

Imagination, Color Theory, and Symmetry

Nancy Walkup

One of the misconceptions I sometimes see about the meaningful integration between science, technology, the arts, engineering, and mathematics (STEAM) is that these concepts should all come together in one lesson or project. In practical terms alone, that would be unwieldy, unworkable, and unnecessary. Instead, in a STEAM classroom, projects connect one or more disciplines through art as they naturally apply. Ideally, over the course of a school year, students would work with all of the STEAM disciplines, just not all at once.

I think I was a STEAM teacher long before it had a name. This lesson I am sharing is one I taught every year for kindergarten and 1st grade since my very first elementary teaching position over 30 years ago. It just made sense to me to incorporate art with math and science in this lesson.

Color Theory and Symmetry

Starting with an introduction to color, I showed students transparent color paddles or gel sheets and demonstrated how they create secondary colors when overlapped in front of a window. (The very first time I did this, a child shouted out, "It's magic!"). I then demonstrated the project before I passed out materials.

Procedures

I gave students 12 x 18 inch Manila paper and crayons and asked them to fold their papers in half, crease the fold, open them up, and write their names on them. If students couldn't write their names (most of my kindergartners couldn't at first), I wrote them for them. You will be passing them back in the next class, so you need those names.

Having previously filled squeeze bottles of red, blue, and yellow paint, I quickly went around the room and squeezed out a blob of each color about the size of a nickel in a triangular formation on one side of the students' opened papers. Don't place the paint too near the edges of the paper; place them closer to the fold. As the art teacher you might instead choose to have a set of squeeze bottles for each table for students to use themselves, but I recommend saving this approach for follow-up experimentation.

Next, I asked students to carefully fold the empty side of the paper like a book and then gently rub it with their hands to spread the paint inside. Then, they quickly used the edge of a ruler to spread the paint further, pressing toward the fold. Finally, students open their papers and see what they have created. To prevent holes in the paper, I reminded them to not open and close the paper too much because it weakens the paper and causes it to tear.

After that, students would share their images with each other and identify any secondary colors where the primary colors overlapped. We talked about symmetry and how one side is the opposite or the reflection of the other. They could clearly see the line of symmetry that splits the full shape created by the paint in half, and those halves were identical. Without prompting, students began talking about what images they could see in their painting. At this point, we set these papers aside to dry in preparation of drawing on them in the next class. If you want students to try another painting where they experiment with placing the paint, they could do that now. These, too, need to be set aside to dry.

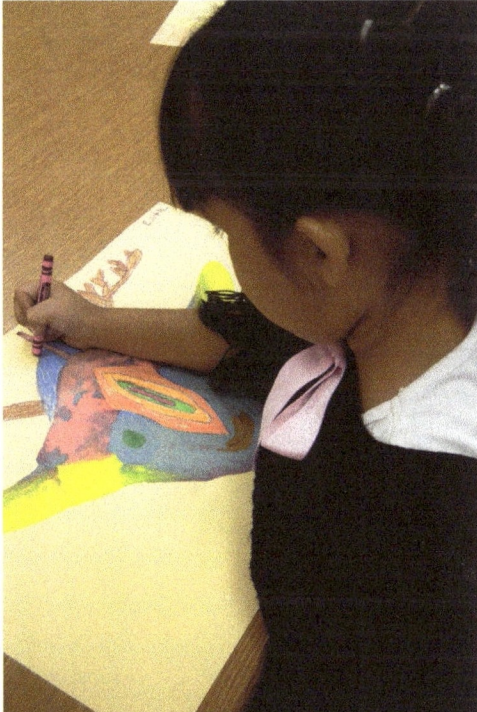

Figures 1 and 2. Children creating symmetrical designs and images from their folded-paper paintings.

If time allows or at the beginning of the next class, you could read aloud a children's book about color, such as *Mouse Paint* by Ellen Stoll Walsh (1995; also available digitally and in a big book), or show a short film clip. The band OK GO has an engaging one made for children, *Three Primary Colors*, that they created for *Sesame Street* (2012). When students return to class, they can add to their pictures by drawing with crayons or oil pastels (see Figures 1 and 2). Since the paint is now dry, they can also draw over it.

Practical Matters

Before beginning this lesson, experiment with the tempera paint you have; some brands are better than others at giving vibrant colors. Manila paper works better than white drawing paper for this process, as it is more absorbent (Figures 3–6). Rubbing the folded papers with a ruler is less likely to tear the paper than just rubbing with the hands. Every child can be successful with this lesson, and it remains one of my favorite lessons for early childhood students.

Materials and Resources

- Primary color paddles or gel sheets
- Manila drawing paper, 12 x 18 inches
- Squeeze bottles of red, yellow, and blue tempera paint
- Rulers
- Crayons or oil pastels

Figures 3–6. Completed symmetrical design works of art. The students were able to point out the magic of art in their artwork through the blending of primary colors to make secondary colors.

Fostering Collaboration

How can you develop STEAM lessons like this with the collaboration of the classroom teacher? At the beginning of every school year, I would ask the classroom teachers to let me know what they would be teaching throughout the year so I could collaborate. The teachers who were most responsive were almost always from kindergarten and 1st grade (we did not have an early childhood program). They seemed to have most of their school year mapped out ahead of time, which was very helpful to me. You can't collaborate with everyone, but don't worry—you are unlikely to get that big a response!

Two other approaches I recommend for fostering collaboration are to learn and use the same vocabulary as the classroom teachers, and to borrow their grade-level readers to discover themes and project ideas to develop. I believe the success of STEAM is through the engagement of art and meaningful connections. It just makes sense.

Nancy Walkup has been the editor of SchoolArts, *a magazine for art educators published since 1901, since 2005. She was also a contributing author, along with Marilyn Stewart, Eldon Katter, and Laura Chapman, for the first edition of* Explorations in Art, *Davis Publications's elementary textbook series.*

References

Sesame Street. (2012, January 30). *Sesame Street: OK Go—Three primary colors* [Video]. YouTube. https://www.youtube.com/watch?v=yu44JRTIxSQ

Walsh, E. S. (1995). *Mouse paint*. Red Wagon Books.

CLOSING

Through these pages and diverse chapters, we have taken a look at a variety of interdisciplinary practices across the curriculum through a STEAM lens. This book has united multiple ideologies from STEAM education; however, it only scratches the surface of the varieties of interdisciplinarity methods of teaching through STEAM. The authors have shared their unique perspectives on STEAM and the interconnectedness between the subject areas. They have also provided a compilation of examples of how it can be implemented in an art room bridging a connection between research and practice. Our goal is for this content to encourage others to put these interdisciplinary methods into practice and to spark the STEAM enthusiast in you as an art teacher, administrator, or academic.

Printed in the USA
CPSIA information can be obtained
at www.ICGtesting.com
LVHW071745310724
786974LV00007B/53